T0328715

An Introduction to
Mathematics for Economics

An Introduction to Mathematics for Economics introduces quantitative methods to students of economics and finance in a succinct and accessible style. The introductory nature of this textbook means a background in economics is not essential, as it aims to help students appreciate that learning mathematics is relevant to their overall understanding of the subject. Economic and financial applications are explained in detail before students learn how mathematics can be used, enabling students to learn how to put mathematics into practice. Starting with a revision of basic mathematical principles the second half of the book introduces calculus, emphasising economic applications throughout. Appendices on matrix algebra and difference/differential equations are included for the benefit of more advanced students. Other features, including worked examples and exercises, help to underpin the readers' knowledge and learning. Akihito Asano has drawn upon his own extensive teaching experience to create an unintimidating yet rigorous textbook.

Akihito Asano is Associate Professor of Economics at the Faculty of Liberal Arts, Sophia University, Tokyo. He has previously held positions at the University of Melbourne and the Australian National University (ANU). In 2008 he received the Award for Teaching Excellence from the College of Business and Economics at the ANU. He currently teaches introductory and intermediate microeconomics, international trade and introduction to game theory to undergraduate students, and mathematical techniques in economics to graduate students.

An Introduction to Mathematics for Economics

AKIHITO ASANO

CAMBRIDGE
UNIVERSITY PRESS

CAMBRIDGE
UNIVERSITY PRESS

University Printing House, Cambridge CB2 8BS, United Kingdom

One Liberty Plaza, 20th Floor, New York, NY 10006, USA

477 Williamstown Road, Port Melbourne, VIC 3207, Australia

314-321, 3rd Floor, Plot 3, Splendor Forum, Jasola District Centre, New Delhi - 110025, India

103 Penang Road, #05-06/07, Visioncrest Commercial, Singapore 238467

Cambridge University Press is part of the University of Cambridge.

It furthers the University's mission by disseminating knowledge in the pursuit of education, learning and research at the highest international levels of excellence.

www.cambridge.org
Information on this title: www.cambridge.org/9780521189460

First published 2013

A catalogue record for this publication is available from the British Library

ISBN 978-1-107-00760-4 Hardback
ISBN 978-0-521-18946-0 Paperback

Contents

Illustrations

Tables

Preface

This book is based on lecture notes I wrote for a first-year compulsory quantitative methods course in the Australian National University (ANU) over a period of seven years. Before I started teaching the course in 2002, an encyclopaedic textbook on introductory quantitative methods that had limited focus on economics was used. However, teaching mathematics out of such a textbook to my students seemed ineffective because many of them disliked studying mathematics unless they saw practical applications. Accordingly, as an economist, I looked for other textbooks in mathematical economics. Many good textbooks were available, but they were too advanced for an introductory course, in terms of both mathematics and economics. Although they contained many applications to economics, they usually assumed that students have learnt some introductory economics. These applications are not straightforward for first-year students with little, if any, background in economics. I decided to write my own lecture notes given this unsatisfactory situation.

Scope

The material in the main text ranges from a revision of high-school mathematics to applications of calculus (single-variate, multivariate and integral) to economics and finance. For example: linear and quadratic functions are introduced in the context of demand and supply analysis; geometric sequences, exponential and logarithmic functions are introduced in the context of finance; single-variate calculus is explained in the course of solving a firm's profit maximisation problem; a consumer's utility maximisation is used to motivate introducing multivariate calculus; and integral calculus is explained in the context of calculating the deadweight loss of taxation. The material can be taught in 13–15 weeks (39–45 hours). To give some flexibility, matrix algebra and an introduction to difference/differential equations are covered in appendices.

Features, approach and style

One of the distinctive features of this book is that, where possible, mathematical techniques are introduced in the context of introductory economics. Many students tend to dislike learning mathematics for its own sake, but this feature allows them to realise that learning introductory mathematics is inevitable in studying economics. The book is self-contained since no knowledge in economics or finance is assumed. Economic and financial applications are explained in detail before students learn how mathematics can be used. For example, in Chapter 4, various notions related to a competitive firm's problem (from microeconomics principles) are explained. Then, motivated by this problem, differential calculus is introduced. Of course the primary objective of the book is for students to learn mathematical techniques, so economic ideas are not explained as comprehensively as in other textbooks on introductory economics.

My notes were originally written as a self-contained workbook on maths applications. The material in the workbook was not presented in an encyclopaedic way – because I wanted to have something I could follow exactly – and was written in a conversational style to make my students feel as if they were studying in my lectures. A typical encyclopaedic quantitative methods textbook covers everything at length. It also means that such a textbook tends to contain a lot of unnecessary detail, which I think is not a desirable feature for an introductory textbook. The spirit of the workbook was 'maths is used to examine economics and finance', and this textbook adopts the same philosophy and the conversational style. I have tried to focus on mathematical ideas that are relevant to our applications in economics and finance, and have tried to remove as much unnecessary detail as possible.

I hope instructors find my approach useful in teaching an introductory quantitative methods course and, where necessary, can provide their students with some details that might be missing from this book – in terms of both economics and mathematics – in their lectures, which I am sure will be appreciated.

Target audience

The book is aimed at first-year economics/finance students – with some high-school maths but little (or even no) background in economics or finance – who are required to take a quantitative methods (calculus) course in their degrees. Any other undergraduate student and/or an MBA student who has no economics background, but who is required to take a quantitative course in economics/finance in their degrees will also find the book useful. Although almost no knowledge of economics and finance is required, it is assumed that students have a knowledge of high-school mathematics up to single-variate calculus.

Calculator policy, etc.

The use of a calculator is strongly discouraged. Arithmetic required in this book is not complicated enough to warrant the use of a calculator. Students who routinely use a calculator – and have difficulty in their arithmetic – should try gradually restraining themselves from relying on it. You won't be able to have a good sense of numbers if you keep relying on a calculator. Moreover, we use numbers everyday when we discuss economics and finance, and it helps a lot to have good arithmetic in understanding what other people are discussing.

Some might argue that a scientific calculator is necessary because sometimes a solution may involve expressions such as $\sqrt{\ }$, log, etc. I have come across many students who are used to – with the help of a scientific calculator – providing an approximate solution to these expressions. I have also seen many students who tend to round numbers to two decimal places even when solutions are in fractions, e.g. instead of writing $\frac{1}{30}$, many tend to write 0.03. On many occasions, from a practical point of view, providing an approximate solution is permissible and could be better than providing an exact solution. For example, if your boss asks you to provide him/her with a forecast of the economic growth rate of a country for the next year, he/she is probably looking for an answer such as '2.83 per cent (or even 2.8 per cent)' rather than '$2\sqrt{2}$ per cent'. The rounding error in this case will be considered trivial to your boss as well as to most people. And indeed, it is handy to have a calculator in this case because it will tell you that $2\sqrt{2} \approx 2.828\,427$ (or even more accurately). But what about rounding top 100-metre sprinters' best records to zero decimal places (in seconds)? It is not practical because too many athletes will be tied at 10 seconds and you won't be able to tell the sprinter with the fastest record. On the other hand, you would round top marathon runners' best records because rounding them to zero decimal places would be enough to rank them quite accurately. Using an approximate solution is therefore considered practical and permissible depending on the context, and at times a scientific calculator may be useful in getting the approximate solution.

However, there is a clear distinction between being practical and being precise, and the latter aspect is more important when you study mathematics. In mathematics we tend to carefully connect many dots to get to a solution. If every one of the dots is connected imprecisely, the solution you arrive at might be quite different to the exact one (the difference may still be trivial depending on the context, but that's not the point here). To be a good user of mathematics, it is important to conduct operations accurately and obtain the exact solution at each of the required steps. In fact, in many cases, you will find that only an exact solution exists. For example, when you end up with $\frac{a}{b}$, where a and b are real numbers, there is no way that you can write it in decimals and round it to a particular number of decimal places! For expressions such as $2\sqrt{2}$, $\frac{1}{30}$ and $\log_e 2$, it is possible to provide approximate solutions, but leave them as they are. As far as learning mathematics is concerned, what we care about most is whether you can actually get the exact solution by following the correct steps. For this reason, you will not need to have a scientific calculator (or even a simple calculator) to study this book.

Acknowledgements

I am indebted to many people who have been involved in the process of making this book a reality. As mentioned in the Preface, this book grew out of the lecture notes that I wrote for the quantitative methods course in the ANU. I wrote my own notes because I couldn't find a suitable textbook. In spirit, I essentially followed in the same footsteps of my former colleagues, Ben Smith, Matt Benge and Rod Tyers, who were teaching a first-year macroeconomics course in rotation at that time. They were dissatisfied with existing textbooks in introductory macroeconomics and decided to write their own lecture notes, which were also known as the *brick* (Ben eventually published his brick as a textbook). I read the brick for the first time when I tutored that course for Rod (in 1998 when I was doing my Ph.D.) and was so surprised how systematically and succinctly their material was put together. I would not have thought of writing my own notes without seeing their teaching, so I would like to thank them for showing me their dedication to teaching good economics.

I'd like to express my gratitude to the many students who took my course and used my notes for giving me positive and encouraging feedback as well as some constructive criticism. Teaching that course was a great learning experience for me as an instructor and it was a privilege to have been able to teach such excellent groups of students. My thanks also go to all the tutors – particularly Shane Evans who provided me with valuable assistance as Head Tutor of the course for several years – for their feedback, support and encouragement.

Many people have helped me turn the lecture notes into this book. I'd like to thank my former colleague at the ANU, Chris Jones, for suggesting that I should publish my lecture notes as a book and for introducing Andrew Schuller to me. I am grateful to Andrew for opening up an opportunity for me to discuss this book project with Chris Harrison, Publishing Director of Social Sciences at the Cambridge University Press. I'd like to thank Chris and his editorial and production team for their professional work and continuous support. I'd also like to thank many anonymous reviewers – and again Chris Jones who acted as a non-anonymous reviewer – for providing me with helpful comments and useful suggestions on earlier drafts. Special thanks are due to Rina Miyahara for proof-reading the final manuscript. Of course, I take full responsibility for any remaining errors.

1 Demand and supply in competitive markets

The book centres around the **demand and supply analysis** in **perfectly competitive markets**. To give you an overview of the book, in this chapter these ideas will be briefly explained without the use of mathematics, primarily for readers who have little knowledge of economics. I will also foreshadow various topics that will be covered in the rest of this book and the mathematical techniques that might be used to examine them. I hope it will motivate you to study the subsequent chapters.

Chapter goals By studying this chapter you will

(1) be able to conduct the demand and supply analysis without the use of mathematics; and

(2) have a bird's-eye view of this book.

1.1 Markets

Think about what you bought yesterday. The items you bought might include those that are physically tangible, e.g. potato chips, vegetables and books, as well as those that are intangible in nature such as 'watching a movie in a cinema' and 'having a haircut at a hairdresser's'. Economists call tangible products such as potato chips and vegetables **goods**, whereas they call intangible ones **services**.

Goods and services are traded in **markets**. If you have not studied economics before, note that the word 'markets' is a technical term (a jargon) and may be different from how you use it everyday. When you hear the term 'market' you might imagine something like a fish market or a fruit market because we are familiar with these markets. But in economics a 'market' is a much broader idea. For example, consider an ice-cream stand in a football stadium. In economics, it constitutes a market for ice-cream because ice-cream is traded at the stand. Another example of a market is book stores on the Internet (such as Amazon.com) where books are traded. Essentially, the market for a good (or a service) is a set of buyers and sellers who potentially engage in trading it, given a particular time and a location.

Thousands of goods and services are traded in markets. In the following, we shall focus on one of them – say, sausages – and examine how the **price** and **quantity** traded in the sausage market are determined.

1.1.1 Perfectly competitive markets

Suppose you are selling sausages. Imagine a situation where (a) many other sausage sellers are around you and they all charge the same price; and (b) there are many people in the market who are willing to pay that price to buy sausages. That is, so long as you charge that price, people will buy as many sausage as you want to sell.

To think about how you might decide what price to charge, start with the situation where you charge the same price as others. Now, would you consider charging a higher price? Well, it is not a good idea because if you did, people would buy sausages from other sellers and would not buy any sausages from you. Then, would you consider charging a lower price? It is not a good idea, either. There are many people who buy sausages from you if you charge the same price as others; so why would you want to do worse by charging a lower price?

In this situation, it seems you have no option but to accept the price other sellers charge. Why can you not affect the price of the sausage? It is because there are so many other sausage sellers in the market. When your sausage supply is only a tiny proportion relative to the size of the sausage market, you cannot change the price of the sausage by yourself. Each of the sellers, including you, has no control over the price and hence accepts (takes) the price that stands in the market. Economists call these sellers **price takers**. Similar logic applies to buyers. If each of the sausage buyers is small compared to the size of the entire market, then none of them has influence on the price of a sausage. Each buyer is a price taker in such a situation. You are in this kind of situation when you are shopping in the supermarket.

However, if you are in fresh food (e.g. fruit, vegetable, fish) markets when they are about to close, you find that you have some 'power' to influence the prices of the goods. It is very likely you can bargain the prices down. In such a case, buyers are not price takers. An example of non-price taking behaviour on the seller's side is found in a market where there is only one seller. The seller is called a **monopolist** (or a **monopoly**) and it can set the price as it likes (although the price is likely to be subject to government regulation). Even when there is more than one seller in the market, each of them may have some control over the price they can charge. In the above sausage example, even if there are many more sausage sellers around you, if you supply sausages that are somewhat different from those others provide – e.g. sightly bigger, spicier, healthier – then you can charge a higher price than your competitors (and consumers who have particular tastes will pay more to buy sausages from you).

In any event, in this book we will *not* focus on situations where sellers and/or buyers have control over the price. It means that our focus will be the market where *homogeneous* goods are traded. There are many sellers as well as many buyers in this market and hence each of them behaves as a price taker. The market that satisfies these two conditions – (a) homogeneous goods and (b) price taking sellers and buyers – is called the **perfectly competitive market**. Now let us look at how buyers and sellers might behave when the price of a sausage is given.

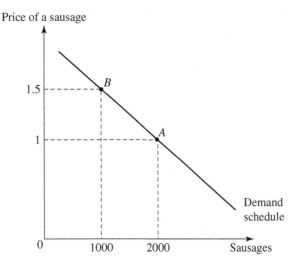

Figure 1.1 The market demand for sausages.

1.2 Demand and supply schedules

1.2.1 Market demand

The **market demand schedule** for sausages depicts, for each and every price of a sausage, the quantity of sausages buyers in the market are willing to buy (in a particular time, per day for example).

The market demand schedule for sausages is depicted in Figure 1.1. On the vertical axis of the diagram, the sausage price is shown, whereas on the horizontal axis, the quantity of sausages is shown. The diagram indicates that when the market price of sausage is given as $1 (remember, buyers take this price as given), buyers wish to buy 2000 sausages (Point *A* in Figure 1.1). In other words, the quantity demanded is 2000 when the price of sausage is $1. Now suppose the price has risen to $1.50 (and again buyers must take this new price as given), what will occur to the quantity of sausages buyers would like to buy? You would think it'd go down, yes?

Now that sausages have become more expensive than before, buyers might want to substitute the sausages and buy something else, such as pizzas. Such an effect is called the **substitution effect**. In addition, an increase in the sausage price has effectively made buyers poorer, if other things – prices of other goods and buyers' income levels – are held constant. We say that the buyers' purchasing power has gone down. With lower purchasing power, buyers tend to purchase less sausages.[1] Such an effect is called the **income effect**. Both these effects give rise to a decline in the quantity demanded when the price rises.

---

1 To avoid confusion for readers who have studied introductory economics before, I note that I am assuming that a sausage is a normal good. If you are unfamiliar with this notion, don't worry about this footnote. It is not essential for following the main text.

The diagram captures these effects and shows that the quantity demanded has decreased to 1000 when there is a 50-cent increase in the price (Point *B* in the figure). The demand schedule for sausages can be constructed by going through this exercise for every price, and you will end up obtaining a downward sloping schedule as in Figure 1.1. So an important lesson that we have learnt here is that the demand schedule slopes downwards; this is called the **law of demand**.

By how much does the buyers' demand for sausages change when there is a change in the price? Sausage sellers are interested in the answer to this question because it affects their revenue from selling sausages. When all the sellers decided to raise the price by 50 cents, if the quantity of sausage demanded did *not* change, their revenue would increase. However, as the law of demand suggests, they will not be able to sell as many sausages as before, and hence it is unclear whether the revenue will rise or fall. In Chapter 2 we introduce some basic mathematical concepts, which include functions. An example of a function is the **demand function**, which mathematically represents the demand schedule we have just discussed. The question as to the change in the sellers' revenue is more complex and we will have to put off the investigation until Chapters 4 and 5, where we learn about **differential calculus**. Differential calculus is crucial in conducting economic analysis. As an application of differential calculus, we will introduce **price elasticity of demand**, which is closely related to the sellers' revenue problem we have discussed above.

In fact, what is behind the demand schedule is more complex than you might think. We briefly mentioned in the above discussion how buyers might choose a good over another provided the prices for those goods and their income levels. It is easy to imagine that a change in the price of a sausage will affect the quantity of sausages demanded, but the prices of other goods and income levels are also important determinants of the sausage demand. How does the consumer decides how much of each good to purchase? In Chapter 6, we use this buyers' consumption choice problem as a motivation to learn the mathematical notion called **multivariate calculus**.

1.2.2 Market supply

The **market supply schedule** in Figure 1.2 depicts, for each and every price of a sausage, the quantity sellers in the market are willing to provide (in a particular time, per day for example).

As in the diagram for the demand schedule, we have price on the vertical axis and quantity on the horizontal axis. The diagram indicates that when the market price is $1 (remember, sellers are price takers), they wish to sell 1000 sausages (Point *C* in Figure 1.2). Another way to put it is that the quantity supplied is 1000 when the price of sausage is $1. Now suppose the price rises to $1.50 (and again sellers take this new price as given), what will happen to the quantity of sausages sellers would like to supply, holding other things – such as sellers' sausage production technology, how much it costs to hire a worker, etc. – constant?

When everything else is held constant – in Latin, *ceteris paribus* – an increase in the price of a sausage (by 50 cents in this case) will increase the quantity of sausages supplied in the market. Not only will the existing suppliers want to supply more sausages than before, but some new sellers who did not supply them before might find it worthwhile

Price of a sausage

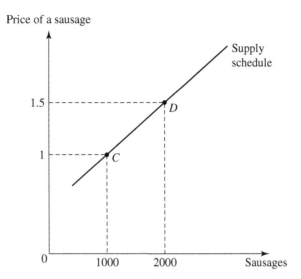

Figure 1.2 The market supply for sausages.

to supply them now that they each sell for $1.50. In the diagram it is shown that the quantity of sausages supplied rises to 2000 when the price increases to $1.50 (Point D in Figure 1.2). The supply schedule of sausages – the upward sloping schedule in Figure 1.2 – can be constructed by obtaining the quantity supplied for all the other prices. The fact that the supply schedule slopes upwards is called the **law of supply**.

As we learned in the beginning, there are many sellers in a competitive market and each of them supplies sausages. It means that the market supply must be the sum of the supply of these individual sellers. In Chapter 4 we will study an individual seller's decision making problem, which is to choose the quantity of supply given the price so as to maximise **profits**. It is called the **profit maximisation** problem and we will learn how to **differentiate** a function in the course of solving this problem. In Chapter 7 we will demonstrate how we can aggregate the individual seller's supply schedules to obtain the market supply schedule.

1.3   Market equilibrium

Now let us put the two schedules together in Figure 1.3.

Both the market demand and supply schedules for sausages are depicted. Remember that each of the buyers is a price taker and so is each of the sellers. The diagram indicates that when the market price of a sausage is given as $1, buyers wish to buy 2000 sausages (Point A in Figure 1.3), but sellers wish to sell 1000 sausages (Point C). The horizontal distance CA (measured in sausages) is 1000 and it means the quantity demanded exceeds the quantity supplied by 1000 sausages if the price is $1. We say that there is an **excess demand** for them. We can also say that there is a **shortage** of sausages. What would you expect to occur when there is excess demand?

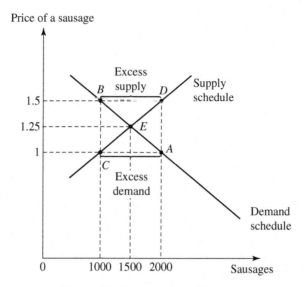

Price of a sausage

Figure 1.3 The market equilibrium.

Well, you'd probably expect the price to rise. But how do we reconcile it with the price taker assumption? The assumption is that *each* seller cannot raise the price because they will lose all their sales given other sellers are not deviating from the current price. Here the trick is to think as follows; we suppose *all* the sellers agree to increase the price by a little bit *at the same time*. When sellers realise that there are desperate buyers who would pay a bit more to buy sausages (rather than missing out on them), they decide to raise the price as a group, which creates an upward pressure on the price. There will be an upward pressure on the price from the buyers' side as well. Namely, the buyers who do not want to miss out on sausages will offer a higher price (if they can), which the sellers have no reason to decline.

Let us see what might occur if the price is $1.50. Now buyers wish to buy 1000 sausages (Point *B*), but sellers wish to sell 2000 sausages (Point *D*). So there is **excess supply**, which is represented by the horizontal distance *BD*. The quantity supplied exceeds the quantity demanded by 1000 sausages if the price is $1.50. This time there will be a downward pressure on price. That is, realising the excess supply, buyers as a group bid down the price, which sellers tend to accept so as to unload the excess supply.

We have looked at the cases where the amount buyers want to buy does not coincide with the amount sellers would like to supply. Now focus on Point *E* in Figure 1.3 where the price of a sausage is $1.25. The demand schedule indicates that buyers wish to buy 1500 whereas the supply schedule shows that sellers would like to provide 1500 to the market. So under this price, the amount buyers want to buy coincides with the amount sellers would like to supply. When this occurs we say that the sausage market **clears** and that the market is in **equilibrium**. It is the situation where (a) each of the buyers and sellers is doing what they want to do; and (b) the quantity demanded equals the quantity supplied, i.e. the market clears. Unlike in the previous cases, buyers and sellers have no reason to change their behaviour under this situation and hence the price and the quantity of sausages traded stay intact. Point E is called the equilibrium point and the corresponding price and quantity are called the **equilibrium price** and the **equilibrium quantity**, respectively.

What do you think might occur to the equilibrium price and quantity if the government decides to collect a certain amount of a tax from the sellers per sausage sold? It seems that sellers will suffer from this arrangement, but what about the sausage buyers? Will there be any effect on them? It turns out that the buyers also tend to suffer from the tax, despite the fact it is the sellers who pay the tax legally. To study the effect of the taxation, we typically rely on the ideas of **consumer surplus** and **producer surplus**, which measure the welfare of buyers and sellers, respectively, in dollars. To obtain these measures we need to study how to obtain the area under the demand and supply schedules. We will study the mathematical technique that allows us to do it – **integral calculus** – in Chapter 7.

1.4 Rest of this book

As foreshadowed above, the main economic applications that involve the use of calculus will be covered in Chapters 4–7. However, it does not mean the next two chapters are unimportant. Chapter 2 recaps some basic ideas in mathematics – numbers, equations, functions, logic, etc. – and demand and supply analysis will be conducted in a more mathematical fashion. In Chapter 3, some more ideas of basic mathematics – most notably, the exponential function and the logarithmic function – will be studied in the context of introductory finance. These chapters are completely free from the use of calculus and will hopefully consolidate your mathematical background before you delve into the main economic applications that utilise calculus in Chapters 4–7.

2 Basic mathematics

This chapter deals with some fundamental mathematical rules and ideas we will use in the rest of the book. It is very important that you become comfortable with them. Going through the basic material may be a tedious experience for you, but much of the confusion in studying mathematics that I know appears to stem simply from a lack of appreciation of these mathematical conventions (if so, what a pity...), so I will spend some time on them.[1]

To become a good user of a foreign language, we need to know some grammar as well as a bit of slang of that language. Sometimes one gets lost completely during conversations because of the use of slang. For example, if I received a letter saying, 'There is a BBQ party; BYO', I would bring my own drink since I know what BYO means. However, some of you whose native language is not English may have to consult with their dictionaries in order to figure out what BYO means.

Learning mathematics has a similar flavour. You will need to know the basic rules as well as some advanced techniques that stand on them. As you don't expect you can master a foreign language overnight, you also should not expect that you can master mathematics overnight. You will need to work hard in order to learn mathematics. The reward from it, though, should be fairly large. If you have studied a foreign language and have been able to communicate with people – who you otherwise wouldn't have been able to – using it, you know how fun and exciting it is.

OK then, put your head down and let's go through the material together. If you have a sound knowledge of high-school mathematics, you may be able to skip the basic material and jump to Section 2.10 where we see how mathematics can be applied to conduct the demand and supply analysis.

Chapter goals By studying this chapter you will

(1) recap basic ideas in mathematics that will be used in the rest of the book;
(2) be able to conduct demand and supply analysis (with mathematics);
(3) be able to carry out comparative static analysis and interpret its results; and
(4) be able to interpret implication statements, and explain the difference between necessary and sufficient conditions.

---

[1] In writing this section, I have drawn a lot of material from M. Timbrell, *Mathematics for Economists* (Basil Blackwell, 1985). I have also benefited a lot from R. G. Bartle and D. R. Sherbert, *Introduction to Real Analysis* (Wiley, 1999).

2.1 Numbers

To begin with, I will discuss numbers. The numbers we use to count things, i.e. $1, 2, 3, \ldots$ are called **natural numbers** (or **positive integers**). If we sum two natural numbers, we have another natural number (say, $5 + 8 = 13$). However, if we subtract one natural number from a smaller one (say, $5 - 8$), we end up with a negative of a natural number ($5 - 8 = -3$). The negative of natural numbers, that is, $-1, -2, -3 \ldots$ are called **negative natural numbers** (or **negative integers**). The set of these two types of numbers and *zero* are called **integers**.

Now, what occurs if we multiply an integer by another? We obtain an integer. For example, $5 \cdot 8 = 40$ or $3 \cdot (-7) = -21$. Note that $\cdot$ in between two numbers implies a multiplication symbol $\times$, i.e. $5 \cdot 8 = 5 \times 8 = 40$. Sometimes we even omit '$\cdot$' if it is not confusing. For instance, if we multiply two numbers x and y, we can write the product as $x \times y$, $x \cdot y$ or xy. Of course, you should avoid writing 58 to represent $5 \cdot 8$ because people will no doubt interpret it as 'fifty-eight'.

In any event, let's turn to division. If we divide an integer by another (with one exception, which we will see shortly), we obtain a different type of number called **fraction**. For instance, $3 \div 2 = \dfrac{3}{2}$. The set of fractions and integers is called **rational numbers**. We will introduce other types of numbers in due course.

2.1.1 We cannot divide a number by zero!

Suppose you have \$120 in your pocket and are thinking about going to a rugby game in the local stadium. Tickets cost \$12 per person. How many friends can you invite? Well, 120 divided by 12 gives 10, so you can invite 9 people (10, if you are not going with them). OK, but what if tickets cost \$0? How can we divide 120 by 0? Obviously there is no sensible number for this question, because you can choose any number of people to take (so long as the stadium does not collapse because of overcrowding!). Mathematics disallows imprecision as such by simply excluding the idea of dividing a number by zero. Consider an expression $x \div (y - z)$. This expression is completely fine so long as $y \neq z$. If $y = z$, then it becomes $x \div 0$, which is not allowed.

2.1.2 Reciprocal

Consider a number x. So long as $x \neq 0$ we can divide 1 by x to create a new number $\dfrac{1}{x}$. It is called the **reciprocal** of x. You can see that $x \cdot \dfrac{1}{x} = 1$, which says that the product of a number and its reciprocal is unity.

2.2 Fractions, decimal numbers and the use of a calculator

We have seen that all the rational numbers can be represented as the ratio of two integers, but they can be represented in many different ways. For example:

$$\frac{3}{10} = \frac{30}{100},$$

$$\frac{5}{16} = \frac{3125}{10\,000}.$$

However, they can also be written as:

$$\frac{3}{10} = 0.3,$$

$$\frac{5}{16} = 0.3125.$$

These numbers, 0.3 or 0.3125, are called **decimal numbers**. The advantage of using decimal numbers is that we can compare numbers very easily. It is obvious that $\frac{3}{10}$ is smaller than $\frac{5}{16}$, once we see that the former is 0.3 and the latter is 0.3125. However, it is not really an advantage. We can always find any common denominator of the two numbers and compare their numerators. In the above example, if we use 10 000 as the denominator, the numerator for $\frac{3}{10}$ is 3000, which is smaller than 3125, so we can reach the same conclusion rather easily.

In contrast, the downside of using decimal numbers is quite notable, which I'd like to emphasise. It is important to appreciate that many fractions actually do not have a nice and short decimal number representation. For example:

$$\frac{1}{3} = 0.333\,33\ldots$$

You can see that 3 is repeating infinitely. This number can be represented as $0.\dot{3}$, meaning that 3 is repeating. The representation is actually nice and short, but that is not the point here, as you will see as you read through the rest of the section. This kind of number is called an **infinite decimal**, whereas numbers such as 0.3 and 0.3125 are called finite decimals.

A rational number is either a finite decimal or an infinite decimal that repeats. There are some infinite decimal numbers that do not repeat. They cannot be represented by any fraction of two integers and are called **irrational numbers**. Examples of irrational numbers include: π, $\sqrt{2}$, $\sqrt{3}$, etc. It will be proven in Section 2.12 that $\sqrt{2}$ is an irrational number.

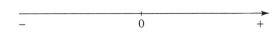

Figure 2.1 The real line.

The problem of using decimal numbers may be serious when it comes to operating a calculator. I will go through an easy exercise to illustrate the point. It will tell us that we need to be careful in using a calculator.

Question   Calculate $39 \times \dfrac{1}{18} \times \dfrac{1}{13}$.

Solution A (using fractions)

$$39 \times \frac{1}{18} \times \frac{1}{13} = \frac{39}{18 \times 13} = \frac{3}{18} = \frac{1}{6}.$$

Solution B (using decimals)

$$39 \times 0.055\,55\ldots \times 0.0769\ldots$$
$$= 39 \times 0.06 \times 0.08$$
$$= 0.1872.$$

Exercise 2.1   A pitfall of using decimal numbers in calculation.

Now, $\dfrac{1}{6} = 0.1666\ldots$ and so you can see that the two methods yield different numbers. Because the infinite decimals $0.055\,55\ldots$ and $0.0769\ldots$ were rounded to two decimal points, Solution B involves a **rounding error**. The error can be trivial or significant depending on the context of the question of the focus, and a small discussion on this matter is provided in the Preface of this book. To avoid the imprecision and, more importantly, to become good with dealing with numbers, I encourage that you restrain yourselves from using a calculator.

Let's get back to the main issue. The numbers we have discussed so far are called the **real numbers**. The real numbers are either rational or irrational numbers. Rational numbers include integers because any integer divided by one is that integer and is represented as a fraction (e.g. $5 = \dfrac{5}{1}$). If we take zero at the centre, and measure positive real numbers as the distance to the right and negative real numbers as the distance to the left, then we can arrange all the real numbers on what we call the **real line**, as shown in Figure 2.1.

2.3   Some algebraic properties of real numbers

Numbers obey certain rules in mathematics as words do in language. There are some basic rules concerning operations of addition (denoted by $+$) and multiplication (denoted by

$\times$ or $\cdot$) of real numbers.[2] I'm sure that you have seen them in school at some stage, but let me just give you a list of them to remind you. In the following, let x, y and z be real numbers.

(1) **Closure** $x + y$ and $x \cdot y$ are also real numbers.

(2) **Communicative**

$$x + y = y + x,$$
$$x \cdot y = y \cdot x.$$

(3) **Associative**

$$(x + y) + z = x + (y + z),$$
$$(x \cdot y) \cdot z = x \cdot (y \cdot z).$$

(4) **Identity**   0 is a real number such that $x + 0 = x$ for all the real numbers x. 1 is a real number such that $x \cdot 1 = x$ for all the real numbers x.

(5) **Inverse**   For any real number x, there is a real number y such that $x + y = 0$, where we write such y as $-x$. For any non-zero real number x, there is a real number z such that $x \cdot z = 1$ where we write such z as $\dfrac{1}{x}$ (and you should realise that this is the reciprocal explained earlier).

(6) **Distributive**

$$x \cdot (y + z) = xy + xz,$$
$$x \cdot (y - z) = xy - xz.$$

A quick remark for readers who have not studied mathematics for a long time. Recall that operations inside brackets have to be conducted first. If there are no operations in brackets, multiplications have to be conducted before additive operations.

2.4   Equalities, inequalities and intervals

Once we have established the real line, we can compare a real number with another one. If a number x lies to the right (left) of a number y, then we say that x is greater (smaller, respectively) than y, and express the relation as $x > y$ ($x < y$, respectively). In contrast to these **inequalities**, if numbers x and z lie at exactly the same position, we say that x is **equal** to z, and we express the relation as $x = z$.

By combining these inequalities and equalities, we can describe **intervals**. For example, $0 < x < 1$ implies that x can take any values between 0 and 1, not including either 0 or 1. The expression $x \in (0, 1)$ carries the same information. The interval where neither of the end points is included is called an **open interval**. If both of the end points are included, then the interval is called a **closed interval**. For example, $0 \leq x \leq 1$ implies that x can take

---

2 Note that subtraction (denoted by $-$) and division (denoted by $\div$) are their inverse operations, respectively.

any values between 0 and 1, including both 0 and 1; $x \in [0, 1]$ is an alternative expression for this interval (notice the difference in the type of brackets used). If $0 \leq x < 1$, then it implies that x can take any values between 0 and 1, including 0 but not including 1. This is sometimes written as $x \in [0, 1)$, and is called a **half-open interval**. Intervals that contain ∞ are called **infinite intervals**. For example, to represent all the non-negative real numbers, we can write $0 \leq x < \infty$ or $x \in [0, \infty)$. The set of all the real numbers can be written as $-\infty < x < \infty$ or $x \in (-\infty, \infty)$.

2.4.1 Absolute values

Now, it follows from the definitions of inequalities that $-100 < 1$ (it seems rather obvious, but try explaining why it is so). However, if we were to measure the distance from the centre of the real line, zero, clearly -100 is further away from zero than 1 is. In other words, if we ignore the minus sign, -100 has a greater magnitude than 1 does. We use an **absolute value** to show the magnitude of a number a, which is written as $|a|$. In the above example, $|-100| > |1|$. The interval $-2 < a < 2$ can be expressed using the absolute value as $|a| < 2$.

2.5 Powers

You will encounter the **power** of numbers in mathematics everywhere. Let us begin with the definition of a power. If we multiply a number q by the same number, the expression will be $q \times q$. Another way of expressing it is q^2, where the superscript 2 is a power showing that two qs are to be multiplied together. In a sense, the power expression is like slang in a language; expressing the same thing in a different way. Just like you need to know slang to be an expert in a particular language, you need to know the power expression if you want to communicate well with others using mathematics.

In any case, let us go through the following process to see if we can learn something about the power expression. We know that multiplying a number by unity yield that number itself, so let us express q^2 as "a 1 multiplied by q twice,"

$$q^2 \equiv 1 \times q \times q.$$

By the same token, we can define q to various powers:

$$q^3 \equiv 1 \times q \times q \times q,$$
$$q^1 \equiv 1 \times q,$$
$$q^0 \equiv 1.$$

Two things are worth noting. First, q is actually q^1 but the superscript 1 is omitted for simplicity. Second, whatever the value q takes, we find that $q^0 = 1$.

We can extend this analysis to division and find out what negative powers look like. Namely, for non-zero q:

$$q^{-1} \equiv 1 \div q = \frac{1}{q},$$
$$q^{-2} \equiv 1 \div q \div q = \frac{1}{q^2},$$

and so,

$$q^{-m} = \frac{1}{q^m}.$$

Now we know that q^{-m} is a reciprocal of q^m.

2.5.1   The basic power rule

There is only one basic power rule you need to remember because other rules follow this one. The important rule is:

$$q^m \cdot q^n = q^{m+n}. \tag{2.1}$$

Question   Simplify $q^4 \cdot q^3$.

Solution

$$\begin{aligned}
q^4 \cdot q^3 &= (q \cdot q \cdot q \cdot q) \cdot (q \cdot q \cdot q) \\
&= q \cdot q \cdot q \cdot q \cdot q \cdot q \cdot q \\
&= q^{4+3} \\
&= q^7.
\end{aligned}$$

Exercise 2.2   Applying the power rule (2.1).

Now, using rule (2.1) we can deduce the following:

$$q^m \cdot q^{-n} = q^{m+(-n)} = q^{m-n}.$$

Note that $q^{-n} = \frac{1}{q^n}$. Together, we have the following:

$$q^m \div q^n = \frac{q^m}{q^n} = q^{m-n}. \tag{2.2}$$

Question   Simplify $q^6 \div q^3$.

Solution

$$\begin{aligned}
q^6 \div q^3 &= \frac{q^6}{q^3} \\
&= \frac{q \cdot q \cdot q \cdot q \cdot q \cdot q}{q \cdot q \cdot q} \\
&= q^{6-3} \\
&= q^3.
\end{aligned}$$

Exercise 2.3   Applying the power rule (2.2).

Suppose now that $y = q^4$. What is y^3 in terms of q? This can be solved by directly applying the definition of the power:

$$y^3 = \left(q^4\right)^3 = q^4 \cdot q^4 \cdot q^4 = q^{4+4+4} = q^{4\times3} = q^{12}.$$

In general, we have:

$$\left(q^m\right)^n = q^{mn}. \tag{2.3}$$

2.5.2   Non-integer powers, particularly $\dfrac{1}{2}$

Up to this point, m and n were implicitly treated as integers and hence numbers were raised to some integers. But numbers need not be raised to integers only and the power rules can be applied for non-integers as well. To delve into this issue, let us look at the following statement: $q^n = y$. It follows from rule (2.3) that:

$$q^n = y^{\frac{1}{n}\times n} = \left(y^{\frac{1}{n}}\right)^n,$$

and hence:

$$q = y^{\frac{1}{n}} \equiv \sqrt[n]{y}.$$

The above identity says that 'q is the nth root of y'.

There are two special (or frequently used) ns. When $n = 2$, we say 'q is the **square root** of y'. It follows from the convention that q^2 is called q-squared. As you may know, we can simply write it as $q = \sqrt{y}$ (instead of $\sqrt[2]{y}$). In turn, when $n = 3$, we say 'q is the **cube** (or **cubic**) **root** of y'. It again follows from the convention that q^3 is called q-cubed.

Two remarks should be made regarding this introduction of non-integer powers. First, the number defined by a statement may *not* be *unique*. For example, 9 can be written as $9 = 3 \times 3 = 3^2$ as well as $9 = (-3) \times (-3) = (-3)^2$. So the statement $q^2 = 9$ can mean either $q = 3$ or $q = -3$. In general, we write it as $q = \pm3$. Second, if we consider a statement such as $q^2 = -16$, we realise that there exists no 'real' number q that satisfies the statement. Mathematicians get away with this problem by 'imagining' that such numbers exist, and we introduce these **imaginary numbers** in the next section. But before that, let me discuss a little about some conventions regarding the square root.

2.5.3   Some conventions on the square root

There are two conventions concerning the square root that I want you to follow. Using a language metaphor, I would say that your mathematics will become more fluent by following these conventions.

The first convention is the following. When we end up with an expression with a square root of 'a number multiplied by a squared number', simplify the expression so that the number inside the squared root cannot be expressed as 'a number multiplied by a squared number'. For example, do not leave the expression $\sqrt{4}$ as it is. It be expressed as $\sqrt{2^2}$ and hence can be simplified to 2. A little more complicated example is $\sqrt{120}$. You should not leave it as it is. This number can be (and should be) simplified to $2\sqrt{30}$.

The second convention is relevant when you end up with a fraction and the denominator includes a square root. If it occurs, do not leave the square root on the denominator. It is considered fine (or fluent, if you like) to have squared roots on the numerator, but not on the denominator. For example, when you end up with $\dfrac{1}{\sqrt{2}}$, then do not leave it. Multiplying both the numerator and the denominator by the same number will not change the value of the expression, so let us use $\sqrt{2}$ and see what occurs. The expression has now become $\dfrac{\sqrt{2}}{2}$ or $\dfrac{1}{2}\sqrt{2}$. You can easily see from this expression that it is 'a half of $\sqrt{2}$', where it is hard to observe something meaningful from the expression $\dfrac{1}{\sqrt{2}}$, which contains a square root on the denominator. The expressions $\dfrac{1}{\sqrt{2}}$ and $\dfrac{\sqrt{2}}{2}$ are value-wise identical, but in order to facilitate communication, we tend to use a more intuitively appealing expression. Since we convert an irrational number on the denominator ($\sqrt{2}$) into a rational number (2), we call this procedure **rationalisation of the denominator**.

2.6 An imaginary number and complex numbers

Suppose (or imagine) that there exists a number called i such that $i^2 = -1$. Such a number i is called an **imaginary number**. Then it follows:

$$(iy)^2 = i^2 y^2 = -y^2.$$

Hence,

$$(\pm 4i)^2 = -16.$$

We have obtained the answer for the question $q^2 = -16$: the answer is $q = \pm 4i$.

We use a combination of real and imaginary numbers, such as $a + bi, d - ci, \dfrac{q - 3i}{4i - 7}$.[3] Such numbers are called **complex numbers**. We will not deal with these numbers in *introductory* economics or finance (obviously they do not make any economic/financial sense on the surface), but nevertheless, it is useful to have the knowledge of where these numbers come from.

2.7 Factorisation: reducing polynomial expressions

We call an expression involving the addition of terms, each having a variable with an unspecified value raised to a different power, a **polynomial expression**. A variable with an unspecified value is called an **unknown**. The process of reducing polynomials to a

---

3 The last expression includes the imaginary number on the denominator. As we avoid having irrational numbers on the denominator, we also avoid having imaginary numbers on the denominator. In this case, by multiplying both the numerator and the denominator by $4i + 7$ we can change the expression to $\dfrac{(3i - q)(4i + 7)}{65}$. It is most unlikely that you will encounter this kind of expression in this book, and hence I will not delve into it any further.

2.7 Factorisation: reducing polynomial expressions

product of two (or simpler) expressions, or **factors**, is called **factorisation**. For example, consider the expression $3x - 6$, where x is the unknown. The expression can be reduced to $3(x - 2)$. Both 3 and $x - 2$ are factors of $3x - 6$. In general, $ax + ab = a(x + b)$, where in the example $a = 3$ and $b = -2$.

There are some well-known rules for factorising polynomials when the highest power the unknown is raised to is two. I list them in the following.

Rule 1 $cdx^2 + (ad + bc)x + ab = (cx + a)(dx + b)$.

Rule 2 $x^2 + (a + b)x + ab = (x + a)(x + b)$.

Rule 3 $x^2 + 2ax + a^2 = (x + a)^2$.

Rule 4 $x^2 - 2ax + a^2 = (x - a)^2$.

Rule 5 $x^2 - a^2 = (x + a)(x - a)$.

Note that if you set $c = 1$ and $d = 1$ in Rule 1, you can obtain Rule 2. You can obtain Rules 3–5 as special cases of Rule 2.

When the highest power is three, things become a little more complicated. Let us think about the following polynomial expression:

$$2x^3 - x^2 - 2x + 1 = (x - 1)(2x - 1)(x + 1).$$

There is virtually only one tip you need to know in conducting this factorisation. That is the following.

> If you observe a particular number, say x^*, that reduces the expression to zero (i.e. the expression becomes zero if you plug in x^* to x), then you know that one of the factors must be $(x - x^*)$.

In the above expression, for example, if we plug in $x^* = 1$ to x, then the expression reduces to zero: $2(1)^3 - (1)^2 - 2(1) + 1 = 2 - 1 - 2 + 1 = 0$. Therefore, $(x - 1)$ is one of the factors of $2x^3 - x^2 - 2x + 1$ as you can see.

Knowing the tip I have given above, however, is not enough. We know $(x - 1)$ is one of the factors of $2x^3 - x^2 - 2x + 1$, but how can we verify that $2x^3 - x^2 - 2x + 1$ can be factorised as $(x - 1)(2x - 1)(x + 1)$? Once you find out one of the x^*s, you need to carry out the rest of the factorisation. I demonstrate how it can be done in the following.

Question A Factorise $2x^3 - x^2 - 2x + 1$.

Solution We already know that one of the factors is $x - 1$ so it must be true that:

$$2x^3 - x^2 - 2x + 1 = (x - 1)(\text{some polynomial expression}).$$

What is 'some polynomial expression' in the above brackets? We know that the highest power x is raised to in that expression is 2, because the product of it and $x - 1$ must be $2x^3 - x^2 - 2x + 1$, which contains an x^3 term. Hence let us denote that polynomial expression as $ax^2 + bx + c$:

$$2x^3 - x^2 - 2x + 1 = (x - 1)(ax^2 + bx + c).$$

If we expand the right hand side (RHS) of this equation, we have:

$$(x - 1)(ax^2 + bx + c) = ax^3 + (b - a)x^2 + (c - b)x - c.$$

Now compare $ax^3 + (b - a)x^2 + (c - b)x - c$ with $2x^3 - x^2 - 2x + 1$, which need to be equal. For them to be equal, it is obvious that $a = 2$ and $c = -1$. It follows that $b = 1$. Therefore, we have obtained the polynomial expression we are looking for. It turns out to be $2x^2 + x - 1$:

$$2x^3 - x^2 - 2x + 1 = (x - 1)(2x^2 + x - 1).$$

However, we have not finished yet because $2x^2 + x - 1$ can be further factorised as $(2x - 1)(x + 1)$. So, in the end, we get:

$$2x^3 - x^2 - 2x + 1 = (x - 1)(2x - 1)(x + 1).$$

Question B   Factorise $2x^3 - 5x^2 + 4x - 1$.

Solution   One of the factors is $x - 1$ because $x = 1$ reduces the above expression to zero. So it must be true that:

$$2x^3 - 5x^2 + 4x - 1 = (x - 1)(ax^2 + bx + c).$$

If we expand the right hand side (RHS) of this equation, we have:

$$(x - 1)(ax^2 + bx + c) = ax^3 + (b - a)x^2 + (c - b)x - c.$$

By looking at $ax^3 + (b - a)x^2 + (c - b)x - c$ and $2x^3 - 5x^2 + 4x - 1$, we can deduce that $a = 2$, $c = 1$, and $b = -3$. Accordingly, we have:

$$2x^3 - x^2 - 2x + 1 = (x - 1)(2x^2 - 3x + 1).$$

Together with the fact that $2x^2 - 3x + 1 = (2x - 1)(x - 1)$ we get:

$$2x^3 - x^2 - 2x + 1 = (x - 1)^2(2x - 1).$$

Exercise 2.4   Factorisation.

Now that you know how to factorise, you can simplify many seemingly complicated expressions, such as $\dfrac{2x^3 - 5x^2 + 4x - 1}{2x^3 - x^2 - 2x + 1}$.

$$\frac{2x^3 - 5x^2 + 4x - 1}{2x^3 - x^2 - 2x + 1} = \frac{(x - 1)^2(2x - 1)}{(x - 1)(2x - 1)(x + 1)}$$

$$= \frac{x - 1}{x + 1}.$$

2.8 Equations

An equality in which one or more unknowns appear is called an **equation**. We are interested in solving an equation, which is assigning to the unknown(s) a value (or a set of values) that satisfies the equality. For example, $x = \dfrac{1}{2}$ is the simplest form of equations, but the solution is so obvious (and hence it is not different from a mere statement). However, $2x - 1 = 0$ is an alternative representation of that statement, and it is represented in the form of what we call a **linear equation**.

2.8.1 A linear equation

We can solve an equation by applying the same operations on the both sides of equality, because the relationship between the two sides will not be affected by such operations.

$$ax + b = 0, \tag{2.4}$$

where $a \neq 0$. Equation (2.4) is called the linear equation (because the highest power of x is raised to is one). It is quite obvious that the solution to this equation is $x = -\dfrac{b}{a}$. So, if $2x - 1 = 0$, then $x = \dfrac{1}{2}$.

2.8.2 Higher order equations; in particular, a quadratic equation

Equations in which the highest power x is raised to is greater than 1, are called higher order equations. If the highest power x is raised to is two, it is called a **quadratic equation**. If the highest power x is raised to is three, then we call it a **cubic equation**. If the highest power x is raised to is four, that equation is called a **quartic equation** (but you will hardly see that in this book).

All these equations can be solved quite simply if they can be factorised. For example, in Section 2.7, we showed the following factorisation:

$$2x^3 - x^2 - 2x + 1 = (x + 1)(x - 1)(2x - 1).$$

Hence if we have an equation $2x^3 - x^2 - 2x + 1 = 0$, we can factorise the left hand side (LHS) of the equation, and it becomes:

$$(x + 1)(x - 1)(2x - 1) = 0.$$

The LHS is equal to zero if $x + 1 = 0$, $x - 1 = 0$ or $2x - 1 = 0$. Hence the xs that solve the equation are $x = -1$, $x = 1$ and $x = \dfrac{1}{2}$.[4]

However, solving an equation will not be that easy all the time. Factorisation is not always possible and, even if it is, sometimes it is very difficult to find factors by the method we have discussed. Here we will discuss some techniques for solving the quadratic equation and will introduce a simple rule.[5] We start with the general form of the quadratic

----

4 You should now be able to see the reason why we could conclude that $(x - x^*)$ is one of the factors of an expression if x^* reduces the value of it to zero.

5 For higher order equations other than the quadratic equation, there are no generally applicable rules except for factorisation. When solutions cannot be found by hand, we can resort to numerical simulations.

equation:

$$ax^2 + bx + c = 0, \tag{2.5}$$

where $a \neq 0$. By conducting some basic operations, we can rearrange it as follows:

$$ax^2 + bx + c = 0$$

$$x^2 + \frac{b}{a}x + \frac{c}{a} = 0$$

$$\underbrace{x^2 + \frac{b}{a}x + \frac{b^2}{4a^2}}_{\text{1st term}} + \underbrace{\frac{c}{a} - \frac{b^2}{4a^2}}_{\text{2nd term}} = 0$$

$$\underbrace{\left(x + \frac{b}{2a}\right)^2}_{\text{1st term}} = \underbrace{\frac{b^2 - 4ac}{4a^2}}_{-\text{2nd term}}.$$

This procedure is called **completing the square**. On the third line of the above procedure, note that $\frac{b^2}{4a^2}$ is added to the LHS of the equation to complete the square of $\left(x + \frac{b}{2a}\right)$. Of course, to retain the equality, note also that $\frac{b^2}{4a^2}$ is subtracted from the LHS at the same time. In any event, once we complete the square, we can solve the equation:

$$\left(x + \frac{b}{2a}\right) = \pm\frac{\sqrt{b^2 - 4ac}}{2a}$$

$$x = \frac{-b \pm \sqrt{b^2 - 4ac}}{2a}.$$

Hence $x = \dfrac{-b \pm \sqrt{b^2 - 4ac}}{2a}$ represents the solutions of any quadratic equation. One thing to note here: there are two possible values for x, one when a positive root is used in the above calculation, and the other when a negative root is used. One exception is where $b^2 - 4ac = 0$. In that case, the expression inside the square root is zero, and so x collapses to $x = -\dfrac{b}{2a}$. The value of the two solutions is identical in this case.

The solutions of the quadratic equation are often referred to as roots of the equation. When $b^2 - 4ac = 0$, we say that the equation has repeated roots. When $b^2 - 4ac > 0$, we say that the equation has two (distinct) real roots. I will give you some examples.

Question A Solve the following equation: $x^2 - 2x + 1 = 0$.

Solution

$$x^2 - 2x + 1 = 0$$
$$(x - 1)^2 = 0$$

$$x = \frac{-(-2) \pm \sqrt{(-2)^2 - 4 \cdot 1 \cdot 1}}{2}$$

$$= \frac{2 \pm \sqrt{0}}{2}.$$

Either way we get $x = 1$.

Question B Solve the following equation: $x^2 - 2x - 6 = 0$.

Solution

$$x = \frac{-(-2) \pm \sqrt{(-2)^2 - 4 \cdot 1 \cdot (-6)}}{2}$$

$$= \frac{2 \pm \sqrt{4 + 24}}{2}$$

$$= \frac{2 \pm \sqrt{28}}{2}$$

$$= \frac{2 \pm 2\sqrt{7}}{2}.$$

Therefore $x = 1 \pm \sqrt{7}$.

Exercise 2.5 Solving quadratic equations.

But what if $b^2 - 4ac < 0$? Then, the value inside the square root is a negative number, and we know that we cannot take the square root of a negative number unless we use complex numbers (remember that $i^2 = -1$). So the solution to this type of quadratic equation involves the imaginary i, and we say that the equation has two complex roots. Basically, when you find a negative number inside the square root, by definition of the imaginary i, we can make the inside positive and put the i after the square root. The following example should illustrate the point.

Question Solve the following equation: $x^2 - 2x + 8 = 0$.

Solution

$$x = \frac{-(-2) \pm \sqrt{(-2)^2 - 4 \cdot 1 \cdot 8}}{2}$$

$$= \frac{2 \pm \sqrt{4 - 32}}{2}$$

$$= \frac{2 \pm \sqrt{-28}}{2}$$

$$= \frac{2 \pm \sqrt{28}i}{2}$$

$$= \frac{2 \pm 2\sqrt{7}i}{2}.$$

Therefore $x = 1 \pm \sqrt{7}i$.

Exercise 2.6 Solving a quadratic equation that has two complex roots.

The above three examples are related to the quadratic functions we will see in the next section.

2.9 Functions

A variable y is said to be a **function** of another variable x if there is a *rule* that associates with each possible value of x *exactly one* value y. For example, we can express the rule that has to hold regarding the temperature in Centigrade (x) and the temperature in Fahrenheit (y) as the following:

$$y = \frac{9}{5}x + 32. \tag{2.6}$$

Here the temperature in Fahrenheit (y) is a function of the temperature in Centigrade (x). It has to be emphasised that functions are defined for particular values of x. For this example, the function is only true for $x > -273$ (because it is absolute zero, and a temperature below that is not possible, as far as our knowledge is concerned). The set of values that x can take is called the **domain**, and is an important part of the definition of a function.[6] If the domain is not specified, it generally means that x can be any real numbers.

The corresponding set of values of y, when the domain is given, is called the **range**. In the above temperature example, the range is $y > -459.4$.

As it was mentioned previously, we cannot divide any number by zero. Hence in defining a function such as $y = \frac{1}{x}$, we need to be careful about specifying the domain. This function is not defined when $x = 0$, so we should define it as:

$$y = \frac{1}{x}, \ x \neq 0.$$

2.9.1 Implicit and inverse functions

In Equation (2.6), we defined the temperature in Fahrenheit (y) as a function of the temperature in Centigrade (x), but we can do it the other way round as well. Namely, by multiplying the both sides of Equation (2.6) by $\frac{5}{9}$ and rearranging it, we obtain:

$$x = \frac{5}{9}(y - 32), \ y > -459.4. \tag{2.7}$$

If we denote Equation (2.6) by the mathematical statement $y = f(x)$ (meaning that y is a function of x), then Equation (2.7) can be written by the **inverse function**, $x = f^{-1}(y)$. Note that f refers to the functional relationship between the argument x and the value of

---

6 In mathematics, the term **set** is used to describe any collection of distinct items, which are called **elements**. For example, the '(French) suits of playing cards' is a set that consists of four elements: spades, hearts, diamonds and clubs. It is an example of a **finite set** whose number of elements is finite (four in this example). On the other hand, the set of x that satisfies $x > -273$ contains an infinite number of elements. Such a set is called an **infinite set**.

the function y, and f^{-1} refers to the reverse procedure necessary to return us to the value of x. It is different from y^{-1}, which simply means a reciprocal of y, $\frac{1}{y}$.

It is worth noting that an inverse function does *not* always exist. Even when it does, finding it may be difficult. In our temperature example, it exists and was easy to find.

Equations (2.6) and (2.7) can also be written as the following:

$$5y - 9x - 160 = 0. \tag{2.8}$$

It is not explicitly stated which variable is a function of the other, although it is implicit in Equation (2.8). For this reason, this function is called an **implicit function**.

2.9.2   A little note on functional notation

You should become familiar with functional notation. In the previous subsection, I used the mathematical statement $y = f(x)$ to imply that y is a function of x; in which case, $f(x)$ is the function per se, and y is the value it takes for a given value of x. Sometimes we need to consider many different functions. To distinguish one function from another, we use different letters (symbols), for instance, $C = g(Y)$, $A = \phi(t)$, $h = h(K)$. Note that in the last one, h is used for both the function itself and the value it takes for a given value of K. It may be confusing, but we sometimes do it to economise the use of letters and symbols.

When we consider the value taken by the function, say $y = f(x)$, when x takes a particular value a, we specify that value function takes as $f(x = a)$, or more simply, $f(a)$. We shall attempt the following exercise to become familiar with functional notation.

Question Suppose $f(x) = (2x - 1)^3$. Express $f(0)$, $f(1)$, $f\left(a + \frac{1}{2}\right)$, and $f\left(-a + \frac{1}{2}\right)$. Show that $f(0) \cdot f\left(-a + \frac{1}{2}\right) = f(1) \cdot f\left(a + \frac{1}{2}\right)$.

Solution

$$f(0) = (0 - 1)^3 = -1$$

$$f(1) = (2 - 1)^3 = 1$$

$$f\left(a + \frac{1}{2}\right) = (2a + 1 - 1)^3 = 8a^3$$

$$f\left(-a + \frac{1}{2}\right) = (-2a + 1 - 1)^3 = -8a^3$$

$$f(0) \cdot f\left(-a + \frac{1}{2}\right) = (-1) \cdot (-8a^3) = 8a^3,$$

$$f(1) \cdot f\left(a + \frac{1}{2}\right) = 1 \cdot 8a^3 = 8a^3.$$

Exercise 2.7   Functional notation.

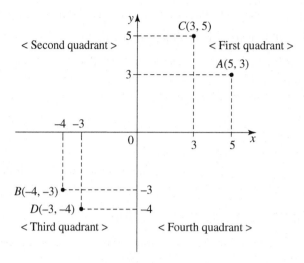

Figure 2.2 The coordinate plane.

The last part of the solution to this exercise warrants a bit of explanation. You can show that two expressions are equal (or not) in two ways. One is to calculate each expression separately (as in the solution above) and check if the two expressions are identical. The other is to calculate the difference between one expression and the other. If the difference is zero, then you have shown that the two expressions are equal (otherwise you have shown that they are not equal). Never start your solution by writing down the equality of the two expressions, i.e. assuming that they are equal. If you assume something that you want to show, then your answer is destined to be tautological.

2.9.3 Coordinate plane

Much of economic analysis relies on the use of diagrams on which various schedules, such as demand and supply schedules, are drawn. In the following subsections (and in Chapter 3), we will introduce various types of function and describe them on diagrams. As a preparation, we will first establish the coordinate plane and related ideas.

Recall the real line we discussed previously. If we place another real line on top of it and pivot one of them anti-clockwise around zero, then we have two real lines intersecting perpendicularly at the zeros as in Figure 2.2. The plane made by these two lines (just imagine placing a piece of paper on the two lines) is called the **coordinate plane**. The horizontal line is called the **horizontal axis** and the other one is called the **vertical axis**. The intersection of the two axes is called the **origin**.

Let us think of the case where x is taken on the horizontal axis and y is taken on the vertical axis. When you draw the coordinate plane, it is important that you write down what you take on the two axes. Otherwise people who see it have no idea what you are trying to explain. Once you take the variables on the two axes, though, we can make the full use of the convenient feature of the coordinate plane, i.e. we can represent all points that lie on it. Take Point A in Figure 2.2 as an example. The question you ask is 'what are the horizontal and the vertical distances to that point from the origin?'. The horizontal distance is 5 and it is to the positive direction of x, and the vertical distance is 3, which is again to the positive direction of y. So we can describe that point as (5, 3) or $A(5, 3)$. The horizontal distance comes *first* in the brackets and the vertical distance enters *second*.

What about B? The horizontal distance from the origin is 4 to the *negative* direction of x, and the vertical distance is 3 to the *negative* direction of y. Hence Point B is described as $(-4, -3)$. All the points that lie on the plane can be described, like these examples, by the **coordinates** or the **ordered pair**. It is called the *ordered* pair because the order is important (*first* and *second* are italicised for that reason). Points C and D on Figure 2.2 correspond to the ordered pairs (3, 5) and $(-3, -4)$, respectively, and you can see that they are different from Points A and B. Let me just note here that the three words, 'coordinates', 'ordered pair' and 'point' will be used interchangeably in this book.

The two axes divide the coordinate plane into four regions, which are called **quadrants**. We often refer to the **first quadrant** in which all the points (x, y) display $x > 0$ and $y > 0$. The position of each quadrant is given in Figure 2.2. In passing, points on either of the axes do not belong to any quadrant.

2.9.4   Linear functions: a straight line

Suppose the function $f(x)$ is given as

$$f(x) = ax + b, \tag{2.9}$$

where a and b are the real numbers and $a \neq 0$. This function is called the **linear function**. If you take x on the horizontal axis and $f(x)$ on the vertical axis and plot all points $(x, f(x))$ on the coordinate plane, what will you come up with? The curve you see on the coordinate plane is called the **graph** of this function. A little more formally, the graph of a function is the set of all ordered pairs $(x, f(x))$.

In fact, the graph of a linear function is a **straight line**. Let me show you an example of sketching a graph of a linear function. We use the following linear function: $C(q) = 10q + 30$. The coordinate plane we look at therefore is the $(q, C(q))$ plane.

First we can figure out the points where the function intersects the horizontal and the vertical axes. They are called the **horizontal intercept** and the **vertical intercept**, respectively. For the horizontal intercept, the value of the function is zero, so by solving $0 = 10q + 30$ we get $q = -3$. So the horizontal intercept is $(-3, 0)$. The vertical intercept is (0, 30) because when $q = 0$, $C(0) = 30$. Why do we care about these intercepts? It is because to determine a straight line, we only need to obtain two points that are on it, and these intercepts are easy ones to obtain. In any event, we can now sketch the line we want, as in Figure 2.3.

Note that, by specifying the two intercepts on the diagram, we are implicitly specifying the **slope** of the function, which is $a = 10$. It is because we can figure out the slope of the function from these two points. Namely, when the run of the function is 3, the rise of it is 30. The slope of a line is given by the dividing the rise by the run, so we get 10 as the slope.

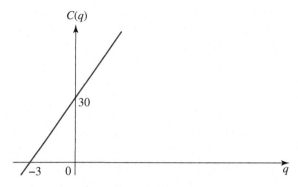

Figure 2.3 $C(q) = 10q + 30$.

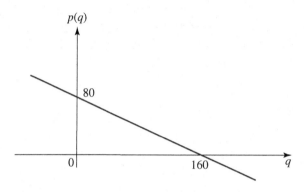

Figure 2.4 $p(q) = -\frac{1}{2}q + 80$.

Now the graph of a different linear function $p(q) = -\frac{1}{2}q + 80$ is given in Figure 2.4. Can you graph the function by yourself? Which variables are on the axes?

Drawing a straight line that goes through the two intercepts works as long as b takes a non-zero value. But when $b = 0$, the horizontal and vertical intercepts are identical – yes, it is the origin – so it is obvious that you cannot graph the function in the same manner. Since you know that the function goes through the origin in this case, one more thing you need to specify in the graph is the slope of the function (which is a) (or another point that the graph goes through, which will enable us to figure out the slope of the function). For example, Figure 2.5 shows the graph of $f(x) = x$.

You can see that the figure is not to scale. However, by specifying the coordinates (1, 1), I can understand that the slope of the straight line is unity. This line is often referred to as the **45-degree line**. It is because the angle made by the horizontal axis and this line is 45 degrees. Since the graph is not to scale, the perceived angle is less than 45 degrees.

What happens when $a = 0$ in Equation (2.9)? It becomes $f(x) = b$. This says that the function takes a value b no matter what the value of x is. In terms of the graph, the straight line is parallel to the horizontal axis (the graph will coincide with the horizontal axis when $b = 0$). On the other hand, the expression $x = b$ means that x takes a value b no matter

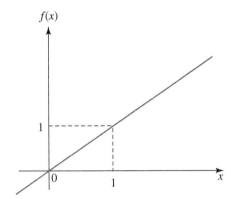

Figure 2.5 $f(x) = x$.

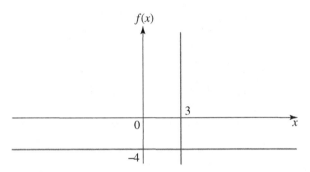

Figure 2.6 $f(x) = -4$ and $x = 3$.

what the value of y is. Hence, the graph of $x = b$ is a straight line parallel to the vertical axis (when $b = 0$, the line coincides with the vertical axis). Note that for this case y is not a function of x (why?). In Figure 2.6 $f(x) = -4$ and $x = 3$ are depicted.

2.9.5   Quadratic functions: a parabola

Suppose the function $f(x)$ is given as

$$f(x) = ax^2 + bx + c, \tag{2.10}$$

where a, b, and c are real numbers and $a \neq 0$. This function is called the **quadratic function**. The quadratic function as in Equation (2.10) can be represented by a **parabola** on the coordinate plane, and it is important that you illustrate it properly. However, we need to wait until Chapter 5 (when we study curve sketching) to discuss exactly why the graph of a quadratic function displays a parabola, and so for the time being, let us just accept that it does.

It turns out that a parabola will be symmetric about a vertical line, and the point where this line cuts the parabola is called the **vertex**. It also turns out that the vertical line is given by $x = -\dfrac{b}{2a}$ and that the vertex is given by the coordinates $\left(-\dfrac{b}{2a}, c - \dfrac{b^2}{4a} \right)$. To demonstrate them we begin with completing the square of Equation (2.10):

$$f(x) = ax^2 + bx + c$$

$$= a\left(x^2 + \frac{b}{a}x\right) + c$$

$$= a\left(x^2 + \frac{b}{a}x + \frac{b^2}{4a^2}\right) + \left(c - \frac{b^2}{4a}\right)$$

$$= \underbrace{a\left(x + \frac{b}{2a}\right)^2}_{\text{1st term}} + \underbrace{\left(c - \frac{b^2}{4a}\right)}_{\text{2nd term}}.$$

Now suppose $a > 0$. Then, $f(x)$ takes the minimum value $c - \dfrac{b^2}{4a}$ when $x = -\dfrac{b}{2a}$. Because, if $x = -\dfrac{b}{2a}$, then the first term is equal to zero, which otherwise takes a positive value. It is also easy to show that $f(x)$ is symmetric about a vertical line $x = -\dfrac{b}{2a}$, because the function takes the same value $f\left(-\dfrac{b}{2a} \pm z\right) = az^2 + \left(c - \dfrac{b^2}{4a}\right)$ when $x = -\dfrac{b}{2a} + z$ and $x = -\dfrac{b}{2a} - z$. In summary, we can deduce the following results.

> The graph of the quadratic function $f(x) = ax^2 + bx + c$, if $a > 0$,
>
> (1) is a parabola that opens *upwards*;
>
> (2) is symmetric about a vertical line $x = -\dfrac{b}{2a}$; and
>
> (3) takes a *minimum* at the vertex, $\left(-\dfrac{b}{2a}, c - \dfrac{b^2}{4a}\right)$.

Question Draw the graph of $g(q) = q^2 + 4q$.

Solution First we complete the square:

$$g(q) = q^2 + 4q$$
$$= (q^2 + 4q + 4) - 4$$
$$= (q + 2)^2 - 4.$$

So $g(q)$ is a parabola that opens upwards and is symmetric about $q = -2$. $g(-2) = -4$, so the vertex is $(-2, -4)$.

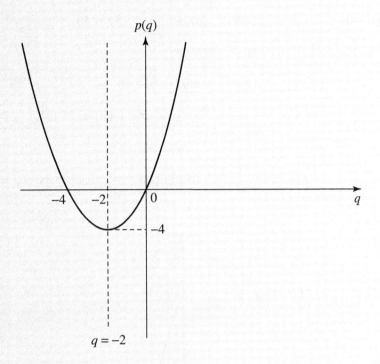

You can see that there is one vertical intersect, $(0, 0)$, which is the origin. It can be obtained by setting $q = 0$. The origin is also one of the horizontal intersects, where the other one is $(-4, 0)$ because of the symmetric nature of the parabola. Alternatively, you can solve $g(q) = 0$, *i.e.* $q^2 + 4q = 0$ to obtain the horizontal intercepts.

Exercise 2.8   The graph of $g(q) = q^2 + 4q$.

Now, by following the same logic as before, for the case where $a < 0$, we can state the following.

The graph of the quadratic function $f(x) = ax^2 + bx + c$, if $a < 0$,

(1) is a parabola that opens *downwards*;

(2) is symmetric about a vertical line $x = -\dfrac{b}{2a}$; and

(3) takes a *maximum* at the vertex, $\left(-\dfrac{b}{2a}, c - \dfrac{b^2}{4a} \right)$.

Question Draw the graph of $p(q) = -\frac{1}{2}q^2 - 8q + 40$.

Solution First we complete the square:

$$p(q) = -\frac{1}{2}q^2 - 8q + 40$$

$$= -\frac{1}{2}\left(q^2 + 16q + 64\right) + 32 + 40$$

$$= -\frac{1}{2}(q + 8)^2 + 72.$$

So $p(q)$ is a parabola that opens downwards and is symmetric about $q = -8$. $p(-8) = 72$, so the vertex is $(-8, 72)$.

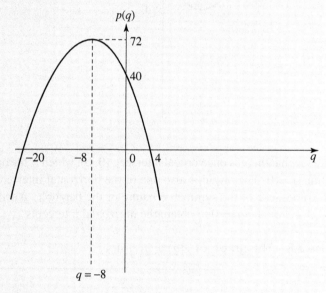

The vertical intercept is $(0, 40)$. The horizontal intercepts can be obtained solving $p(q) = 0$. They are $(-20, 0)$ and $(4, 0)$.

Exercise 2.9 The graph of $p(q) = -\frac{1}{2}q^2 - 8q + 40$.

2.9.6 Quadratic functions and quadratic equations

Recall that quadratic equations can have two distinct roots, repeated roots or two complex roots. Let us explain these three types of quadratic equations diagrammatically now that we have learnt how to graph quadratic functions. To start with, consider the LHS of the equations we saw in exercises in Subsection 2.8.2 as quadratic functions. That is, we consider three functions: $f(x) = x^2 - 2x + 1$, $g(x) = x^2 - 2x - 6$ and $h(x) = x^2 - 2x + 8$. Taking x on the horizontal axis, we can draw the graphs of these three

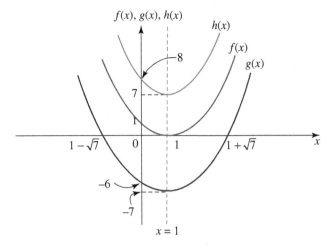

Figure 2.7 Diagrammatic representation of the solutions to a quadratic equation.

quadratic functions. An important point here is that solving these quadratic equations is identical to obtaining the horizontal intercepts of the relevant quadratic functions (why?).

We can see in Figure 2.7 that the quadratic function may or may not have horizontal intercepts. This corresponds to the fact that the quadratic equation may or may not have real roots. For example, we have seen previously that the quadratic equation $x^2 - 2x + 8 = 0$ does not have any real roots (it has two complex roots; see Subsection 2.8.2). The corresponding quadratic function, $h(x) = x^2 - 2x + 8$, as you can see in Figure 2.7, does not have horizontal intercepts. The two horizontal intercepts of the quadratic function $g(x) = x^2 - 2x - 6$ are $1 - \sqrt{7}$ and $1 + \sqrt{7}$. You should recall that these are the solutions to the quadratic equation $x^2 - 2x - 6 = 0$.

Hence, in drawing the graph of a quadratic function, you should be able to specify not only the vertical intercept, but also the horizontal intercepts (if they exist).

2.9.7 Rational functions

A function that is expressed as a ratio of two polynomial expressions is called a **rational function**. For example,

$$f(x) = \frac{ax + b}{cx^2 + dx + e},$$

where $cx^2 + dx + e \neq 0$ is a rational function, where the numerator is linear and the denominator is quadratic.

The particular rational function we often use in economics is the function

$$f(x) = \frac{a}{x},$$

where $a > 0$ and $x \neq 0$. The graph of this function turns out to be a **rectangular hyperbola**, which we will draw in the next figure. We will again put off the discussion as to *why* the graph shapes like that until Chapter 5.

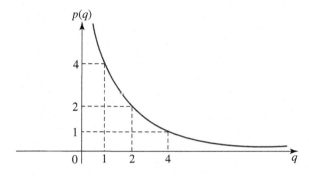

Figure 2.8 The graph of $p(q) = \dfrac{4}{q}$.

Denoting $f(x) = y$, note that the above function can be rearranged as $xy = a$. It means the product of the two variables x and y is always constant at a. Note also that neither x nor y can be zero (if either is zero, the product of the two can never be a positive number). This means that the function never cuts the axes. Instead, the curve approaches the axes *asymptotically*. That is, the curve will come closer and closer to the horizontal axis as x becomes larger and larger; and will become closer and closer to the vertical axis as y becomes larger and larger. In this case, the horizontal and vertical axes are called the **asymptotes** of the function.

2.9.8   A function of a function

Consider a function $y = f(t)$. In this, y is a function of t. Suppose that t is also a function of another variable, say x, so we can write $t = g(x)$. Then it is obvious that the value of y now depends upon the value of x, and this relationship is expressed as $y = f(g(x))$. The function defined this way is called a function of a function. We may also view it as a decomposition of a function $y = f(g(x))$ into $y = f(t)$ and $t = g(x)$.

We can make two important remarks from the following exercise. First, the decomposition of a function is unlikely to be unique. Second, the order in which you substitute functions matters.

Question A   Take two functions: $y = f(t) = 2t^2$ and $t = g(x) = 3x^2$. Express y in terms of x.

Solution $y = f(g(x)) = 2(3x^2)^2 = 2 \cdot 9x^4 = 18x^4$.

Question B   Take two functions: $y = h(t) = t$ and $t = k(x) = 18x^4$. Express y in terms of x.

Solution $y = h(k(x)) = 18x^4$.

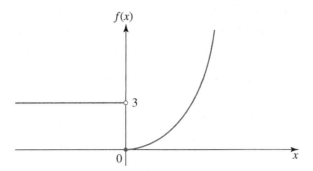

Figure 2.9 Case-defined function.

Question C   Take two functions: $f(x) = 2x^2$ and $g(x) = 3x^2$. Obtain $f(g(x))$ and $g(f(x))$.

Solution   The order you substitute functions matters.

$$f(g(x)) = 2(3x^2)^2 = 2 \cdot 9x^4 = 18x^4.$$
$$g(f(x)) = 3(2x^2)^2 = 3 \cdot 4x^4 = 12x^4.$$

Hence $f(g(x)) \neq g(f(x))$.

Exercise 2.10   Decomposing $y = f(x) = 18x^4$.

2.9.9   A case-defined function

The function $f(x)$ might change its expression across various domains. For example, $f(x)$ may be a linear function when x takes negative values ($x < 0$), but quadratic otherwise ($x \geq 0$). Because we specify different functions for different cases (domains), we call them **case-defined functions**. The graph of the following function is depicted in Figure 2.9. Note that Point $(0, 3)$ is represented by a white dot but a dark dot is used for Point $(0, 0)$. It means that the former is *not* part of the graph, but the latter is:

$$f(x) = \begin{cases} 3 & \text{if } x < 0, \\ x^2 & \text{if } x \geq 0. \end{cases}$$

2.9.10   Functions of more than one variable: multivariate functions

Up till now, we have been dealing with a function of only one variable, which is called a **univariate function** (or a **single-variate function**). However, there is no reason to think that functions cannot depend upon more than one variable. Such functions are called **multivariate functions**. For example, population density of a country (d) is a function of population (N) and the area (T) of the country:

$$d = a\frac{N}{T},$$

where $a > 0$. We need this **parameter** in case we want to convert a unit into a different one. The above relationship can be represented as $d = f(N, T)$. N and T are called **arguments** of this function. More specifically, we say that N is the **first argument** and T is the **second argument**.

To conclude this subsection, I note that a function can have more than two arguments. In general, we can write $y = f(x_1, x_2, \ldots, x_n)$. It means that y is a function of n arguments, $x_1, x_2, \ldots, x_n$. We will discuss the multivariate function in the context of a consumer's utility maximisation problem in Chapter 6.

2.10 Simultaneous equations: the demand and supply analysis

Now we are able to discuss the demand and supply analysis using mathematics. As explained briefly in Chapter 1, when we describe the quantity demanded for a good (q) as a function of its price (p), it is called the **demand function**. The following is an example of a linear demand function. Note that both q and p have a power of one:

$$q = 160 - 2p. \tag{2.11}$$

You should be able to see that as the price of the good rise, the quantity demanded declines. It is useful to solve Equation (2.11) for p, because in the demand–supply diagram the price is usually taken on the vertical axis. The above equation can be written as Equation (2.12), which we call the **inverse demand function**:

$$p = 80 - \frac{1}{2}q. \tag{2.12}$$

Turning to the supply side, the **supply function** expresses the quantity of the good supplied (q) as a function of its price (p). For example, if we postulate a linear relationship between them, we may describe the supply function as follows:

$$q = -80 + 2p. \tag{2.13}$$

If we solve Equation (2.13) for p, it becomes:

$$p = 40 + \frac{1}{2}q. \tag{2.14}$$

This function is called the **inverse supply function**.

We saw in Chapter 1 that, in the competitive market for a particular good, demand and supply interact with each other, and as a consequence the price and the quantity traded are determined. We use the following numerical example to describe how they are determined. In doing so, we will distinguish the quantity demanded from the quantity supplied; we denote the former by q^D and the latter by q^S:

$$p = -q^D + 5. \tag{2.15}$$

$$p = 3q^S - 7. \tag{2.16}$$

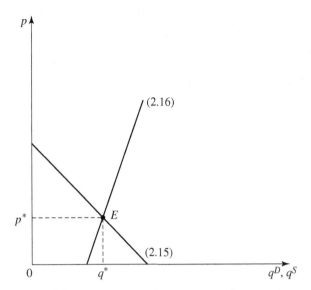

Figure 2.10 Inverse demand and inverse supply functions.

Equations (2.15) and (2.16) are the inverse demand function and the inverse supply function, respectively.

In Figure 2.10, we can see that two curves intersect at Point E. This is where quantity demanded (q^D) is equal to quantity supplied (q^S). As we discussed in Chapter 1, this point is called **equilibrium**. The price that equates demand and supply is called the **equilibrium price** and is often denoted by p^*.

I also explained in Chapter 1 that Point E is called equilibrium because there is no incentive for any parties to move from it once the price is set there. The other side of the same coin is that at any other price levels than p^*, incentives for both buyers and sellers to move from the status quo exist. If you can explain the incentives, then you may skip reading the following two paragraphs. Otherwise, let us recap them.

Suppose that the current price is above the equilibrium price, i.e. $p > p^*$. If this is the case, as we can see in Figure 2.10, there is an **excess supply** of the good. Under this situation, sellers tend to lower the price in order to unload extra goods, and at the same time, buyers tend to bid the price down realising the excess supply. As a result, q^D will rise, q^S will fall, and the excess supply will be reduced. The excess supply is eliminated when the price equals p^*. On the other hand, if the current price is below the equilibrium price, i.e. $p < p^*$, there is an **excess demand** of the product. This shortage leads buyers to bid the price up. Sellers who realise the shortage will also raise the price. The increase in the price will continue until it reaches the equilibrium price.

In summary, at any price levels other than p^*, there are incentives for both buyers and sellers to move (bid the price up/down). The only price where they have no incentive to move is p^*, which is the equilibrium price level where the quantity demanded is equal to the quantity supplied.

Here, our objective is to explore how we go about achieving equilibrium. In equilibrium, quantity demanded equals quantity supplied, so let us denote it by $q^D = q^S = q$. Then, Equations (2.15) and (2.16) will become the following:

$$\begin{cases} p = -q + 5 \\ p = 3q - 7. \end{cases} \tag{2.17}$$

We call this set of equations a **system of two linear equations** in the variables (or unknowns) p and q. We need to find values of p and q that satisfy both equations simultaneously. These are called **solutions** of the system. As we can see in the previous diagram, a point of intersection gives a solution of this system.

Before we delve into obtaining the solution of this system of equations, let us discuss the types of solution. If there are two *linear* equations and two unknowns, there are three situations that may occur.

(1) Two lines may be the same. In this case, the coordinates of any points of the line are a solution of the system: there are **infinitely many solutions**.
(2) Two lines may be parallel and have no points in common: there is **no solution**.
(3) Two lines may intersect at exactly one point. In this case, we say that this system has a **unique solution**.

We will look at numerical examples for these three cases in turn.

Case 1 (Infinitely many solutions)   Solve the following system of equations:

$$\begin{cases} y = 2x & (2.18) \\ 4x - 2y = 0. & (2.19) \end{cases}$$

Note that Equation (2.19) reduces to $y = 2x$, which is Equation (2.18). So Equations (2.18) and (2.19) represent the same straight line and therefore 'any points of $y = 2x$' are a solution of the system. The line $y = 2x$ (and $4x - 2y = 0$) is depicted in Figure 2.11. You can also express the solution as '$(x, y) = (k, 2k)$ for any real number k'.

Case 2 (No solution)   Solve the following system of equations:

$$\begin{cases} y = 2x + 1 & (2.20) \\ -2x + y = -4. & (2.21) \end{cases}$$

These two equations are sketched in Figure 2.12. Notice that both equations have the same slope but their vertical intercepts are different. Having the same slope means that they are **parallel** to each other, and if they go through a different vertical intercept, then we can conclude that they will never intersect. It means that there is no (x, y) that satisfies both equations simultaneously. Hence, 'no solution' is the answer to the question.

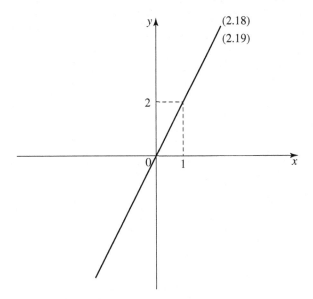

Figure 2.11 Infinitely many solutions.

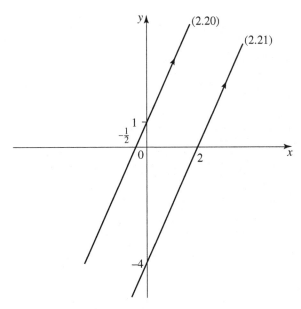

Figure 2.12 No solutions.

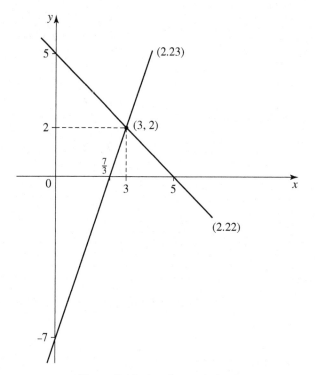

Figure 2.13 A unique solution.

Case 3 (A unique solution) Solve the following system of equations:

$$\begin{cases} y = -x + 5 & (2.22) \\ y = 3x - 7. & (2.23) \end{cases}$$

Note that this system is the same as system (2.17) (our demand and supply story) except different variables are used. It is easy to obtain the solution of this system. If (x, y) satisfies Equation (2.23), then y equals $3x - 7$ so let us substitute $3x - 7$ into y in the other equation, namely Equation (2.22). It yields:

$$3x - 7 = -x + 5.$$

So $x = 3$ is the solution to this equation. Substituting $x = 3$ into Equation (2.22) (or into Equation (2.23)), we get $y = 2$. Hence the solution to the above system is $(x, y) = (3, 2)$. This method of obtaining the solution of the system of two linear equations involves eliminating the variable y by substituting y (expressed in terms of x and a constant) into y of the other equation. Hence it is called the method of **elimination by substitution**.

There is one more method you can use to obtain the solution of the system of two linear equations. Consider the following system:

$$\begin{cases} 2y - 3x = 8 & (2.24) \\ -3y + 2x = -7. & (2.25) \end{cases}$$

You could solve this system by using the method of elimination by substitution. For example, if we solve Equation (2.24) for y, we get $y = \frac{1}{2}(3x + 8)$. Substituting it into y in Equation (2.25) will yield an equation in x only, and you can solve it for x. Some of you might find taking these steps tedious, and for those of you, I introduce another method.

Let us multiply the both sides of Equation (2.24) by 3 (remember, multiplying the both sides of the equality by the same number retains the equality). We also multiply the both sides of Equation (2.25) by 2 (not 3). Then we get the following system:

$$\begin{cases} 6y - 9x = 24 \\ -6y + 4x = -14. \end{cases}$$

The reason we multiplied both sides of the two equations as above is to create the terms $6y$ and $-6y$. Now consider adding each side of the two equations. On the LHS, we have $6y - 9x + (-6y + 4x) = -5x$ (the $6y$s cancel out and get eliminated). The RHS is $24 + (-14) = 10$, so we get $-5x = 10$. It follows that $x = -2$. Substituting it back to one of Equations (2.24) or (2.25) yields $y = 1$. Hence the solution of the system is $(x, y) = (-2, 1)$. This method involves eliminating one variable by adding one equation to the other, so it is called the method of **elimination by addition**. You can use either of these two methods to solve a system of two linear equations.

In any event, let's get back to our demand and supply analysis. By solving the simultaneous equation, we have shown that the equilibrium price for our problem is $p^* = 2$. At this price, demand is equal to supply ($q^* = 3$). The important features of our problem are that both of the equations are linear and that there is a unique solution.

However, in general, as we have seen, systems of equations may not have a solution, or even when it exists, it may not be unique. Furthermore, in more complicated systems (remember, we have looked only at a system of two linear equations), solutions may be difficult to find. Linear equations are the easiest to solve, but there is no reason for equations to be linear. In general, we cannot find analytical solutions for systems of non-linear equations, and hence we often resort to numerical simulations. You need not worry about this case in this book, but just be aware of the fact that there are a number of systems of equations that are analytically unsolvable.

Some non-linear systems are, however, solvable. Let us look at the following demand and supply model. Suppose that the inverse supply function of apples is described as follows (we use the same notation as before):

$$p = q^S + 2. \tag{2.26}$$

Suppose also that the inverse demand function for apples is given by the following:

$$p = 8 - (q^D)^2. \tag{2.27}$$

Note that p is linear in q^S in the first equation, but is non-linear in q^D in the second one (p is a quadratic function of q^D). When we determine the equilibrium levels of price

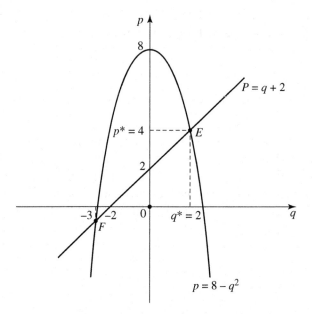

Figure 2.14 A system of non-linear equations.

and quantity, we need to solve the following **non-linear system of equations**:

$$\begin{cases} p = q + 2 \\ p = 8 - q^2. \end{cases} \tag{2.28}$$

Question Use the method of elimination by substitution to solve the non-linear system of equations given as above.

Solution Substituting the second equation into the first one yields:

$$8 - q^2 = q + 2.$$

Rearranging this equation gives the following quadratic equation:

$$q^2 + q - 6 = 0.$$

We can factorise it as follows:

$$(q + 3)(q - 2) = 0.$$

Therefore, $q = 2, -3$.

Exercise 2.11 A system of non-linear equations.

There are two solutions, $q = 2$ and $q = -3$. These correspond to Points E and F, respectively, in Figure 2.14. If you were doing a course in mathematics you may be able to stop here. But we are studying economics and, in the current context, the latter solution does not make any sense. The only relevant solution in this problem is $q^* = 2$. The market equilibrium level of price can be obtained by substituting this value back in to either

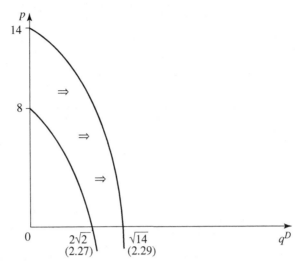

Figure 2.15 A shift of the demand curve (schedule).

the inverse demand function or the inverse supply function: it should be easy to see that $p^* = 4$.

2.10.1 Comparative statics

Suppose that the inverse demand function for apples has changed to the new one as follows:

$$p = 14 - (q^D)^2. \tag{2.29}$$

Figure 2.15 depicts two demand schedules: Equations (2.27) and (2.29). You can see the shift in the demand schedule to the right. Note that at each and every price, more apples will be demanded.

Various events may cause the shift. An increase in buyers' income may be one of them. Keeping other things constant, with more income buyers may want to buy more apples than before *at each and every price* of an apple. Another event that may give rise to the rightward shift in the demand schedule is an increase in the price of bananas (not apples). Suppose everything (including the price of apples and buyers' income) remained the same except for the price of bananas. If apples were close substitutes for bananas, people would substitute away from bananas and would consume more apples (again at each and every price of an apple).

One way to capture the effect of a change in the price of a substitute (or a change in buyers' income levels) is to change a parameter value of the inverse demand function. What we are interested in is to know how this change in a parameter value affects the equilibrium level of price and quantity. In general, we call this exercise **comparative static analysis**: it examines how the equilibrium values of the variables in question might change if one of the parameters in the question changed. We conduct comparative static analysis below and see how the equilibrium price and quantity should be affected.

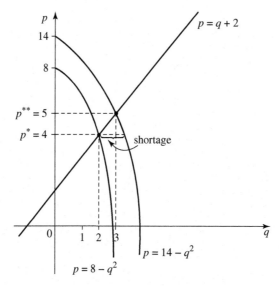

Figure 2.16 Comparative statics.

Question   Explain why the equilibrium price cannot stay the same if there is the change in the demand as explained above. Obtain the new equilibrium price.

Solution   If the price of apples stayed the same as the original equilibrium price, which is 4, there would be an excess demand (or a shortage) of apples. This leads apple buyers to bid the price up. Apple sellers who realise the shortage will also raise the price. The increase in the price of apples will continue until the excess demand becomes zero, i.e. until it reaches the new equilibrium price.

The new system of equations is

$$\begin{cases} p = q + 2 \\ p = 14 - q^2 \end{cases}$$

Substituting the second equation into the first one yields:

$$14 - q^2 = q + 2.$$

Rearranging this equation gives the following quadratic equation:

$$q^2 + q - 12 = 0.$$

We can factorise it as follows:

$$(q + 4)(q - 3) = 0.$$

Therefore, $q = 3, -4$. We ignore the negative solution and hence $q^{**} = 3$. The new equilibrium price is $p^{**} = 5$. This exercise is described in Figure 2.16.

Exercise 2.12   Comparative statics.

2.11   Logic

In the course of your study of economics and finance, you will be required to construct your argument in a logical manner, especially to prove that your argument is correct. Well, it may sound trivial but doing so is not always easy. In closing this chapter, we briefly study **logic** and **proofs**. What is discussed in this section may seem simple and easy in the beginning, but please don't be fooled by that. We shall cover some subtle issues that require you to think carefully.

2.11.1   Statements

In the 2006 FIFA World Cup (WC2006), Australia played Japan in the group stage. I was watching it on TV with my Australian friends and I was very excited when Japan scored first in the first half. It looked (to me) as if Japan was never going to lose, so I said to my friends, 'I think the match won't finish with 1-0, the final score will be 3-1'. What I meant to say – but didn't say – was '3-1 to Japan', and my friends seemed to interpret it that way. Well, in the end, to my disappointment, Australia scored three goals in the second half and my friends were happy to tell me that '3-1, you were right!'.

'Australia defeated Japan in WC2006.'

This is an example of a **statement**. When a declarative (*objective*) sentence can be classified as either 'true' or 'false', but not both, we call it a statement. While the above statement is indeed true, what about the following?

'This textbook is great!!'

In an everyday conversation, you might call it a statement, but whether you think my textbook is great is your personal (subjective) opinion. Therefore, in a mathematical sense, it is not regarded as a statement. While I hope the above opinion is popular amongst the readers, I shall introduce another one.

'10 000 000 000 000 000 001 is a multiple of 7.'

Don't worry if you cannot immediately tell whether it is true or false; perhaps none of us can! But we know that it can not be both true and false. So long as we know that we can classify it as either 'true' or 'false', we can call it a statement.

Some statements are sometimes true but false other times. For example, if we confine x to be real numbers,

$$'x^2 = 4'$$

is true when $x = \pm 2$, but false otherwise (so the above statement is false if it is meant to be for all the real xs).

Let us denote one statement by P and another statement by Q. We say that two statements P and Q are **logically equivalent** if P is true (false) exactly when Q is true (false, respectively). When P and Q are logically equivalent, we write $P \equiv Q$. For example,

$$\text{`}x \text{ is Japan'} \equiv \text{`}x \text{ is beaten by Australia in WC2006'}[7]$$
$$\text{`}2x - 1 = 0\text{'} \equiv \text{`}x = \frac{1}{2}\text{'}.$$

2.11.2 Combinations of statements

New statements can be created by combining some statements. For example, we can negate a statement P by writing as follows

$$\text{`not P' (or } \neg P).$$

This statement is called a **negation** of the statement P. Trivially, the above negation is true when P is false (and is false when P is true).[8]

Now, consider the following statement:

$$\text{`}x^2 = 4\text{'}.$$

This statement is true if $x = \pm 2$, i.e. x has to be either 2 or -2 for the statement to be true. This condition can be denoted by:

$$\underbrace{x = 2}_{P} \text{ or } \underbrace{x = -2}_{Q}. \tag{2.30}$$

If we let $x = 2$ be P and $x = -2$ be Q, statement (2.30) is called the **disjunction** of P and Q. For the disjunction 'P or Q' to be true, either P or Q (or both) has to be true. In contrast, when we have a statement 'P and Q' we call it the **conjunction** of P and Q. For the conjunction to be true, both P and Q have to be true. For example, the conjunction '$100 < 1$ and $100 < 1000$' is false (because '$100 < 1$' is false) but the disjunction '$100 < 1$ or $100 < 1000$' is true (because '$100 < 1000$' is true).

2.11.3 Implications

Some combinations of statements are particularly important: you will use them frequently in many disciplines that require analytical skills. They are called the **implications**. An implication statement is denoted by:

$$P \Rightarrow Q,$$

and we read it as 'P **implies** Q' (or 'Q **is implied by** P'). For example, consider the following:

$$\text{`If } \underbrace{\text{I am in Tasmania}}_{P}, \text{ then } \underbrace{\text{I am in Australia}}_{Q}\text{'} \tag{2.31}$$

or

$$\text{`}\underbrace{\text{I am in Tasmania}}_{P} \Rightarrow \underbrace{\text{I am in Australia}}_{Q}\text{'}.$$

---

7 The only team Australia beat in WC2006 was Japan.
8 Using the negation twice we obtain $P \equiv \text{not}(\text{not}\,P)$. This is called the **Principle of Double Negation**.

Statement P is called the **hypothesis** (or **assumption**), whereas statement Q is called the **conclusion** of the implication. Suppose P is true, then you are in Tasmania, therefore you must be in Australia, implying that Q is true. Therefore, statement (2.31) is true. It would be false if Q were something like, 'I am in Japan'.

2.11.4 Contrapositive and converse

It is known that the implication $P \Rightarrow Q$ is logically equivalent to the following implication:

$$\text{`(not}Q) \Rightarrow (\text{not}P)\text{'}.$$

It is called the **contrapositive** of $P \Rightarrow Q$. For example, the contrapositive of statement (2.31) is:

$$\text{`If } \underbrace{\text{I am not in Australia}}_{\text{not } Q} \text{, then } \underbrace{\text{I am not in Tasmania}}_{\text{not } P} \text{'.} \tag{2.32}$$

The equivalence between a statement and its contrapositive is a very useful result, which we shall see in the next section.

We can form another statement by exchanging P and Q in the implication $P \Rightarrow Q$, that is:

$$\text{`}Q \Rightarrow P\text{'}.$$

It is called the **converse** of $P \Rightarrow Q$. Therefore the converse of statement (2.31) is:

$$\text{`If } \underbrace{\text{I am in Australia}}_{Q} \text{, then } \underbrace{\text{I am in Tasmania}}_{P} \text{'.} \tag{2.33}$$

You should realise that this statement (2.33) is not necessarily true, although (2.31) is true. Indeed, you can be in Australia without being in Tasmania. So . . . , be careful. When an implication is true, it does not necessarily mean that the converse of it is also true. It probably sounds quite obvious now that you have read this section, but history tells us that many students frequently get confused by directions of implications.

Of course, for some true implications, their converses may also be true. For example, consider the following:

$$\text{`If } \underbrace{x = y}_{P} \text{, then } \underbrace{x - y = 0}_{Q} \text{'.} \tag{2.34}$$

Statement (2.34) is a true implication statement. In words, it says that if two numbers are equal, the difference of the two numbers is zero. For this statement, the converse of it is also true:

$$\text{`If } \underbrace{x - y = 0}_{Q} \text{, then } \underbrace{x = y}_{P} \text{'.} \tag{2.35}$$

In words, it says that if the difference of two numbers is zero, then the two numbers are equal. When both $P \Rightarrow Q$ and $Q \Rightarrow P$ occur as above, we write it as $P \Leftrightarrow Q$ and read 'P **if and only if** Q'. Some people use the expression 'P iff Q', where 'iff' stands for 'if and only if'. There is a significant distinction between 'if' and 'iff'. In any case,

'$P \Leftrightarrow Q$' is true exactly when statements P and Q are both true, or both false (convince yourselves of this using statement (2.34)).

2.11.5 Necessary and sufficient conditions

When the statement '$P \Rightarrow Q$' is true, we say that 'P is a **sufficient condition** for Q'. Consider an implication we saw previously:

'If $\underbrace{\text{I am in Tasmania}}_{P}$, then $\underbrace{\text{I am in Australia}}_{Q}$'.

To be in Australia, you don't really need to be in Tasmania. You can be in other states/territories so long as it is in Australia. So, if I were to let someone else know that you are in Australia, specifying the state Tasmania would *not* be absolutely *necessary*. But if I say that you are in Tasmania, then that is *sufficient* for someone else to figure out that you are in Australia.

When $P \Rightarrow Q$ is true, we say that 'Q is a **necessary condition** for P'. For you to be in Tasmania, you cannot be outside Australia. It is absolutely *necessary* that you are in Australia. However, your being in Australia is not *sufficient* for me to conclude that you are in Tasmania. You might be in Queensland, New South Wales, or in some other states/territories.

Finally, when $P \Leftrightarrow Q$ is true, we say that 'P is a **necessary and sufficient condition** for Q' (or equivalently, we say 'Q is a necessary and sufficient condition for P'). You should be able to apply this terminology to explain implications (2.34) and (2.35).

2.11.6 Quantifiers

We introduce **quantifiers** to close the section in logic. Consider the two following statements:

'For any real number x, $x^2 = 9$.'
'There exists a real number x such that $x^2 = 9$.'

Whilst the former is false, the latter is true. As for the former statement, the word 'any' implies that the statement has to be true if we plug in any arbitrarily chosen real number to x. If you choose x to be zero, since $0 \neq 3$, you can see that the statement is false. Whereas for the latter statement, for it to be true, we just have to show the existence of a real number that satisfies $x^2 = 9$. Indeed, both $x = 3$ and $x = -3$ meet the statement.

The former statement involves the use of the **universal quantifier** 'for every (or for any)', and hence the statement encompasses all the real numbers (and this is why the statement is false: $x = 0$ is no good, for example). The latter statement, in contrast, involves the phrase 'there exists', which is called the **existential quantifier**. This means that statement is concerned with at least one real number (and this is why the statement is true: $x = 3$ will do).

We can deduce important and strong lessons from the above example. If a statement includes the universal quantifier, to show that the statement is false, it suffices to produce a *single* **counter example** (for the statement 'For any real number x, $x^2 = 9$', $x = 0$ is one of many counter examples). But when a statement includes the existential quantifier, and you want to show that the statement is *false*, you need to show that *every single example* fails to meet the statement (which is obviously more difficult). Mathematicians use particular notation for these quantifiers. Whilst $\forall$ denotes 'for every' $\exists$ denotes 'there exists.' Using them, we can rewrite the previous statements, respectively, as

$$\text{`}\forall x \in (-\infty, \infty),\ x^2 = 9\text{'}$$

$$\text{`}\exists x \in (-\infty, \infty),\ x^2 = 9\text{'}.$$

Let me conclude this section by saying that it is important to make a precise statement. A statement '$\exists x,\ x^2 = -9$' reads 'There exists an x such that $x^2 = -9$', but what kind of number is x? If it means a real number, then the statement is false. But if it means a complex number, then the statement is true because both $x = 3i$ and $x = -3i$ meet it. Usually, we are concerned only about the real numbers (or just non-negative numbers) in economics, and so long as everyone has that common ground, it may be fine to assume that people will interpret x as a real number. But if you are unsure how things will be interpreted, you had better specify all the details precisely. Had I said to my friends, 'the final score will be 3-1 to Japan' then they wouldn't have said to me, 'you were right!'. Instead, they would have said, 'you were wrong mate, it was 3-1 to us!' (but I am sure I would've been equally upset).

2.12 Proofs

In this section, we introduce several ways to *prove* implications. To start with, we will define some peculiar types of integers that we will use in our discussion.

Definition 2.1 (Even and odd numbers)   An integer n is called an even number if there is an integer m such that $n = 2m$. An integer that is not even is called an odd integer and can be denoted by $n = 2m + 1$.

Definition 2.2 (Prime number)   A natural number m (not including 1) is called a prime number if *whenever* m can be written as the product $m = a \cdot b$ of two natural numbers, then $a = 1$ or $b = 1$.

I think Definition 2.1 is straightforward to understand, but some readers may have trouble understanding Definition 2.2. According to Definition 2.2, 4 is not a prime number. This is because 4 can be written as the product $4 = 2 \cdot 2$, and for this product, neither $a = 1$ nor $b = 1$ holds. Notice that 'whenever' in the definition is italicised: 4 can also be written as the product $4 = 1 \cdot 4$, in which case $a = 1$, but for a number to be a prime number, either $a = 1$ or $b = 1$ needs to occur *whenever* the number is written as the product $a \cdot b$. In contrast, 5 is a prime number because the only ways to write it as the product are $5 = 1 \cdot 5$ and $5 = 5 \cdot 1$, and so either $a = 1$ or $b = 1$ will occur when 5 is written as $a \cdot b$. More plainly put, a prime number has no divisors except for 1 and the number itself.

Now, we go into the main story. Consider the following (implication) statement.

Let m be an even integer and p be any integer. Then $m \cdot p$ is an even integer.   (2.36)

You think the statement is true (don't you?), perhaps after trying out some numbers. But how can you be absolutely sure that it is true? How can you rule out the possibility that somebody comes to you with a counter example? The only way to be absolutely sure that you are right is to *prove* that the statement is true. What do we mean by proving (mathematically) that a particular statement is false (or true)?

A **proof** is a process of deducing an irrefutable conclusion from accepted assumptions. These assumptions may come from three sources. Firstly, the assumptions may be given specifically in the statement of the question. For example, statement (2.36) has two assumptions. One is that m is an even integer and the other is that p is any integer.

Sometimes these assumptions together with a chain of logic may lead to the conclusion you want. But when these assumptions are not enough, we need to introduce the second group of assumptions. They are assumptions that are generally accepted as true – in mathematics these are called **axioms** – and we use them without proving that they are true. For instance, for any real numbers a, b and c, nobody will refuse accepting the following four properties of equality.

$$a = b \text{ and } b = c \Rightarrow a = c. \tag{2.37}$$
$$a = b \Rightarrow a + c = b + c. \tag{2.38}$$
$$a = b \Rightarrow a \cdot c = b \cdot c. \tag{2.39}$$
$$a = b \text{ and } c = d \Rightarrow a \cdot c = b \cdot d. \tag{2.40}$$

Thirdly, statements that have been proven previously will be accepted as true by every-one, so they can also be used as assumptions when necessary.

In the following, I demonstrate how we can prove statement (2.36) using a **direct proof** (or the **direct method**). Subsequently I shall introduce a few other proof methods, which you will frequently use.

2.12.1 Direct method

Suppose there are two statements P and Q, and you are sure that P implies Q, but you cannot see immediately how Q necessarily occurs when P occurs. In statement (2.36), P is 'm is an even integer and p is an integer' and Q is '$m \cdot p$ is an even integer'.

One way to prove $P \Rightarrow Q$ is to make a detour. You may be able to see that P necessarily leads to A, that is $P \Rightarrow A$. You may also be able to see that A will cause B, so $A \Rightarrow B$. You are also convinced that Q will occur when B occurs, i.e. $B \Rightarrow Q$. You have completed a string of statements as follows:

$$P \Rightarrow A \Rightarrow B \Rightarrow Q.$$

By the **Law of the Syllogism**, you have $P \Rightarrow Q$ and the proof is done.[9]

We shall see how this method is applied to the proof of statement (2.36). The statement to be proven is called the **proposition**, and hence we will call it later, Proposition 2.1. Before going into the proof of it, though, we need to state one result regarding the product of two integers.

Lemma 2.1   Let a and b be integers. Then the product $a \cdot b$ is also an integer.

Non-essential propositions that are used to prove the main proposition are called **lemmas**, and we will use Lemma 2.1. to prove the proposition in question.

Proposition 2.1   Let m be an even integer and p be any integer. Then $m \cdot p$ is an even integer.

Before starting the proof, it is useful to write down all the assumptions (which are specific to the statement):

$$m \text{ is an even integer}$$

$$p \text{ is an integer.}$$

Proof   Because m is an even integer, there exists an integer q such that $m = 2q$ (recall the definition of an even integer).

Using Equation (2.39) (which is accepted by everybody), we have

$$m \cdot p = (2q) \cdot p.$$

Using the associative rule (which is accepted by everybody), we have

$$m \cdot p = 2 \cdot (q \cdot p).$$

By definition of an even integer, we can say that $m \cdot p$ is an even integer (because $q \cdot p$ is an integer due to Lemma 2.1). Q.E.D.

Note 1   Propositions that have been proven are called **theorems**. (So now the above proposition can be called Theorem 2.1.)

Note 2   Q.E.D. stands for *quod erat demonstrandum* (in Latin it means 'which was to be demonstrated'. Write either Q.E.D. or put ■ (a black square) after the proof in order to show that it is the end of the proof.

Exercise 2.13   Direct method.

---

[9] The Law of the Syllogism states that if both $A \Rightarrow B$ and $B \Rightarrow C$ are true, then $A \Rightarrow C$ is true. Don't worry about the terminology. If you can construct the string of statements, then you can say that your proof is done.

2.12.2 Contrapositive proofs

Sometimes proving a statement turns out to be a very simple task. Consider the following proposition. Can you prove it? The key is to think about the contrapositive of the proposition.

Proposition 2.2   Let m and p be integers, and suppose $m \cdot p$ is odd. Then both m and p are odd.

Proof   The contrapositive of the proposition is, 'If at least one of the integers m and p is even, then $m \cdot p$ is an even integer'. This is what we have proven in Section 2.12.1. The proposition and the contrapositive are logically equivalent, and hence we have proven that the proposition is true.   ■

Exercise 2.14   Contrapositive proof.

Since the above proposition has been proven, we can call it Theorem 2.2. Now, in the theorem we can consider a special case where $p = m$. We have already shown that the proposition is true including this special case, so it has to be true for this special case as well. Let us write down the proposition when $p = m$ (just replace p with m).

Proposition   Let m and m be integers, and suppose $m \cdot m$ is odd. Then both m and m are odd.

Clearly this proposition sounds a little clumsy, and so I rewrite it as follows.

Corollary 2.1   Let m be an integer, and suppose m^2 is odd. Then m is odd.

Notice that the term, **corollary**, is used. It is a proposition that immediately follows a theorem (without a need for proof because it is so trivial), or a special case of a theorem as the one we just saw above. Unsurprisingly, you will not find any proof after corollaries.

2.12.3 Proof by contradiction (indirect method)

You need to be especially comfortable with this method because it is perhaps the most popularly and commonly used method of all (and hence you will surely encounter it in your future studies). It is called **proof by contradiction** or *reductio ad absurdum*.

The idea of this method is the following. Suppose you want to prove $P \Rightarrow Q$. It may sound ridiculous, but we start with supposing that Q is false. If such a supposition leads to a contradiction of (1) P itself, (2) one of axioms, or (3) previously established propositions, then it must have been incorrect to have supposed that Q is false. Hence, if we find a contradiction, then we can conclude that Q must be true.

I provide two illustrative examples of proof by contradiction in the following. In the first example, I will show that the converse of Corollary 2.1 is also true (remember that the converse of a true statement is not necessarily true). The proven converse statement will be referred to as Lemma 2.2, because it will be used to prove the main result in the second example. The second example is one of the classic examples of *reductio ad absurdum* where $\sqrt{2}$ is proven to be irrational. I have tried to emphasise which of the accepted assumptions I am using in each step even when it is trivial.

Lemma 2.2   Let m be an integer, and suppose m^2 is even. Then m is even.

Proof   We start with negating the conclusion. Suppose m is not even, that is suppose m is odd.

Then there is an integer n such that $m = 2n + 1$ by definition of odd integers. Therefore,

$$m^2 = (2n + 1)^2 = 4n^2 + 4n + 1.$$

This can be rearranged as:

$$m^2 = 2(2n^2 + 2n) + 1.$$

Since $(2n^2 + 2n)$ is an integer, this implies that m^2 is odd (by definition).

But it *contradicts* to the assumption (of the lemma itself) that m^2 is even.

Therefore our initial supposition was incorrect, and we have proven that m is even. ■

Exercise 2.15   Proof by contradiction.

Theorem $\sqrt{2}$ is an irrational number.

Proof   We again start with negating the conclusion. Suppose $\sqrt{2}$ is not irrational, that is suppose $\sqrt{2}$ is rational (because it has to be either rational or irrational).

Then by the definition of rational numbers we can express $\sqrt{2}$ as a ratio of two integers,

$$\sqrt{2} = \frac{m}{n}.$$

More importantly, we can choose integers m and n, so that at least one of them is not even. This is because when both of them are even, by definition of even integers, we can factor 2 out of the numerator and the denominator of the fraction (and keep doing that until one (or both) of them becomes odd). So, to summarise, we have:

$$\sqrt{2} = \frac{m}{n} \text{ and at least one of } m \text{ and } n \text{ is not even.}$$

Now, using Equation (2.40):

$$\sqrt{2} \cdot \sqrt{2} = \frac{m}{n} \cdot \frac{m}{n}.$$

And so by the power rules:

$$2 = \frac{m^2}{n^2}.$$

Using Equation (2.39), we have:

$$2n^2 = m^2. \tag{2.41}$$

This implies that m^2 is even by definition. By Lemma 2.2, m is even.

By definition of an even integer, we can express m using some integer p as:

$$m = 2p.$$

Again using Equation (2.40) we get,

$$m \cdot m = (2p) \cdot (2p).$$

Using the power rules as well as communicative and associative properties of the real numbers, we get the following:

$$m^2 = 2(2p^2).$$

Applying Equation (2.37) to the above equation and Equation (2.41) (more simply, substituting the above equation into Equation (2.41)) yields:

$$2n^2 = 2(2p^2).$$

Using Equation (2.39) we have

$$\frac{1}{2} \cdot 2n^2 = \frac{1}{2} \cdot 2(2p^2).$$

So we have

$$n^2 = 2p^2.$$

This equation implies that n^2 is even by definition. By Lemma 2.2, n is even.

Together with the established result that m is even, we have both m and n even. This is a *contradiction* because we have supposed that at least one of m and n is not even.

Therefore our initial supposition was incorrect, and we have proven that $\sqrt{2}$ is irrational. ∎

Exercise 2.16 $\sqrt{2}$ is irrational.

2.13 Additional exercises

1. **(Numbers)** Which of the following statements are true? Note that i is an imaginary number.

   (1) -4 is a rational number.

   (2) i^2 is an integer.

   (3) 0 is an integer.

   (4) $-\dfrac{1}{3}$ is a rational number.

2. **(Elementary algebra, especially powers)** Which of the following statements are true?

   (1) $\dfrac{\frac{1}{x}}{y} = \dfrac{y}{x}$.

   (2) $\dfrac{x+y}{y+x} + \dfrac{x-y}{y-x} = 0$.

   (3) $\dfrac{x^{15} \cdot x^3}{x^{15}} = x^3$.

   (4) $\dfrac{\sqrt{36}}{\sqrt{9}} = 2$.

   (5) $\sqrt{80} = 4\sqrt{5}$.

   (6) $(-1)^3 - (-3)^2 + (\sqrt[3]{5})^3 = 13$.

3. **(Equalities, inequalities and intervals)** Which of the following statements are true?

   (1) $|-100| = |300 - 200|$.

   (2) $x^3 < 0$ for any $x < 0$.

   (3) $x^4 > 0$ for any $x \in (-\infty, \infty)$.

   (4) If $x \in (-1, 7)$, then $|x - 3| > 4$.

   (5) If $x \in (-2, 6)$, then $|x - 2| \le 4$.

   (6) $(x - a)^2 = -(a - x)^2$.

   (7) $(x - a)^3 = -(a - x)^3$.

4. **(Factorisation)** Factorise the following polynomial expressions.

   (1) $x^2 + 11x + 10$.

   (2) $x^2 + 6xy + 9y^2$.

   (3) $9x^2 + 3x - 2$.

   (4) $xy - yz + zx - y^2$.

   (5) $x^2 + 3xy + 9y - 9$.

(6) $2x^3 + 11x^2 - 7x - 6$.

(7) $x^4 - x^3 - 7x^2 + x + 6$.

5. **(Functions)** Which of the following statements are true?

   (1) If $f(x) = 2x$, then $f(2a - 3) - f(a + 1) = f(a - 4)$.

   (2) If $f(x) = 3^x$, then $f(a + 1) - f(a - 2) = f(a)$.

   (3) If $f(x) = (-2)^x$, then $\dfrac{f(a - 1)}{f(a - 4)} = 8$.

6. **(Equations)** Where possible, solve the following equations (where relevant, consider complex solutions).

   (1) $(2x - 1)(x - 3) = 0$.

   (2) $x^2 - 5x + 6 = 0$.

   (3) $3x^2 + 5x - 2 = 0$.

   (4) $x^2 + 6x + 12 = 0$.

   (5) $5x^2 - 6x + 2 = 0$.

   (6) $x^3 - 4x^2 + 5x - 2 = 0$.

   (7) $x^3 - 2x^2 + 2x - 1 = 0$.

7. **(Functions and equations)** Let $f(x) = 3x + 1$ and $g(x) = -x^2 - x$. Is it true that $f(g(x)) = g(f(x))$ for any $x \in (-\infty, \infty)$? If not, is there any particular real value of x, which satisfies the above equation?

8. **(Demand and supply model)** For the following demand and supply functions of a product, state the economically sensible values of price and quantity for which each of them are defined. Draw the market diagram for this product with price shown on the vertical axis. What are the equilibrium price and quantity? Carefully explain why the price you obtained is the equilibrium price.

$$\begin{cases} q^S = -5 + 3p, \\ q^D = 20 - 2p. \end{cases}$$

9. **(Demand and supply model)** Consider the following demand and supply functions for a product.

$$\begin{cases} q^S = -5 + 3p, \\ q^D = 9 - 2p^2. \end{cases}$$

Draw the market diagram for this product with price shown on the vertical axis. Find the economically meaningful solution for the equilibrium price and quantity.

10. **(Comparative statics)** Information on a coffee market is given as below:

$$\begin{cases} q^S = 20p - 100, \\ q^D = \dfrac{6000}{p}, \end{cases}$$

where p is the price of coffee per tin and q is the quantity of coffee in tins.

2.13 Additional exercises

(a) Draw two functions on a diagram restricting your attention to $p \in [0, \infty)$ and $q \in [0, \infty)$.

(b) Obtain the market equilibrium. What occurs if the price of coffee per tin is $15?

(c) Suppose the demand function has changed to $q^D = \dfrac{3000}{p}$. Provide an economic explanation of this change and list a few reasons as to why it might have occurred.

(d) Obtain the new market equilibrium. What would happen if the price of coffee per tin stayed the same as the equilibrium price you obtained in (b)?

11. **(Logic)** We want to make the following statements true. Fill in the (underlined) blank with 'iff' where possible. Otherwise, fill in the blank with 'if' or 'only if'.

(1) $x = 1$ _____ $x^2 = 1$.

(2) $6x - 9 = 15$ _____ $x = 4$.

(3) $x = -1$ _____ $x^2 + 2x + 1 = 0$.

(4) $x = \sqrt{25}$ _____ $x = 5$.

(5) $x(x + 6) < 0$ _____ $x > -6$.

(6) $x^2 > 9$ _____ $|x| > 3$.

(7) $x^2 < 49$ _____ $x < 7$.

(8) $x(x^2 + 1) = 0$ _____ $x = 0$.

(9) $x^2 > 0$ _____ $x > 0$.

(10) $x^2 + y^2 = 0$ _____ $xy = 0$.

12. **(Logic)** Which of the following statements are equivalent to the following statement in italics: *If tennis is cancelled, then it is raining.* [**Note.** We are not concerned about the veracity of the statement.]

(a) If it is raining, then tennis is cancelled.

(b) It can be raining only if tennis is cancelled.

(c) If it is not raining, then tennis is not cancelled.

(d) A necessary condition for tennis to be cancelled is that it is raining.

(e) A sufficient condition for it to be raining is that tennis is cancelled.

(f) If tennis is not cancelled, then it is not raining.

13. **(Proof)** Using the direct method, prove the following statements.

(1) The sum of two odd numbers is even.

(2) The sum of an odd and an even number is odd.

14. **(Proof)** Prove the following statements by contradiction.

(1) When we divide 29 people into 4 groups, at least one of the groups must consist of 8 or more people.

(2) If x is rational, $x + \sqrt{2}$ is irrational. [**Hint.** Use the fact that $\sqrt{2}$ is irrational, which has been proven in the text.]

3 Financial mathematics

In this chapter, I will introduce some more ideas of basic mathematics including: limits, summation, a geometric series (or the sum of a geometric sequence), the exponential function and logarithms. For some readers these terms may not sound relevant to either economics or finance, but it turns out that they can be powerful in examining various problems in both economics and finance. For example, when we buy a house, a car, or furniture, we may want to borrow money from a bank. Usually borrowing involves a series of repayments and naturally we are interested in the size of the repayments. How will interest be charged on these repayments? Financial institutions often use a procedure that is called daily compounding in calculating interest payments. By using mathematical techniques we learn in this chapter, it turns out the payments can be calculated in a simple manner. Various other ideas in finance will be introduced in this chapter while we go through some mathematics.

Chapter goals By studying this chapter you will

(1) become familiar with basic mathematical notions used in financial mathematics, such as limits, summation, geometric series;
(2) be able to interpret exponential and logarithmic functions;
(3) be able to calculate the net present value of an investment project and make the correct decision on whether to invest; and
(4) be able to use a time line to visualise an ordinary annuity and express it using the geometric series.

3.1 Limits

We start with considering the following statement:

$$\lim_{x \to a} f(x) = L. \tag{3.1}$$

Equation (3.1) says that L is the **limit** of $f(x)$ as x tends to a, where L and a are both real numbers. It means that the value of the function $f(x)$ becomes very close to L if x is very close to a. You might notice that x can become closer to a either from smaller values or from larger values. The former is called the **left-hand limit** and the latter is called the **right-hand limit**, and they are expressed as Equations (3.2) and (3.3), respectively.

$$\lim_{x \to a^-} f(x) = L. \tag{3.2}$$

$$\lim_{x \to a^+} f(x) = L. \tag{3.3}$$

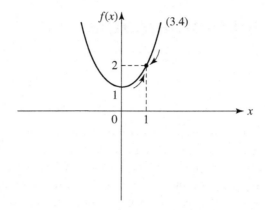

Figure 3.1 Continuous function.

Equation (3.2) means that the value of the function $f(x)$ becomes very close to L if x becomes closer to a from smaller values. Likewise, Equation (3.3) means that the value of the function $f(x)$ becomes very close to L if x approaches a from larger values. Let us see these notions by using some examples.

Let us consider the following function:

$$f(x) = x^2 + 1. \tag{3.4}$$

What is the limit of this function as x approaches 1? It is rather obvious, as $f(x)$ is defined at $x = 1$, i.e. $f(1) = 2$. It does not matter whether x becomes closer to 1 from smaller values or larger values: the value of the function approaches 2. That is:

$$\lim_{x \to 1^-} f(x) = \lim_{x \to 1^+} f(x) = f(1) = 2. \tag{3.5}$$

When the first two equalities of Equation (3.5) holds, we call that the function $f(x)$ is **continuous** at $x = 1$. More formally, continuity of a function can be defined as follows.

Definition 3.1   A function $f(x)$ is continuous at $x = a$, where a is in the domain of f, if the left- and right-hand limits at $x = a$ exist and are equal, i.e.

$$\lim_{x \to a} f(x) = \lim_{x \to a^-} f(x) = \lim_{x \to a^+} f(x),$$

and the limit as x tends to a equals the value of the function at that point, that is,

$$\lim_{x \to a} f(x) = f(a).$$

As we can see in Figure 3.1, the function $f(x)$ is continuous for all x. Roughly speaking, continuous functions are those that can be drawn without removing a pen from paper.

Now, let us look at functions that are not continuous. Consider a function:

$$g(x) = \frac{x^3 - x^2 + x - 1}{x - 1}, \quad x \neq 1. \tag{3.6}$$

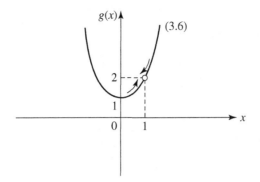

Figure 3.2 A function not continuous.

For an obvious reason, we cannot define the function when $x = 1$. So we are interested in knowing the value this function approaches when x approaches 1. It turns out that both the left- and right-hand limits at $x = 1$ exist and are 2.

When $x \neq 1$, $g(x)$ can be simplified to:

$$g(x) = \frac{(x - 1)(x^2 + 1)}{x - 1} = x^2 + 1, \ x \neq 1.$$

Therefore,

$$\lim_{x \to 1} g(x) = \lim_{x \to 1^-} g(x) = \lim_{x \to 1^+} g(x) = 2.$$

Hence $\lim_{x \to 1} g(x) = 2$, but, the function is not defined at $x = 1$, so we cannot say $\lim_{x \to 1} g(x) = g(1)$. The second part of the definition of continuity is violated, hence the function is not continuous at $x = 1$. The graph of this function is depicted as in Figure 3.2. You should realise that you need to remove your pen from the paper when you are exactly at $x = 1$ because the parabola is disconnected there.

What about the following function?

$$h(x) = \frac{1}{x}, \ x \neq 0. \tag{3.7}$$

Again for an obvious reason, we cannot define the function when $x = 0$. We are interested in knowing the value this function approaches when x approaches 0. We know that when x approaches zero from values greater than zero, the value of the function approaches *positive* infinity. However, if x approaches zero from values smaller than zero, the value of the function approaches *negative* infinity. This is an example where the left- and right-hand limits are not equal. That is, at $x = 0$,

$$\lim_{x \to 0^-} h(x) \neq \lim_{x \to 0^+} h(x).$$

Hence, the first part of the definition of continuity is violated (in fact, the second part as well), hence the function is not continuous at $x = 0$. The graph of this function is depicted as in Figure 3.3.

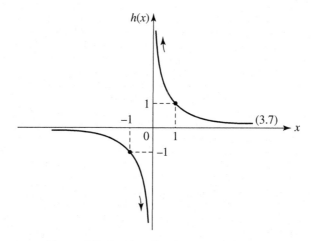

Figure 3.3 Another function not continuous.

3.1.1 Limit rules

I now list the limit rules, which will be assumed knowledge in the rest of the book. Some exercises (with the solution) are provided after the rules.

Limit rules If $\lim\limits_{x \to a} f(x) = L_f$ and $\lim\limits_{x \to a} g(x) = L_g$, then we have the following.

Rule 1 $\quad \lim\limits_{x \to a} \{f(x) + g(x)\} = L_f + L_g.$ $\hfill (3.8)$

Rule 2 $\quad \lim\limits_{x \to a} \{f(x) - g(x)\} = L_f - L_g.$ $\hfill (3.9)$

Rule 3 $\quad \lim\limits_{x \to a} \{f(x) \cdot g(x)\} = L_f \cdot L_g.$ $\hfill (3.10)$

Rule 4 $\quad \lim\limits_{x \to a} \left\{ \frac{f(x)}{g(x)} \right\} = \frac{L_f}{L_g}.$ $\hfill (3.11)$

Rule 5 $\quad \lim\limits_{x \to a} f(g(x)) = f(L_g).$ $\hfill (3.12)$

Here are some questions you can use to practise taking limits.

Question A Find $\lim\limits_{x \to 2} (x - 1)^{100}$.

Solution Well, you will need to spend hours to expand $(x - 1)^{100}$ out, so let us think differently. Just applying Equation (3.12) you get:

$$\lim_{x \to 2} (x - 1)^{100} = \left[\lim_{x \to 2} (x - 1) \right]^{100}$$
$$= 1^{100}$$
$$= 1.$$

Question B   Find $\lim\limits_{x\to 3} \dfrac{x-3}{x^3}$.

Solution   Applying Equation (3.11) yields:

$$\lim_{x\to 3} \frac{x-3}{x^3} = \frac{\lim\limits_{x\to 3}(x-3)}{\lim\limits_{x\to 3} x^3}$$

$$= \frac{0}{27}$$

$$= 0.$$

Exercise 3.1   Applying the limit rules.

3.2   Summation

In economics or finance, it is common to add variables of our interest for particular time periods, say the sum of your monthly pay in 2012. If we denote your pay for January by w_1, February by w_2, and so on, then one way to represent the sum of your pay (W) will be the following:

$$W = w_1 + w_2 + w_3 + w_4 + w_5 + w_6 + w_7 + w_8 + w_9 + w_{10} + w_{11} + w_{12}. \quad (3.13)$$

However, it looks too cumbersome and we do not really want to write it this way every time we need to. Hence, to represent the same idea, we use a **summation operator** $\sum$. Equation (3.13) can now be written as:

$$W = \sum_{t=1}^{12} w_t. \quad (3.14)$$

In Equation (3.14), the $\sum\limits_{t=1}^{12}$ symbol tells you to add w_t for the values of t running from $t = 1$ to $t = 12$, inclusive. This letter t is known to the **running variable**. For this case, t is used for the running variable to represent 'time', but any symbol can be used as long as it is well specified. Hence the following representation also carries the same information as Equation (3.14):

$$W = \sum_{i=1}^{12} w_i. \quad (3.15)$$

In Equations (3.14) and (3.15), the **lower limit** of the summation operator is 1. However, it can take any integer. The **upper limit** of the summation operator, 12 in Equations (3.14) and (3.15), can be any natural number that is greater than the lower limit. For example, the sum of your pay from July to September can be represented by $\sum\limits_{t=7}^{9} w_t$.

3.2.1 Summation rules

Now I list the basic summation rules, which will be assumed knowledge in the rest of the book. All these rules can be deduced by simply writing out sufficient terms, but doing so is very tedious, and it may be better to have these rules in hand from the beginning. Nevertheless, a question will be given that requires you to deduce the second rule, just to emphasise that memorising the rules per se is not the point. This is followed by questions in which you are asked to apply these rules.

Summation rules

Rule 1 $\displaystyle\sum_{i=1}^{n} c = nc.$ (3.16)

Rule 2 $\displaystyle\sum_{i=1}^{n} cx_i = c \sum_{i=1}^{n} x_i.$ (3.17)

Rule 3 $\displaystyle\sum_{i=1}^{n} (x_i \pm y_i) = \sum_{i=1}^{n} x_i \pm \sum_{i=1}^{n} y_i.$ (3.18)

Rule 4 $\displaystyle\sum_{i=1}^{n} x_i = \sum_{i=1}^{k} x_i + \sum_{i=k+1}^{n} x_i.$ (3.19)

Rule 5 $\displaystyle\sum_{i=1}^{n} (x_i \pm y_i)^2 = \sum_{i=1}^{n} x_i^2 \pm 2\sum_{i=1}^{n} x_i y_i + \sum_{i=1}^{n} y_i^2.$ (3.20)

Question Deduce Equation (3.17).

Solution Simply writing out some terms will do:

$$\sum_{i=1}^{n} cx_i = cx_1 + cx_2 + cx_3 + \cdots + cx_{n-1} + cx_n$$
$$= c(x_1 + x_2 + x_3 + \cdots + x_{n-1} + x_n)$$
$$= c\sum_{i=1}^{n} x_i.$$

Exercise 3.2 Deducing Equation (3.17).

Here are some questions for you to practise applying these rules.

Question A Provided that $\displaystyle\sum_{i=1}^{n} x_i = 4$ and $\displaystyle\sum_{i=1}^{n} x_i^2 = 10$, express $\displaystyle\sum_{i=1}^{n} (x_i + 2)^2$ in terms of n.

Solution By applying Equation (3.20):

$$\sum_{i=1}^{n} (x_i + 2)^2 = \sum_{i=1}^{n} x_i^2 + 2\sum_{i=1}^{n} 2x_i + \sum_{i=1}^{n} 4.$$

By applying Equations (3.17) and (3.16):

$$\sum_{i=1}^{n} (x_i + 2)^2 = \sum_{i=1}^{n} x_i^2 + 2\sum_{i=1}^{n} 2x_i + \sum_{i=1}^{n} 4$$

$$= \sum_{i=1}^{n} x_i^2 + 4\sum_{i=1}^{n} x_i + 4n.$$

Substituting in $\sum_{i=1}^{n} x_i = 4$ and $\sum_{i=1}^{n} x_i^2 = 10$ to this expression leads to the solution:

$$\sum_{i=1}^{n} (x_i + 2)^2 = \sum_{i=1}^{n} x_i^2 + 2\sum_{i=1}^{n} 2x_i + \sum_{i=1}^{n} 4$$

$$= \sum_{i=1}^{n} x_i^2 + 4\sum_{i=1}^{n} x_i + 4n$$

$$= 10 + 4 \cdot 4 + 4n$$

$$= 26 + 4n.$$

Question B   Provided that $\sum_{i=1}^{5} x_i = 2$, $\sum_{i=6}^{10} x_i = 4$ and $\sum_{i=1}^{10} x_i^2 = 8$, express $\sum_{i=1}^{10} (x_i + 2)^2$.

Solution   Firstly, by applying Equation (3.19) to $\sum_{i=1}^{5} x_i = 2$, $\sum_{i=6}^{10} x_i = 4$, we get $\sum_{i=1}^{10} = 6$.

Now by applying Equation (3.20):

$$\sum_{i=1}^{10} (x_i + 2)^2 = \sum_{i=1}^{10} x_i^2 + 2\sum_{i=1}^{10} 2x_i + \sum_{i=1}^{10} 4.$$

By applying Equations (3.17) and (3.16):

$$\sum_{i=1}^{10} (x_i + 2)^2 = \sum_{i=1}^{10} x_i^2 + 2\sum_{i=1}^{10} 2x_i + \sum_{i=1}^{10} 4$$

$$= \sum_{i=1}^{10} x_i^2 + 4\sum_{i=1}^{10} x_i + 40.$$

Substituting $\sum_{i=1}^{10} x_i = 6$ and $\sum_{i=1}^{10} x_i^2 = 8$ into this expression leads to the solution:

$$\sum_{i=1}^{10} (x_i + 2)^2 = \sum_{i=1}^{10} x_i^2 + 2\sum_{i=1}^{10} 2x_i + \sum_{i=1}^{10} 4$$

$$= \sum_{i=1}^{10} x_i^2 + 4\sum_{i=1}^{10} x_i + 40$$

$$= 8 + 4 \cdot 6 + 40$$

$$= 72.$$

Exercise 3.3   Applying the summation rules.

3.3) A geometric series

Now I shall introduce a new idea called a **sequence**, which is just a list of numbers. Let us consider the following sequence:

$$2, 6, 18, 54, 162, \ldots$$

If you examine these values, you will find the following.

(1) The sequence starts with an **initial value** of 2; and
(2) the second value is equal to the initial value multiplied by 3, whilst the third value is equal to the second value multiplied by 3, etc. The value of 3 is called the **common ratio**.

More generally, let us denote the initial value and the common ratio by a and i, respectively.[1] Then the sequence (of n terms) can be written as follows:

$$a, ai, ai^2, ai^3, \ldots, ai^{n-2}, ai^{n-1}.$$

This sequence is called a **geometric sequence** (or **geometric progression**) with common ratio i. Note that, for the last term, i is raised to $n - 1$ (not n), and it is because the first term does not include i (or you can interpret that the first term is ai^0, in which case the last term should be ai^{n-1} if the sequence consists of n terms).

The sum of the terms of the geometric sequence is called a **geometric series**. Here, let us consider summing the first n terms of the geometric sequence:

$$\underbrace{a + ai + ai^2 + ai^3 + \cdots + ai^{n-2} + ai^{n-1}}_{n \text{ terms}}.$$

The following shows the steps to obtain the geometric series (you should try remembering the steps instead of the result per se; you can always reproduce the result if you are on top of the relevant steps). Let us denote the geometric series of n terms by Z:

$$Z = a + ai + ai^2 + ai^3 + \cdots + ai^{n-2} + ai^{n-1}. \tag{3.21}$$

Multiplying both sides of Equation (3.21) by i gives the following:

$$iZ = ai + ai^2 + ai^3 + ai^4 + \cdots + ai^{n-1} + ai^n. \tag{3.22}$$

Subtracting each side of Equation (3.22) from the corresponding side of Equation (3.22) gives:

$$Z - iZ = a - ai^n.$$

Solving this equation for Z gives the following:

$$Z = \frac{a(1 - i^n)}{1 - i}. \tag{3.23}$$

[1] Just a note to avoid possible confusion: the i used here is not the imaginary i we learnt in Chapter 2.

Here's a question to consolidate your understanding.

Question   Find the sum of the geometric sequence {2, 6, 18, 54, 162}.

Solution A   Just do it by hand . . .

$$2 + 6 + 18 + 54 + 162 = 20 + 60 + 162 = 242.$$

Solution B   Alternatively, use the geometric series formula where $a = 2$, $i = 3$, and $n = 5$.

$$Z = \frac{2(1 - 3^5)}{1 - 3} = \frac{2}{-2}\left(1 - 3^5\right) = (243 - 1) = 242.$$

Exercise 3.4   Geometric series.

We are now equipped with the basic mathematics to discuss some topics in finance. Two more mathematical notions, however, will need to be introduced eventually.

3.4   Compound interest

Most of us borrow money when we purchase a car, a house, education, etc. Most businesses borrow money when they purchase new equipment or just to keep up the daily operation of their businesses. We call the amount of money we borrow the **(original) principal**. When people borrow money, they have to agree to repay this amount – usually plus some extra – in the future. This extra amount is called the **interest**. These terms are also used when we invest money and earn interest, and our story indeed involves investing money.

Consider the following situation. Suppose you have invested $100 at an interest rate of 10 per cent per annum. Suppose also that interest is compounded annually, i.e. the interest earned by the principal is reinvested so that it, too, earns interest. How much will you obtain by the end of the tenth year?

After one year, the value of investment will be the original principal ($100), plus the interest on the principal ($100 × 0.1):

$$100 + 100 \times 0.1 = \$110.$$

So the interest for the second year is earned for $110, not just $100. At the end of the second year, the value of investment will be the principal at the end of the first year ($110), plus the interest on it ($110 × 0.1):

$$110 + 110 \times 0.1 = \$121.$$

It means that the principal increases each year by 10 per cent. The $121 represents the original principal, plus all accrued interest, and is called the **compound amount**. The difference between the compound amount and the original principal is called the

compound interest. In this example, the compound interest (at the end of the second year) is $121 - $100 = $21.

In general, the compound amount S_t of the principal P at the end of t years at the rate of i (expressed as a fraction or decimal) compounded annually can be expressed as follows.

(1) After the first year:

$$S_1 = P + Pi$$
$$= P(1 + i).$$

(2) After the second year:

$$S_2 = S_1 + S_1 i$$
$$= S_1(1 + i)$$
$$= P(1 + i)(1 + i)$$
$$= P(1 + i)^2.$$

(3) After the third year:

$$S_3 = S_2 + S_2 i$$
$$= S_2(1 + i)$$
$$= P(1 + i)^2(1 + i)$$
$$= P(1 + i)^3.$$

$$\vdots$$

(t) At the end of year t:

$$S_t = P(1 + i)^t. \tag{3.24}$$

Now try the following question.

Question   What is the compound amount of $1000 invested at an annual rate of 6 per cent for 6 years? What are the compound amount and the compound interest? You may round your answer to two decimal places at the end of calculation.

Solution:

$$S_6 = 1000 \cdot (1 + 0.06)^6 \approx 1418.52.$$

$$S_6 - P = 1000 \cdot (1 + 0.06)^6 - 1000 \approx 418.52.$$

Exercise 3.5   Compound interest.

3.4.1 What do we need to do if the compounding period is not annual?

Compounding may not necessarily take place annually. It may take place daily, monthly, quarterly, etc. If compounding takes place quarterly (every three months), we say that there are four **interest periods** or **conversion periods** per year. However, regardless of how often compounding occurs, an interest rate is usually quoted as an annual rate, which is called the **nominal rate**.

The **periodic rate** (of interest) is obtained by dividing the nominal rate by the number of conversion periods per year. For example, if the nominal rate is 8 per cent and compounding occurs quarterly, the periodic rate is $\dfrac{8\%}{4} = 2\%$. In this chapter, unless otherwise stated, all interest rates will be assumed to be nominal rates. We now can generalise Equation (3.24).

The compound amount S_n of the principal P at the end of n interest periods when the periodic rate is r (expressed as a fraction or decimal) can be expressed as follows.

(1) After the first interest period:

$$S_1 = P + Pr$$
$$= P(1 + r).$$

(2) After the second interest period:

$$S_2 = S_1 + S_1 r$$
$$= S_1(1 + r)$$
$$= P(1 + r)(1 + r)$$
$$= P(1 + r)^2.$$

(3) After the third interest period:

$$S_3 = S_2 + S_2 r$$
$$= S_2(1 + r)$$
$$= P(1 + r)^2(1 + r)$$
$$= P(1 + r)^3$$

$$\vdots$$

(n) At the end of nth interest period:

$$S_n = P(1 + r)^n. \tag{3.25}$$

Now try this one.

Question What is the compound amount of \$1000 invested at an annual rate of 6 per cent compounded semi-annually for 6 years? What is the compound interest? You may round your answer to two decimal places at the end of calculation.

Solution Observe that there are 12 interest periods (twice per year for 6 years) and the periodic rate is 3 per cent.

$$S_{12} = 1000 \cdot \left(1 + \frac{0.06}{2}\right)^{6 \times 2} = 1000 \cdot (1 + 0.03)^{12} = 1425.76.$$

$$S_{12} - P = 1000 \cdot (1 + 0.03)^{12} - 1000 = 425.76.$$

Exercise 3.6 Compound interest (but not annually).

We have seen that for a principal of \$1000 at a nominal rate of 6 per cent over a period of 6 years, annual compounding results in a compound interest of \$418.52, and with semi-annual compounding the compound interest is \$425.76. So the important lesson here is: for a given positive nominal rate, the more frequent the compounding, the greater is the compound interest.

3.4.2 The effective rate of interest

If we invest \$1000 (principal) at a nominal rate of 6 per cent compounded semi-annually for one year, it will earn more than 6 per cent that year.

Question How much will you earn in the above situation?

Solution

$$S - P = P\left(1 + \frac{0.06}{2}\right)^2 - P$$
$$= P(1.03)^2 - P$$
$$= \left[(1.03)^2 - 1\right]P$$
$$= (1.0609 - 1)P$$
$$= 0.0609P.$$

Exercise 3.7 The effective rate of interest.

As we show above the compound interest is $0.0609P$, which is 6.09 per cent of P. This means that 6.09 per cent is the rate of interest compounded annually that is actually earned. We call this rate the **effective rate** of interest, or the **yield**. In other words, the effective rate is just the rate of change in the principal over a period of one year. Hence we have shown that the nominal rate of 6 per cent compounded semi-annually is equivalent to an effective rate of 6.09 per cent.

In fact, we can formally state the relationship between the effective rate and the nominal rate in general. Suppose the principal is P and the nominal rate of i is compounded n times a year. Then the compound amount after a year can be denoted by $P\left(1 + \dfrac{i}{n}\right)^n$. If we denote the effective rate by r_e, then by definition of the effective rate, $P(1 + r_e)$ has to equal $P\left(1 + \dfrac{i}{n}\right)^n$. Therefore:

$$1 + r_e = \left(1 + \frac{i}{n}\right)^n.$$

Solving this for r_e we get:

$$r_e = \left(1 + \frac{i}{n}\right)^n - 1. \tag{3.26}$$

Again, don't just try remembering the result per se. You can always derive Equation (3.26) by yourselves if you understand the notion of the effective rate. Understanding the idea is far more important. The effective rate is quite useful in comparing different compounding methods with different nominal rates. If you convert those into the effective rates, comparison becomes possible and we can see which one of the methods will yield more interest in one year. Now you should be able to answer the following question.

Question   If you have a choice of investing money at 6.3 per cent compounded annually or 6.125 per cent compounded quarterly, which one should you prefer? You may round your answer (expressed as a percentage) to two decimal places at the end of calculation.

Solution

The effective rate for the first option:

$$r_e = \left(1 + \frac{0.063}{1}\right)^1 - 1$$
$$= 0.063.$$

By definition, it is 6.3 per cent.

The effective rate for the second option:

$$r_e = \left(1 + \frac{0.061\,25}{4}\right)^4 - 1$$
$$= \left(\frac{4.061\,25}{4}\right)^4 - 1$$
$$\approx 1.0627 - 1$$
$$= 0.0627.$$

It is 6.27 per cent. Hence the first option is preferred.

Exercise 3.8   Comparing the effective rates.

3.5 The exponential function: how can we calculate the compound amount of the principal if interest is compounded continuously?

Question Express in terms of t the compound amount of $1000 invested for t years at a nominal rate of 10 per cent if interest is compounded (1) annually (2) semi-annually (3) quarterly (4) monthly (5) daily and (6) *continuously*.

(1) Annually:

$$S = 1000 \times (1 + 0.1)^t$$
$$= \$1000(1.1)^t.$$

(2) Semi-annually:

$$S = 1000 \times \left(1 + \frac{0.1}{2}\right)^{2t}$$
$$= \$1000(1.05)^{2t}.$$

(3) Quarterly:

$$S = 1000 \times \left(1 + \frac{0.1}{4}\right)^{4t}$$
$$= \$1000(1.025)^{4t}.$$

(4) Monthly:

$$S = 1000 \times \left(1 + \frac{0.1}{12}\right)^{12t}$$
$$= 1000 \times \left(\frac{12.1}{12}\right)^{12t}$$
$$= \$1000\left(\frac{121}{120}\right)^{12t}.$$

(5) Daily

$$S = 1000 \times \left(1 + \frac{0.1}{365}\right)^{365t}$$
$$= 1000 \times \left(\frac{365.1}{365}\right)^{365t}$$
$$= \$1000\left(\frac{3651}{3650}\right)^{365t}.$$

$$\vdots$$

(6) When $m \to \infty$:

$$S = 1000 \times \left(1 + \frac{0.1}{m}\right)^{mt}$$

$$= \text{How much?}$$

Exercise 3.9 Towards continuous compounding.

Our focus is (6): we want to obtain the value of S when m approaches infinity. We say interest is compounded **continuously** in this case. Recall the idea of the limits introduced in Section 3.1. Using the limit we can describe what we want:

$$S = \lim_{m \to \infty} \left\{ 1000 \times \left(1 + \frac{0.1}{m}\right)^{mt} \right\}. \tag{3.27}$$

How do we move on from here? We introduce a new mathematical idea to deal with this problem. It will turn out that the term $\lim_{k \to \infty} \left(1 + \frac{1}{k}\right)^k$ has a lot to do with solving this problem, so let us investigate it in detail. To begin with, it may be useful to see what values $\left(1 + \frac{1}{k}\right)^k$ takes for a given k.

As we can observe in Table 3.1, $\left(1 + \frac{1}{k}\right)^k$ increases as k increases, but at a decreasing rate. A Swiss mathematician Leonhard Euler found that $\left(1 + \frac{1}{k}\right)^k$ approaches an irrational number as k approaches infinity. The number is approximately equal to 2.718 28. In mathematics it is denoted by e and referred to as **Euler's e**.

$$\lim_{k \to \infty} \left(1 + \frac{1}{k}\right)^k = e. \tag{3.28}$$

We will discuss a little more about the function that involves Euler's e later. For now, let us get back to Equation (3.27) and solve for S. To use Equation (3.28), we rearrange Equation (3.27) in the following manner and obtain Equation (3.29):

$$1000 \times \left(1 + \frac{0.1}{m}\right)^{mt} = 1000 \times \left(1 + \frac{0.1}{0.1k}\right)^{0.1kt},$$

where $k = 10m$. Hence,

$$S = \lim_{m \to \infty} \left[1000 \times \left(1 + \frac{0.1}{m}\right)^{mt} \right]$$

$$= \lim_{k \to \infty} \left\{ 1000 \times \left[\left(1 + \frac{1}{k}\right)^k \right]^{0.1t} \right\}. \tag{3.29}$$

Table 3.1. Values of $\left(1 + \dfrac{1}{k}\right)^k$.

k	$\left(1 + \dfrac{1}{k}\right)^k$
1	$\left(1 + \dfrac{1}{1}\right)^1 = 2^1 = 2$
2	$\left(1 + \dfrac{1}{2}\right)^2 = 1.5^2 = 2.25$
3	$\left(1 + \dfrac{1}{3}\right)^3 = \left(\frac{4}{3}\right)^3 \approx 2.37$
4	$\left(1 + \dfrac{1}{4}\right)^4 = 1.25^4 \approx 2.44$
$\vdots$	$\vdots$
100	$\left(1 + \dfrac{1}{100}\right)^{100} = 1.01^{100} \approx 2.704\,81$
$\vdots$	$\vdots$
1000	$\left(1 + \dfrac{1}{1000}\right)^{1000} = 1.001^{1000} \approx 2.716\,92$
$\vdots$	$\vdots$

Notice that $k \to \infty$ in Equation (3.29). Since $k = 10m$, if $m \to \infty$, then $k \to \infty$. Using the limit rules you learned in Section 3.1, we can boil Equation (3.29) down to Equation (3.30):

$$S = \lim_{k \to \infty} \left\{ 1000 \times \left[\left(1 + \frac{1}{k}\right)^k \right]^{0.1t} \right\}$$

$$= 1000 \times \lim_{k \to \infty} \left[\left(1 + \frac{1}{k}\right)^k \right]^{0.1t}$$

$$= 1000 \times \left[\lim_{k \to \infty} \left(1 + \frac{1}{k}\right)^k \right]^{0.1t}. \tag{3.30}$$

Finally, using the definition of e in Equation (3.28), we can obtain the compound amount of \$1000 compounded *continuously* at a nominal rate of 10 per cent over t years:

$$S = 1000 \times \left[\lim_{k \to \infty} \left(1 + \frac{1}{k}\right)^k \right]^{0.1t}$$

$$= 1000e^{0.1t}. \tag{3.31}$$

The above analysis tells us the following: to obtain the compound amount S of a principal of P dollars after t years when a nominal interest rate i is compounded continuously, we need to calculate:

$$S = P \lim_{k \to \infty} \left[\left(1 + \frac{1}{k} \right)^k \right]^{it}$$

$$= Pe^{it}. \tag{3.32}$$

Question What is the compound amount of $100 invested at a nominal rate of 5 per cent compounded continuously for (a) 1 year (b) 5 years?

Solution

(a) $S = 100e^{0.05}$.
(b) $S = 100e^{0.25}$.

Exercise 3.10 The compound amount under continuous compounding.

3.5.1 The effective rate under continuous compounding

We can calculate the effective rate under continuous compounding as we derived Equation (3.26). Recall that the effective rate is the equivalent rate compounded annually (it shows the rate of change in the principal in a year). If we denote it by r_e, then the principal P will accumulate to $P(1 + r_e)$ after one year. By definition, this has to be equal to the compound amount under continuous compounding for one year ($t = 1$) at a nominal rate i, Pe^i.

$$P(1 + r_e) = Pe^i$$
$$1 + r_e = e^i$$
$$r_e = e^i - 1. \tag{3.33}$$

Question Find the effective rate that corresponds to an annual rate of 5 per cent compounded continuously.

Solution

$$r_e = e^{0.05} - 1.$$

Exercise 3.11 The effective rate under continuous compounding.

3.5.2 The natural exponential function

We have seen that the compound amount (S) of the principal (P) under continuous compounding is expressed using an irrational number e, e.g. $S = Pe^{0.05t}$. Suppose the

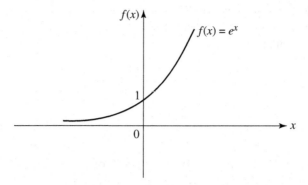

Figure 3.4 A graph of the natural exponential function.

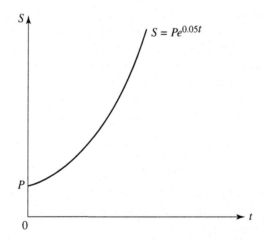

Figure 3.5 The compound amount increases at an increasing rate.

75

3.6 Logarithms: how many years will it take for my money to double?

principal P is given (so it is not a variable), and suppose we vary t to see how S changes. Then we can see that S is a function of t (e is a number so it is not a variable). We have not seen this type of function before, so let us discuss it a little.

Consider a function:

$$f(x) = \alpha^x, \tag{3.34}$$

where $\alpha > 0, \alpha \neq 1$, and if the exponent x is any real number, we call this function an **exponential function** with **base** α. In financial mathematics, as we have seen, we are particularly interested in the case where the base is equal to e. That is:

$$f(x) = e^x. \tag{3.35}$$

This function, which is the exponential function with base e, is called the **natural exponential function**. The graph of the natural exponential function is depicted in Figure 3.4.

The vertical intercept is $(0, 1)$ because $f(0) = e^0 = 1$. You can also see that as x increases $f(x)$ increases *at an increasing rate*. At this stage, it suffices to convince yourself that the graph is shaped as illustrated in the figure, perhaps by plotting several points (you can use the fact that $e \approx 2.7$). We will learn how to properly sketch the exponential function in Chapter 5.

What is more important is to relate the exponential function to our problem in finance. As we have seen, the compound amount (S) of the principal (P) under continuous compounding at a nominal rate of 5 per cent is expressed as $S = Pe^{0.05t}$. If we take t on the horizontal axis and S on the vertical axis, the graph of S will look like the one in Figure 3.5. S starts with the original principal P (when $t = 0$) and increases at an increasing rate as t increases. Why at an increasing rate? It is just because the interest is *compounded*.

3.6 Logarithms: how many years will it take for my money to double?

Recall that when we have a function $y = f(x)$, the inverse function $x = f^{-1}(y)$ may exist, and we saw in Section 2.9 that it can be found nicely in some cases (as in the temperature example). What is the inverse function of the natural exponential function, $y = f(x) = e^x$? As yet, we have no device to express x in terms of y in this case, so we shall introduce a new notion as follows:

$$x = \log_e y. \tag{3.36}$$

This function is called the **logarithmic function** with **base** e (remember, we were looking at the exponential function with base e), or we just call it the **natural logarithmic function**. It is an inverse function of $y = e^x$.

Most of the time, we write $x = \log_e y$ in an alternative way:

$$x = \ln y. \tag{3.37}$$

In fact, we can also define logarithmic functions with other bases as follows.

> **Definition 3.2** The logarithmic function with base α, where $\alpha > 0$ and $\alpha \neq 1$, is denoted by $\log_\alpha$ and is defined by:
>
> $$x = \log_\alpha y \text{ if and only if } y = \alpha^x.$$
>
> Alternatively we can write:
>
> $$x = \log_\alpha y \Leftrightarrow y = \alpha^x. \tag{3.38}$$

Let us do some simple exercises.

Question Obtain x.

(1) $x = \log_2 16$.
(2) $x = \log_{10} 1$.
(3) $x = \ln e^2$.
(4) $x = \ln 1$.

Solution

(1)

$$x = \log_2 16$$
$$2^x = 16$$
$$x = 4.$$

(2)

$$x = \log_{10} 1$$
$$10^x = 1$$
$$x = 0.$$

(3)

$$x = \ln e^2$$
$$x = \log_e e^2$$
$$e^x = e^2$$
$$x = 2.$$

(4)

$$x = \ln 1$$
$$x = \log_e 1$$
$$e^x = 1$$
$$x = 0.$$

Exercise 3.12 Exponentials and logarithms.

3.6 Logarithms: how many years will it take for my money to double?

Two bases are commonly used for the logarithm. One is the one we have discussed, e, the natural logarithm (ln). The other is 10. We call $\log_{10}$ the **common logarithm** (since we use a decimal system of numbers, it is likely to be the most common value for the base). Most scientific calculators will have the facilities of $\log_{10}$ and ln but, as discussed in Preface, it is irrelevant in the spirit of the book. When you end up with expressions including e and/or ln, leave it as long as further simplification is not possible.

3.6.1 Logarithm properties

The logarithmic function has many important properties. I will list those, and they will be assumed knowledge for the rest of the book. I will show in the following exercise that the first property must hold, but will leave the rest for you to show, since it can be done in a similar fashion. Some exercises are provided after the list of properties.

Logarithm properties

Property 1

$$\log_a x + \log_a y = \log_a(xy). \tag{3.39}$$

Property 2

$$\log_a x - \log_a y = \log_a\left(\frac{x}{y}\right). \tag{3.40}$$

Property 3

$$\log_a x^b = b\log_a x. \tag{3.41}$$

Property 4

$$\log_a x = \left(\log_a b\right) \cdot \left(\log_b x\right). \tag{3.42}$$

Property 5

$$\log_a x = \frac{1}{\log_x a}. \tag{3.43}$$

Question Show that Equation (3.39) holds.

Solution Let $\log_a x = m$ and $\log_a y = n$. So the LHS of Equation (3.39) is $m + n$. Note also that $a^m = x$ and $a^n = y$ by the definition of the logarithm, and hence $xy = a^m a^n = a^{m+n}$.

In the meantime, the RHS of Equation (3.39) is: $\log_a(xy) = \log_a(a^{m+n})$. By the definition of the logarithm, it is equal to $m + n$.

Hence we have shown that the LHS and the RHS of Equation (3.39) are equal.

Exercise 3.13 Deducing Equation (3.39).

Here are some exercises for you to get used to logarithms.

Question Express x in terms of a and b, provided that $\log_{10}2 = a$ and $\log_{10}3 = b$.

(1) $x = \log_{10}2000$.

(2) $x = \log_{10}\dfrac{1}{9}$.

Solution

(1)

$$x = \log_{10}2000$$
$$= \log_{10}2 + \log_{10}100$$
$$= a + 2.$$

(2)

$$x = \log_{10}\frac{1}{9}$$
$$= \log_{10}1 - \log_{10}9$$
$$= 0 - \log_{10}3^2$$
$$= -2\log_{10}3$$
$$= -2b.$$

Exercise 3.14 Logarithm calculation.

In passing, the graph of the natural logarithmic function $y = \ln x$ is depicted in Figure 3.6. Again, at this stage, it suffices to convince yourself that the graph is shaped as shown in the figure by plotting several points. We will learn how to properly sketch the logarithmic function in Chapter 5. The horizontal intercept is $(1,0)$ because $\ln 0 = 1$. The value of the function y increases as x increases but at a decreasing rate. If you imagine that there is a mirror on the line $y = x$, the graph of the natural logarithmic function $y = \ln x$ is a mirror image of its inverse function $y = e^x$.

3.6.2 How many years will it take for my money to double?

Now that we know how to deal with the logarithms, we are able to tell how many years it will take for our money to double, given the information about compounding. Let us think how many years it will take for our money to double at the effective rate of 5 per cent.

Recall first that the effective rate is the equivalent rate compounded annually. If we denote the principal by P, then the compound amount over t years can be written as $P(1 + 0.05)^t$. This has to be equal to twice as much as P, which is $2P$, in which case:

$$2P = P(1 + 0.05)^t. \tag{3.44}$$

79

3.6 Logarithms: how many years will it take for my money to double?

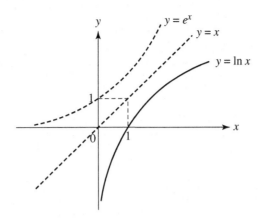

Figure 3.6 A graph of the natural logarithmic function.

Rearranging this equation yields:

$$1.05^t = 2. \tag{3.45}$$

Taking (the natural) logarithms of the both sides of this equation yields:

$$\ln 1.05^t = \ln 2. \tag{3.46}$$

Now, using one of the logarithm properties, we rearrange the left hand side of this equation in order to solve for t:

$$t \ln 1.05 = \ln 2. \tag{3.47}$$

Hence:

$$t = \frac{\ln 2}{\ln 1.05} \text{ (years).} \tag{3.48}$$

This is the answer and you can stop here. If you have a scientific calculator, you can check that the value of t in (3.48) is roughly 14.21. Remember this value in reference to the next exercise.

Question How many years will it take for our money to double if interest is compounded quarterly at a nominal rate of 5 per cent?

Solution

$$2P = P\left(1 + \frac{0.05}{4}\right)^{4t}$$

$$\ln 2 = 4t \ln 1.0125$$

$$t = \frac{\ln 2}{4 \ln 1.0125}$$

$$\approx 13.95.$$

The answer shows us that it will take (approximately) 13.95 years for our money to double if interest is compounded quarterly at a nominal rate of 5 per cent. Recall that if interest is compounded annually at 5 per cent (the example we saw above) it takes (approximately) 14.21 years for our money to double.

This finding is consistent with our discussion on the compound interest in the previous section. Given a positive nominal rate, recall that, the more frequent the compounding, the greater is the compound interest. It follows that, given a positive nominal rate, the more frequent the compounding, the less time it will take for our money to double. Hence, in this question, it does not take as long as 14.21 years to double our money.

Exercise 3.15 Doubling funds.

3.7 Present values

3.7.1 $100 today is different from $100 in two years' time

If you have $100 today, you can deposit it in a savings account and earn interest. We have seen that if the savings account pays 10 per cent compounded annually, by the end of the second year your account is worth

$$\$100 \times (1 + 0.1)^2 = \$121.$$

It implies that $100 you receive today is worth more than $100 you may receive two years later. In the above context, we say that $121 is the **future value** of $100, and $100 is the **present value** of $121.

In general, for the periodic rate of r over n interest periods, the principal P will be accumulated to the compound amount $S = P(1 + r)^n$. Hence, by simply applying one of the power rules, we can conclude that, for the periodic rate of r over n interest periods, for the compound amount to be S, the principal P that must be invested is given by:

$$P = S(1 + r)^{-n}. \tag{3.49}$$

P is called the present value of S. The present value is sometimes referred to as the **present discounted value** or just the **discounted value**. The process of converting the future value into the present value is referred to as **discounting**.

Try the following simple question.

Question A Find the present value of $1000 due after three years if the interest rate is 8 per cent compounded quarterly. You may round your answer to two decimal places.

Solution

$$1000\left(1 + \frac{0.08}{4}\right)^{-12} = 1000(1.02)^{-12}$$
$$\approx 788.49.$$

Question B Suppose I owe you two sums of money: $1000, due in one year, and $600, due in two years. What do you think of my following offer? 'Instead, I'll pay you $1450 today (because that's better for you than receiving $1000 one year later and $600 two years later).' The interest rate of 8 per cent is compounded quarterly. You may round your answer to two decimal places.

Solution

Using the present value (PV)

$$\text{PV of the two sums} = 1000(1 + 0.02)^{-4} + 600(1 + 0.02)^{-8}$$
$$\approx 1435.94.$$

So it is better to accept the offer of $1450 today.

Using the future value (FV) at the end of the second year

$$\text{FV of \$1450 today} = 1450 \cdot (1 + 0.02)^8$$
$$\approx 1698.91.$$

$$\text{FV of the two sums} = 600 + 1000 \cdot (1 + 0.02)^4$$
$$\approx 1682.43.$$

So, of course, we get the same result: it is better to accept the offer of $1450 today. It does not matter at which time you evaluate the two options. You just need to make sure that you compare their same time values.

Exercise 3.16 The present value and future value.

3.7.2 The net present value and cash flows

If a business investment generates payments in the future, these payments are called **cash flows**. The **net present value** (*NPV*) of the cash flows is defined as the sum of *present values* of the cash flows minus the principal (initial investment). If $NPV > 0$, we conclude that the investment is profitable. The reasoning will be provided after the following exercise.

Question A Suppose you invest $12\,000$ in a business that generates cash flows at the end of years, 3, 4 and 5, as indicated in Table 3.2. Assume that if you deposit money with a bank, interest is compounded annually at 7 per cent. Find the net present value (*NPV*) of the cash flows. You may round your answer to two decimal places.

Solution

$$NPV = 5000(1.07)^{-3} + 4000(1.07)^{-4} + 4000(1.07)^{-5} - 12\,000$$
$$= 9985.02 - 12\,000 < 0.$$

Hence the investment is not profitable.

Table 3.2. Cash flow schedule.

Year	3	4	5
Cash flows	$5000	$4000	$4000

Question B Think about the same question as above, but assume instead that, if you deposit money with a bank, interest is compounded annually at 2 per cent. Find the net present value (*NPV*) of the cash flows. You may round your answer to two decimal places.

Solution

$$NPV = 5000(1.02)^{-3} + 4000(1.02)^{-4} + 4000(1.02)^{-5} - 12\,000$$
$$= 12\,029.92 - 12\,000 > 0.$$

Hence the investment is profitable.

Exercise 3.17   Net present value.

In Question A, the investment turns out to be unprofitable ($NPV < 0$). Let us think about why it is the case. What is your outside option? The only option given in the question is to deposit your initial cash outlay at the bank. That is, if you didn't invest in this business, you *could have* earned 7 per cent compound interest for 5 years at the bank. In other words, by investing in the business, you are forgoing an opportunity of earning the interest return on your deposit at the bank. We say that there is an **opportunity cost** of investing this money in the business, and it is equal to the interest return forgone. When the nominal rate is 7 per cent, that cost turns out to be too large.

In contrast, in Question B, the investment turns out to be profitable ($NPV > 0$). It shows that investing in this business is a cheaper way of producing that income stream than depositing in the bank. The opportunity cost of investing in this business is forgoing the interest return from the bank deposit, which is 2 per cent. This is considerably lower than 7 per cent in Question A, and indeed it turns out that the opportunity cost is low enough for you to prefer investing in the business rather than depositing in the bank.

3.8   Annuities: what is the value of your home loan?

The major personal financial transactions in our lives involve a series of repayments or payments. In finance, a series of repayments or payments is called an **annuity**. For example, most people use a loan to purchase their home and then make a series of regular repayments to pay off this loan. We call the value of this loan the **present value of an annuity**. An opposite example can be found in a superannuation scheme. People make regular payments (contributions), and on retirement they receive these payments

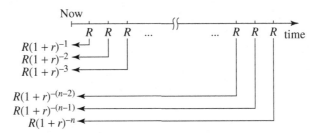

Figure 3.7 A time line 1.

and the interest on them. The total value of these payments and the interest is called the **future value of an annuity**. In this section we will discuss these two types of annuity in turn.

3.8.1 Present value of an ordinary annuity

Consider the following situation. You decided to use a loan to purchase your home at the beginning of Period 1. You are now committed to make n times of repayments to a bank. Each time, you are repaying R dollars. The repayments will start at the end of Period 1, and will occur at the end of each period until the end of Period n. We say that the **term** of this annuity is n periods and each of the n periods is called the **repayment period**.

We also assume that compounding takes place at the end of each repayment period. Such an annuity is called an **ordinary annuity**. When compounding takes place at the beginning of each period, it is called an **annuity due**, but it is not going to be our focus. Note that when compounding takes place at the end of each repayment period, the compounding period and the repayment period coincide. In such a case, the annuity is called a **simple annuity**. Whereas when these periods do not coincide – e.g. when you make annual repayments when interest is compounded continuously – the annuity is called a **general annuity**. We will not deal with general annuities in this book, so our focus in the following will be **ordinary simple annuity**.

Now suppose the periodic rate is denoted by r. The present value of an annuity (A) is the sum of the present values of all the repayments, which can be written as follows:

$$A = R(1+r)^{-1} + R(1+r)^{-2} + R(1+r)^{-3} + \cdots + R(1+r)^{-(n-1)} + R(1+r)^{-n}.$$

$$(3.50)$$

The use of a **time line** helps you visualise this equation. In Figure 3.7, a time line is drawn. It describes how all the repayments are discounted to their present values. R repaid at the end of Period 1 is discounted back one period to $R(1+r)^{-1}$, R repaid at the end of Period 2 is discounted back two periods to $R(1+r)^{-2}$, and so on. You can see that the RHS of Equation (3.50) is merely the collection of them.

It can be observed that the right hand side of Equation (3.50) is the geometric series of n terms with the initial value $R(1+r)^{-1}$ and the common ratio $(1+r)^{-1}$. So you should be able to apply the geometric series formula and simplify Equation (3.50).

Question Simplify Equation (3.50).

Solution

$$A = \frac{R(1+r)^{-1}\left[1-(1+r)^{-n}\right]}{1-(1+r)^{-1}}$$

$$= \frac{R\left[1-(1+r)^{-n}\right]}{(1+r)\left[1-(1+r)^{-1}\right]}$$

$$= \frac{R\left[1-(1+r)^{-n}\right]}{(1+r)-1}$$

$$= R \cdot \frac{1-(1+r)^{-n}}{r}.$$

Exercise 3.18 Simplifying Equation (3.50).

So, the present value A of an ordinary annuity of R dollars per repayment period for n periods at the interest rate of r per period can be written as

$$A = R \cdot \frac{1-(1+r)^{-n}}{r}. \qquad (3.51)$$

Here's an exercise for you.

Question Find the present value of an annuity of \$50 per month for 3 years at an interest rate of 6 per cent compounded monthly. You may round your answer to two decimal places.

Solution Substituting in Equation (3.51), we set $R = 50$, $r = 0.005$, and $n = 36$. Therefore:

$$A = 50 \cdot \frac{1-(1+0.005)^{-36}}{0.005}$$

$$\approx 1643.55 \text{ (dollars)}.$$

Exercise 3.19 The present value of an ordinary annuity.

3.8.2 Future value of an annuity

We turn to discuss the future value of an ordinary annuity. In short, it is the sum of the compound amounts of all payments (we will visualise it shortly). Let us consider the following situation.

You will deposit money in your savings account n times. Each time, you are depositing D dollars. Suppose the periodic rate is denoted by r. The deposit will start at the end of

3.8 Annuities: what is the value of your home loan?

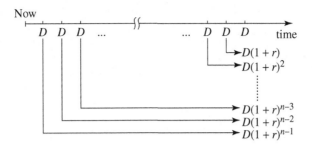

Figure 3.8 A time line 2.

Period 1, and will occur at the end of each period until the end of Period n. Compounding takes place at the end of each period as we are looking at an ordinary annuity.

The future value of the annuity S can be written as follows:

$$S = D + D(1+r) + D(1+r)^2 + D(1+r)^3 + \cdots + D(1+r)^{n-2} + D(1+r)^{n-1}.$$

$$(3.52)$$

Again the use of a time line helps you visualise this equation. In Figure 3.8 we describe how all the repayments are discounted (forward) to their future values. We start with D deposited at the end of Period n, which needs no discounting. D deposited at the end of Period $n-1$ is discounted forward one period to $D(1+r)$, D deposited at the end of Period $n-2$ is discounted forward two periods to $D(1+r)^2$, and so on. The RHS of Equation (3.52) is merely the collection of these values discounted forward.

Again, S is the geometric series of n terms with the initial value D and the common ratio $(1+r)$. Using the geometric series formula, you should be able to simplify S.

Question Simplify Equation (3.52).

Solution

$$S = \frac{D\left[1 - (1+r)^n\right]}{1 - (1+r)}$$

$$= \frac{D\left[1 - (1+r)^n\right]}{-r}$$

$$= \frac{D\left[(1+r)^n - 1\right]}{r}.$$

Exercise 3.20 Simplifying Equation (3.52).

So the future value S of an ordinary annuity of D dollars per payment period for n periods at the interest rate of r per period can be written as:

$$S = D \cdot \frac{(1+r)^n - 1}{r}.$$

$$(3.53)$$

Here's an exercise for you.

Question Find the future value of an annuity of $50 at the end of every three months for 3 years at an interest rate of 8 per cent compounded quarterly. What is the compound interest? You may round your answer to two decimal places.

Solution

$$S = 50 \cdot \frac{(1 + 0.02)^{12} - 1}{0.02}$$

$$\approx 670.60 \text{ (dollars)}.$$

Compound interest: $670.60 - 12 \times 50 = 70.60$.

Exercise 3.21 The future value of an ordinary annuity.

3.9 Perpetuity

Financial assets that yield regular payments for an infinite number of periods are called **perpetuities**. An example of a perpetuity is a particular type of a **bond**. A bond is a promise by the issuer to pay the holder a fixed sum (a **redemption value**) at a specified **maturity date** and to make interest payments (**coupon interest** payments) at regular intervals. So a bond that has no maturity date or redemption value and which pays coupon interest forever is a perpetuity (we will look at this in the example shortly).

In fact, a perpetuity can be considered as an ordinary annuity with an infinite duration. Despite this, we can show that the present value of a perpetuity approaches a certain value, $\frac{R}{r}$. To check this, we use the present value formula as in Equation (3.51). The present value of a perpetuity can be obtained by taking the limit, $\lim\limits_{n \to \infty} A$:

$$\lim_{n \to \infty} A = R \lim_{n \to \infty} \frac{1 - (1 + r)^{-n}}{r}$$

$$= \frac{R}{r} \lim_{n \to \infty} \left[1 - (1 + r)^{-n} \right]$$

$$= \frac{R}{r} - \frac{R}{r} \lim_{n \to \infty} (1 + r)^{-n}$$

$$= \frac{R}{r} - \frac{R}{r} \lim_{n \to \infty} \frac{1}{(1 + r)^{n}}.$$

The second term of the RHS approaches zero because $(1 + r)$ is greater than unity (the denominator approaches infinity and the numerator is constant at unity, so the ratio approaches zero). Therefore, the present value of a perpetuity approaches $\frac{R}{r}$.

Question Suppose the government guarantees that all holders of a bond will be paid $100 at the end of each quarter forever. If interest of 8 per cent is compounded quarterly, what are the future and the present values of this perpetuity?

Solution

$$PV = \frac{100}{0.02} = 5000.$$

Exercise 3.22 The present value of a perpetuity.

3.10 Additional exercises

1. **(Limits)** Find the following limits where possible.

(1) $\displaystyle\lim_{x \to 2} \frac{x^2 + x - 6}{x - 2}$.

(2) $\displaystyle\lim_{x \to \infty} \frac{x^2 + x - 6}{x - 2}$.

(3) $\displaystyle\lim_{x \to 3} \frac{x - 3}{x^2 - 6x + 9}$.

(4) $\displaystyle\lim_{x \to -2} \frac{x^2 - 4}{x^2 + 12x + 20}$.

(5) $\displaystyle\lim_{x \to \infty} \frac{12x}{x^8 - 4x^4 - 17}$.

2. **(Summations)** Express the following sums using a summation operator.

(1) $1 + 3 + 5 + 7 + 9$.

(2) $1 + 4 + 9 + 16 + 25 + 36 + \cdots + n^2$.

(3) $2x + 4x^2 + 8x^3 + 16x^4 + 32x^5$.

(4) $a_{i1}b_{1j} + a_{i2}b_{2j} + \cdots + a_{in}b_{nj}$.

3. **(The geometric series)** Find the sum to infinity of the following series. [**Hint.** Do it in two steps. Step 1: describe the sum assuming there are n terms. Step 2: think what will happen to this sum when n approaches infinity, i.e. $n \to \infty$.]

(1) $243, 81, 27, 9, 3, 1, \ldots$

(2) $1, 2, 4, 8, 16, 32, \ldots$

(3) $1, \dfrac{1}{1+r}, \dfrac{1}{(1+r)^2}, \dfrac{1}{(1+r)^3}, \ldots$, where $r > 0$.

(4) $\dfrac{1}{1+r}, -\dfrac{1}{(1+r)^2}, \dfrac{1}{(1+r)^3}, -\dfrac{1}{(1+r)^4}, \ldots$, where $r > 0$.

Table 3.3. Net cash flows.

End of year	Project Constant Cash flow	PV at 5%	PV at 10%
1	50		
2	50		
3	50		
4	50		
5	50		

End of year	Project Increasing Cash flow	PV at 5%	PV at 10%
1	0		
2	20		
3	50		
4	100		
5	100		

4. **(The effective rate)** What is the effective rate of interest? Denote the principal by P, the nominal rate by i, and the number of compounding periods per year by n. Carefully derive the effective rate r_e. If \$2000 is accumulated to \$6000 over a period of 6 years in an account where interest is compounded daily, how can we obtain the effective rate? You may use the following information at the end of your calculation: $3^{\frac{1}{6}} \approx 1.20$.

5. **(The effective rate and the nominal rate)** If a major credit-card company has a finance charge of 1 per cent per month on the outstanding debt, obtain the nominal rate compounded monthly. Also, obtain the effective rate. You may use the following information at the end of your calculation: $1.01^{12} \approx 1.13$.

6. **(Doubling the money)** How many years will it take for our money to double if interest is compounded continuously at a nominal rate of 2 per cent? Express your answer using the natural logarithm. Calculate it using the information that $\ln 2 \approx 0.7$. How many years will it take for our money to double if interest is compounded annually at the same nominal rate? Express it using the natural logarithm. Do you expect this duration to be shorter than the one you obtained under continuous compounding?

7. **(Net present value)** A firm has two investment projects, Constant and Increasing. Cash flows that these projects will generate are given in Table 3.3. Calculate the sum of the present value of cash flows for each project if interest is compounded annually at (a) 5 per cent, and (b) 10 per cent. Suppose both projects require the same amount of initial investment. Give advice to this firm as to which of these projects is better to undertake under (a) and (b). Carefully explain your findings. In calculating, you may round numbers to two decimal places for each of the present values of cash flows.

8. **(Compound interest)** The population growth rate in Fefmland for the 5 years between 1999 and 2003 had been r_1 per annum. Because of a change in policy the population growth rate of Fefmland was r_2 per annum for the 5 years between 2004 and 2008. Express the average population growth rate per annum over the 10-year period between 1999 and 2008 in terms of r_1 and r_2. Here, the average population growth rate per annum, denoted by g, for the 10-year period is defined by the following equation: $P_{1998}(1 + g)^{10} = P_{2008}$, where P_{1998} and P_{2008} are the population of Fefmland in the beginning of 1999 and the end of 2008, respectively.

9. **(Future value of an annuity)** A company called Generous Insurance sells an education policy to parents with new babies. If the nominal rate of 8 per cent is compounded quarterly, what is the size of the payments that must be made by parents at the end of each quarter (so the first payment is made 3 months after the child is born), if they wish to receive $15 000 when their child turns 18? What will the size of the payments be if those must be made at the beginning of each quarter?

10. **(Perpetuity with increasing payments)** Consider the situation where Nasty Bank offers new-home buyers the option of making payments of continually increasing size at the end of each period. That is, instead of payments of R, customers will make payments of:

$$R, R(1 + g), R(1 + g)^2, R(1 + g)^3, \ldots \qquad \text{(IP)}$$

Here, g is an increase in the size of the payment from one period to the next. For example, if the payment increases by 1 per cent from one period to the next, then $g = 0.01$. Assume that the periodic rate is $r > 0$ and $r \neq g$.

Obtain the present value of a perpetuity when we have payments of an increasing size as in (IP). [**Hint.** Recall we obtained the PV of an annuity in the main text when payments are constant (Equations (3.50) and (3.51)). Using the same approach, you need to derive the PV of an annuity when payments are increasing. Think what Equation (3.50) will become if payments are increasing. And then, using the geometric series formula, you can simplify the sum similar to Equation (3.51), which should involve R, r, g and n. Then, take the limit of it when n approaches infinity.] Does it depend on the relative size of r and g? What will the present value be if g is zero? Explain.

4 Differential calculus 1

This chapter deals with differential calculus. Recall that we dealt with *market* supply curves in previous chapters. They were generally assumed to be upward sloping (the law of supply). In this chapter, we will derive an upward sloping supply schedule *of a firm* both intuitively and mathematically. To this end, we will focus on a firm's profit maximisation problem that underlies it.

A firm is an institution that hires factors of production (inputs) and transforms them into goods and services (outputs) using its production technology. Here we consider a firm whose objective is to maximise its profits. Therefore we are interested in obtaining the level of output that maximises the firm's profits. In the course of obtaining the profit maximising level of output, we will introduce differentiation, which is the process of finding the derivative of a function, and will also foreshadow some of the important mathematical notions related to curve sketching that will be covered in the next chapter.

Chapter goals By studying this chapter you will

(1) be able to explain various notions regarding costs;
(2) be able to interpret what it means by differentiating a function; and
(3) be able to set up and solve the firm's profit maximisation problem.

4.1 Cost function

As mentioned before, a **firm** is an institution that hires **factors** of production (**inputs**), such as labour, machines and raw materials, and transforms them into goods and services (**outputs**) by using their production technologies. Our focus will be profit maximising firms, i.e. those whose objective is to maximise their profits. Throughout this chapter, we will also limit our analysis to the **short run**. A short run is the time period in which at least one factor of production is fixed: for example, it is hard to imagine that a new factory is built in a few days. Typically, capital (K) is fixed in the short run. Some other inputs, such as labour and raw materials, can typically be changed in the short run. Here, we assume that only one input is variable in the short run, which we call labour (L), and also assume that only one good is produced. In passing, the other time frame economists frequently use is the **long run**, where all factors of production including capital are variable, but this time period is not of interest to us here.

To figure out the profits the firm might make, it has to know (a) how much its products sell for at the market; and (b) how much it needs to pay to hire factor(s) of production.

Table 4.1. Costs.

q	TC	FC	VC
0	500	500	0
1	700	500	200
2	820	500	320
3	920	500	420
4	1040	500	540
5	1190	500	690
6	1390	500	890
7	1670	500	1170
8	2070	500	1570
9	2640	500	2140
10	3440	500	2940

Because our focus here is on the firms that produce one good using one input (labour), we can rephrase it as follows; the firm has to know how much its product sells for at the market and how much it needs to pay to hire labour. In this chapter, we make an assumption on markets for both inputs and outputs (unless it is explicitly noted otherwise). Namely, we assume that both the goods market and the labour market are competitive: since there are so many parties involved in both of these markets, *no single party has power to change the price by itself.* Under this situation, *each party takes the market price as given.* More specifically, we assume that a firm sells its product at a product price (p) and hires the labour it needs at its market price (w per hour).

Let q and c denote the amount of the good it produces and the **total cost**, respectively. In the short run, the total cost consists of two parts: the **fixed cost (FC)** and the **variable cost (VC)**. The former is the cost of production that does not depend on the quantity of production, i.e. the cost a firm incurs regardless of the production level. The latter is the cost of production that varies with the quantity of production. Therefore:

$$c = FC + VC(q).$$

The notation $VC(q)$ shows that the variable cost VC is a function of q (it depends on q). Accordingly, the total cost also depends on q, so let us write the above relationship as follows:

$$c = C(q) = FC + VC(q). \tag{4.1}$$

$C(q)$ is called the **cost function**: it is a function C that maps quantity of production q to the total cost c.

4.1.1   A numerical example

Table 4.1 shows the various costs of a firm in goods production. Let us plot the information on the following diagram.

The curve plotted in Figure 4.1 is called the **total cost (TC) curve**. The total cost curve described in this figure can be found in most introductory economics textbooks, but some of you might wonder what sort of production technology is represented by this total cost

Table 4.2. The marginal cost.

q	TC	MC
0	500	
1	700	200
2	820	120
3	920	100
4	1040	120
5	1190	150
6	1390	200
7	1670	280
8	2070	400
9	2640	570
10	3440	800

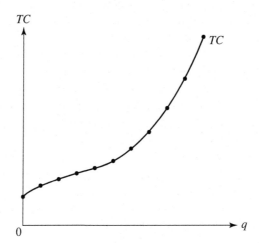

Figure 4.1 A rough sketch of the total cost curve.

curve. To answer this question, we will need to further investigate a firm's production technology. Let us first introduce some measures of costs.

4.2 The marginal cost and the average costs

The **marginal cost (MC)** of production is the change in the total cost when there is *a one-unit change* in the quantity produced. For example, the marginal cost of increasing production from $q = 3$ to $q = 4$ is $120 ($1040–$920). The marginal cost of increasing production from $q = 9$ to $q = 10$ is $800 ($3440–$2640). Note that the marginal cost differs according to the level of production. How does the marginal cost differ from one level of production to another? We can see how the marginal cost changes in the final column of Table 4.2.

Table 4.3. The average cost and the average variable cost.

q	TC	AC	AVC
0	500		
1	700	700	200
2	820	410	160
3	920	307	140
4	1040	260	135
5	1190	238	138
6	1390	232	148
7	1670	239	167
8	2070	259	196
9	2640	293	238
10	3440	344	294

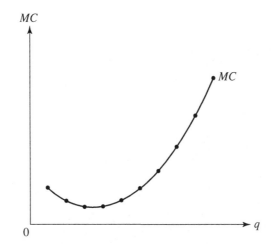

Figure 4.2 A rough sketch of the marginal cost curve.

We can observe that the marginal cost declines at low levels of production (until $q = 3$) and then starts increasing. The graph that plots the marginal cost is called the **marginal cost curve**. The above observation implies that the curve is *U-shaped*.

There are two other important measures of costs. The **average total cost (AC)**, or just the **average cost**, is simply the total cost of production (TC) divided by the quantity produced (q). For example, the total cost of producing 4 units is $1040 so the average total cost is $260 ($1040 divided by 4). The average cost changes according to quantity (see the third column of Table 4.3). It declines initially (until $q = 6$) and then starts increasing. It follows that the **average cost curve** is U-shaped as well.

The **average variable cost (AVC)** is simply the variable cost of production (VC) divided by the quantity produced (q). For example, the variable cost of producing 3 units is $420 so the average variable cost is $140 ($420 divided by 3). The average variable cost also changes with the quantity of production (see the last column of Table 4.3). It declines

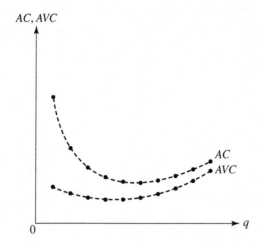

Figure 4.3 A rough sketch of AC and AVC curves.

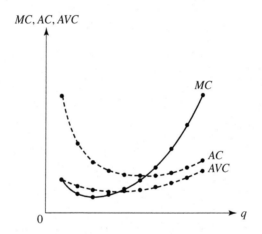

Figure 4.4 A rough sketch of MC, AC and AVC curves.

initially (until $q = 4$) and then starts increasing. This implies that the **average variable cost curve** is also U-shaped. These two curves are depicted in Figure 4.3.

Let us draw MC, AC and AVC curves on the same diagram (Figure 4.4). We have already noted that the three curves are U-shaped. Besides, we should note the following important facts.

(1) When the marginal cost (MC) is less than the average cost (AC), then AC is declining. When MC is greater than AC, then AC is increasing.

(2) When the marginal cost (MC) is less than the average variable cost (AVC), then AVC is declining. When MC is greater than AVC, then AVC is increasing.

The relative positions of these three curves are important. We will prove these facts *mathematically* later in this chapter, but let us try thinking about them intuitively first.

4.2.1 Intuitive explanation

The reason for the above relationship regarding MC, AC and AVC can be seen with an analogy. Imagine that the average age of the students attending a particular class is 20. Suppose one student comes in late and joins the class. Say this student's age is 19. What will happen to the average age of the students in this class? Our intuition suggests that the average age should go down. The logic is simple: this student's contribution to the total number of the age in class is below the average (prior to him joining), so the average age falls inevitably.

Some of you may wonder what the above story has to do with the relationship between 'marginal' and 'average'. If so, you need to think what the 'marginal age' is in this context ('the average age' is rather obvious). Recall that the marginal cost is the change in the total costs when there is a one-unit change in the quantity produced. Then, likewise, we can define the marginal age as the change in the total age (in the class) when *one* student joins the class (i.e. a one-student increase). In the above story, you can see that 19 (the new student's age) is the marginal age because the total age of the class has gone up by 19 when this student has joined the class.

Thus, in the above story, the marginal age (which is 19) is less than the average age (prior to him joining the class, which is 20). In this case, the average age of the class goes down. On the other hand, if the student who joins is 21 instead of 19, then the scenario will be the opposite. This student's age of 21 is greater than the class average of 20, and this above-average contribution by the student increases the average age of the class. In other words, if the marginal age is greater than the average age, then the average age of the class increases when a student with this age joins.

4.3 Production function

Now we get to answering the question we asked at the end of Section 4.1: what explains the shape of the typical cost function? Throughout the discussion here, we call the variable input labour (L) and the fixed input capital (K). It is obvious from Table 4.1 that the fixed cost is $500, which means that to hire capital K the firm has paid $500. It is fixed, so this firm has to pay $500 regardless of how much they produce. To change the level of output in the short run, it can only vary the level of the other input, labour, which costs w per unit. Our interest is to investigate the relationship between the level of output and the level of labour input.

Note that this firm's labour hiring cost corresponds exactly to its variable cost (VC), because labour is the only input that is variable in the short run. Look at Table 4.4. It is identical to Table 4.1 except for the final column where labour input is shown. Suppose that it costs $10 to hire one hour of labour ($w = 10$). Then we can deduce the hours of work (L) that are needed for each level of production (q). For example, in order to produce one unit, the variable cost is $200. It means 20 (200 divided by 10) hours of labour are

Table 4.4. Costs and labour input.

q	TC	FC	VC	L
0	500	500	0	0
1	700	500	200	20
2	820	500	320	32
3	920	500	420	42
4	1040	500	540	54
5	1190	500	690	69
6	1390	500	890	89
7	1670	500	1170	117
8	2070	500	1570	157
9	2640	500	2140	214
10	3440	500	2940	294

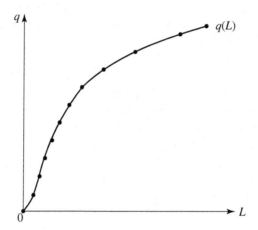

Figure 4.5 A rough sketch of the production function.

required. For 10-unit production, the variable cost is $2940, indicating that 294 (2940 divided by 10) hours have to be put in. Following the same steps, you should be able to figure out how the final column of the table is constructed. The information in the first and the last columns in the table gives us the **production function**: it shows how much output can be produced for each amount of labour input:

$$q = f(L). \tag{4.2}$$

Let us plot the information on a diagram; what does the production function look like? Figure 4.5 shows the plot taking hours of work on the horizontal axis and the level of output on the vertical axis.

We now introduce a new notion called the **marginal product of labour**. The marginal product of labour is the change in the level of output caused by a one-unit increase in labour. We cannot see the marginal product of labour from the table, but can roughly observe on the diagram how it behaves. You should observe the following.

(1) At low levels of production, the marginal product of labour increases.
(2) At high levels of production, the marginal product of labour starts to decline.

The increasing marginal product of labour is also referred to as **increasing returns to labour** whereas the decreasing marginal product of labour is often called **diminishing returns to labour**.

The pattern of the marginal product of labour increasing up to a certain unit of production then declining explains the pattern of the marginal cost decreasing up to a certain unit of production then increasing (which is observed in Section 4.2: remember, the MC curve is U-shaped). If the marginal product of labour is increasing, then the marginal cost is decreasing, and vice versa.

In Section 4.1 we deferred answering the question: what sort of production technology are we looking at? Let us think about the above pattern of the marginal product of labour. For instance, consider working in a restaurant and, to start with, suppose you are the only worker. As a sole worker, you have to do everything – taking orders, all the cooking, serving, etc. – by yourself, yet still you are able to serve a certain number of customers in a day. The marginal product of labour is equivalent to your output (i.e. an increase in the restaurant's total output). Now, if the restaurant hires another worker who has the same skills, then you can imagine that the restaurant's output in a day *more than* doubles. Why? The new worker is as skillful as you are, so if both of you worked independently, then the output should double. That is, the marginal product of the new worker (an increase in the total output caused by the new worker) is the same as yours (i.e. your output when you were the sole worker). But you and the new worker may be able to do better than working independently; both of you can coordinate – e.g. one specialises in cooking and the other in all the other things – and work more effectively as a team. In this case, the marginal product (let me remind you again, it is an increase in the total output caused by the new worker) is greater than yours (an increase in the total output caused by you when you were the sole worker, i.e. your output before the new worker joined). A third worker may allow making the kitchen (and hence the whole restaurant) work more efficiently; two workers may be able to specialise in particular processes in the kitchen while another worker does all the other things in the dining area. The marginal product of the third worker, in this case, is greater than that of the second one.

You may be able to envisage the increasing marginal product described as above up to some level of output but, as you might already have guessed, there may be an end to it; i.e. the diminishing returns to labour may kick in at some stage. Any restaurant has its capacity (it presumably depends on the size of the restaurant, which has to do with the fixed costs) – both in the kitchen and in the dining area – and so the room for further coordination between the workers becomes less and less. At some stage, an additional worker may increase the total output (so the marginal product is positive) but this increase in the total output may be less than that when the previous worker was hired. You may even be able to imagine the case under which the marginal product is negative (i.e. the total output *decreases* when the new worker is hired), although numbers provided in Table 4.4 do not consider this extreme situation.

Table 4.5. The marginal
revenue and marginal cost.

q	MR	MC
3	210	100
4	210	120
5	210	150
6	210	200
7	210	280
8	210	400
9	210	570
10	210	800

The numbers provided in the tables in this chapter (and hence the shapes of the production function and the cost function) represent the production technology described as in the story above. In the following section, we will deduce an upward sloping supply curve for a firm supposing that the firm's production technology is of the above sort; but here is a word of warning before moving on. If you encounter other tables that summarise some production technology, they may *not* necessarily replicate the story described above. For example, the table may represent the case where the marginal product of a particular input is constant (see Question 2 in Section 4.8).

4.4 Firm's supply curve

Now we are in a position to deduce an upward sloping supply curve of a firm. Checking the validity of the following claim turns out to be (almost) equivalent to conducting this task: *a firm in a competitive market (that is, this firm takes the price as given) will choose the quantity such that the price equals the marginal cost.*[1]

Let us investigate why it is the case using our example. Suppose the price of a good in a competitive market is $210. It means that if a firm increases the supply by one unit, its revenue increases by $210 (because that one unit will sell for $210 for sure). This extra revenue resulting from producing and selling one more unit is called the **marginal revenue**. In a competitive market, the marginal revenue – denoted by MR – is the same as the market price (p).

Look at Table 4.5. Suppose you are producing 3 units of output. Should you produce another unit of output? The answer is YES. Because, by producing and selling another unit of output, you will get $210 of marginal benefit, whereas the marginal cost of producing that unit is only $120. You will gain $90 by producing another unit. Hence, it is not profit-maximising to stop producing at 3 units of output. Then, is it profit-maximising for you to stop at producing 4 units of output? The answer is NO. Because, again, by producing and selling another unit of output (the fifth unit), you will get $210 of the marginal revenue,

---

1 I will shortly show that the claim is true only when the price is sufficiently high; hence there is a word 'almost' in the brackets.

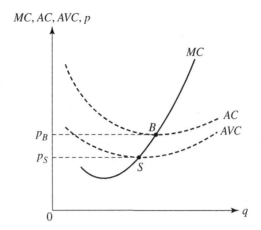

MC, AC, AVC, p

Figure 4.6 A rough sketch of MC, AC and AVC curves.

but the marginal cost of producing that unit is only \$150, and hence you will gain \$60 (you can increase the profits by producing this unit!).

Let us jump to the end of this story. Suppose you are producing and selling 6 units of output. Should you produce the seventh unit? The answer is NO. Because by producing and selling that unit, you will obtain the marginal revenue of \$210 (the market price), but the marginal cost of producing that unit is \$280. You will *lose* \$70 by producing this unit, so it is better for you to stop at the sixth unit production. The profit-maximising output is therefore 6 units.

What the above analysis shows is that a firm increases quantity of production if the marginal revenue is above the marginal cost, and it stops doing so when $MR = MC$.[2] Hence the correctness of the initial claim is verified: *a firm in a competitive market will choose the quantity such that the price equals the marginal cost.*

4.4.1 Not all parts of the *MC* curve are the supply curve

We have shown that the MC curve is, in fact, the supply curve of a firm in a competitive market. The supply curve is the MC curve drawn on a space of (p, q) instead of (MC, q). However, we need to be careful. Only some parts of the MC curve are the supply curve. We will illustrate it here using Figure 4.4 of this chapter (we relabel it as Figure 4.6).

There are two important points in Figure 4.6. One is the intersection of MC and AC curves. Let us denote this point by B. The other is the intersection of MC and AVC curves. We denote this point by S. We take the price (as well) on the vertical axis, and denote the price levels corresponding to Points B and S by p_B and p_S, respectively.

First, let us think what happens if the price of the good is above p_B, that is $p > p_B$. If this is the case, a firm will produce because it makes positive profits. Why? Let us look at a specific example: $p = 400$. Using Tables 4.2 and 4.3, we obtain Table 4.6.

---

2 In the above example, $MR = MC$ does not hold exactly because we are looking at a discrete case, i.e. the change in production is possible by one unit at minimum. We will eventually look at a continuous case where the production can be adjusted by an infinitesimally small amount.

Table 4.6. Firm's profit maximisation when $p = 400$.

q	MC	AC	AVC
3	100	307	140
4	120	260	135
5	150	238	138
6	200	232	148
7	280	239	167
8	**400**	**259**	**196**
9	570	293	238
10	800	344	294

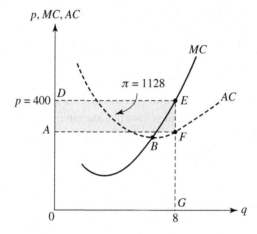

Figure 4.7 A firm makes positive profits: $p > p_B$.

When $p = 400$, this firm will supply 8 units of output (because $p = MC$). What are the profits? Profits are the difference between the total revenue and the total costs. The total revenue is simply the quantity of output sold multiplied by the price per output, so it is \$3200. By definition, the total costs can be calculated by multiplying the average total cost (AC) by quantity produced. The total costs are $8 \times 259 = \$2072$. Hence this firm is making positive profits of \$1128. There is no problem for this firm to supply output where $p = MC$. The situation can be depicted as in Figure 4.7. Note that the total revenue and the total costs correspond to the rectangles $ODEG$ and $OAFG$, respectively. Accordingly, the profits are described by the rectangle $ADEF$.

Second, let us consider the case where the price of the good is p_B, that is $p = p_B$. In this situation, it is easy to show that a firm will produce and is break-even. When $p = p_B$, this firm will choose to produce at Point B, where $p_B = MC$. Denote this quantity by q_B. At this point, note that $p_B = AC$ also holds. The revenue of this firm is $p_B q_B$. The total costs are AC multiplied by q_B, so the firm makes the profits that equal $p_B \cdot q_B - AC \cdot q_B$. This expression collapses down to zero because we are looking at the point where $p_B = AC$. Since the firm is making zero profits (break-even), Point B in the diagram is referred to

Table 4.7. Firm's profit
maximisation when $p = 200$.

q	MC	AC	AVC
3	100	307	140
4	120	260	135
5	150	238	138
6	**200**	**232**	**148**
7	280	239	167
8	400	259	196
9	570	293	238
10	800	344	294

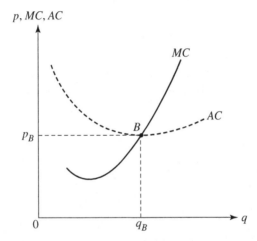

Figure 4.8 A firm is break-even: $p = p_B$.

as the **break-even point**. If the firm is break-even, then it will produce because it is better than not producing. By choosing not to produce, this firm makes negative profits of $500 (fixed costs). Obviously, for this firm, break-even (recovering the fixed costs) is better than making losses. The situation can be depicted in Figure 4.8. The rectangle $Op_B B q_B$ corresponds to both the total revenue and the total costs.

Third, what occurs if the price is below p_B but above p_S, that is $p_S < p < p_B$. If this is the case, a firm will still produce *despite making losses*. Why is this the case? Let us again look at a specific example: $p = 200$.

Looking at Table 4.7 (whose information is again taken from Tables 4.2 and 4.3), we can see that, when $p = 200$, this firm will supply 6 units of output ($p = MC$). What are profits? The total revenue is $1200 whereas the total costs are $6 \times 232 = \$1392$. Hence this firm is making *losses* of $192. This firm, however, will supply 6 units to the market. Again, it is because doing so is better than not producing, under which circumstances it will end up making losses of $500. The situation can be described as in Figure 4.9. The (negative) profits correspond to the rectangle $ADFE$.

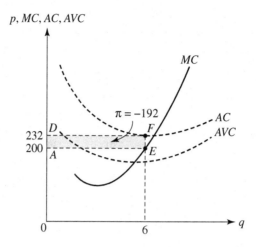

Figure 4.9 A firm makes losses but produces: $p_S < p < p_B$.

Fourth, what happens if the price is equal to p_S, that is $p = p_S$? If this is the case, a firm will be indifferent between producing and not producing.[3] Why?

When $p = p_S$, the firm will choose to produce at Point S, where $p = MC$, so let us denote the quantity by q_S. At this point, note that $p = AVC$ also holds. We know from the previous analysis that the firm's profits can be expressed as $p \cdot q - AC \cdot q$. In the meantime, we also know that $TC = VC + FC$, so dividing both sides of this expression by q gives us $AC = AVC + \dfrac{FC}{q}$. Using this expression, the firm's profits now become $p \cdot q - AVC \cdot q - FC$.

Recall that $p = AVC$ at Point S, so the first two terms of the expression for the profits cancel out. It means that the firm's profits are exactly the negative of the fixed costs, i.e. the firm makes losses exactly equal to \$500 if it produces at Point S (which is the best it can do as long as it wants to produce). These losses are equivalent to the losses this firm will make if they choose not to produce. Hence the firm is indifferent between producing and not producing. The situation can be seen in Figure 4.10. By now you should be able to verify that the (negative) profits are described by the rectangle $p_S ADS$.

Point S in Figure 4.10 is called the **shutdown point** because if the price goes below p_S – the final case – it is better for a firm *not* to produce (shutdown production). When $p < p_S$, if a firm chooses to produce output where $p = MC$ (the best the firm can do if they want to produce), it makes losses, and *the losses are greater than those under zero production*. Therefore, *the firm will not supply in the case when $p < p_S$*. You should attempt Question 3 in Section 4.8 to verify the claim both algebraically and diagrammatically.

In summary, the MC curve is the supply curve of a firm in a competitive market, but only the segment above the shutdown point (the intersection of MC and AVC curves) is relevant. In other words, it is *profit maximising* for a firm to supply a quantity such that price equals the marginal cost if $p \geq p_S$, but to supply zero if $p < p_S$. A firm's supply curve is hence case-defined.

---

3 In economics, if a firm is indifferent in producing and not producing, it is often assumed that it will produce.

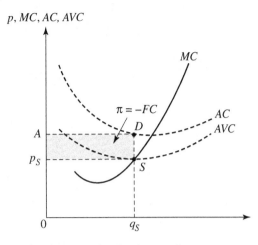

Figure 4.10 The shutdown point: $p = p_S$.

Our next objective is to derive a firm's supply function mathematically when its total cost function is given. To this end, we will introduce some mathematical notions.

4.5   From a one-unit change to an infinitesimally small change

Up to the present, we have been discussing the change in costs of production when the level of production has changed by one unit. Accordingly, we drew various curves we looked at in previous subsections in a *step-wise* fashion. That is, all we could do was to *plot* points and *connect* them.

Hereafter we will focus upon an *infinitesimally small change* in the level of production, and investigate the corresponding change in the production costs.[4] Focusing upon an infinitesimally small change in q motivates us to draw those curves in a different – much smoother – manner. Our first focus is the total cost curve for a firm.

Look at Figure 4.11. Consider that you are producing q_0 units of the goods, i.e. our attention is on Point A. Recall that the cost function is written as $C(q)$, so the total costs for that production level are written as $C(q_0)$. Suppose you increase production by one unit, and now you are producing q_1 units of the goods; obviously $q_1 = q_0 + 1$. At this production level, the total costs are $C(q_1)$. The difference between these two costs, $C(q_1) - C(q_0)$, is the marginal cost when you are producing q_0 units of this good. The next diagram is the enlargement of the cost curve in Figure 4.11. The marginal cost at Point A is equal to the distance BE.

On Figure 4.12, a straight line DJ is drawn. It is *tangent to* the cost curve at Point A. We can see that the marginal cost at Point A, BE, consists of two parts: BD and DE. The

---

4 An example of an infinitesimally small change may be found in wine production. A one-unit increase in wine production can mean an increase in production by 1 litre of wine. Now we are looking at an increase in production, say by 400 millilitres of wine. We are ultimately interested in an increase in production by a drop (an infinitesimally small change) of wine.

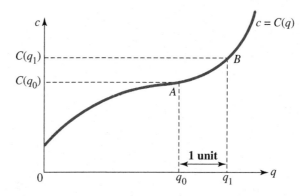

Figure 4.11 The total cost curve.

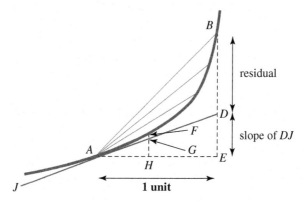

Figure 4.12 Enlargement of Figure 4.11.

important thing to note is that DE is, in fact, the *slope* of the tangent line DJ (why?). Also notice that distance DE (slope of DJ) is quite different from the marginal cost BE (the size of the residual distance BD is large), which is in fact the slope of the secant line AB. So, the above argument can be translated into the following: the slope of the secant line AB (actual marginal cost at Point A) is different from the slope of the tangent line DJ.

Now let us think about a smaller increase in production, say the production level increases by less that one unit. In Figure 4.12, this is shown as a movement from Point A to Point F. You should be able to realise that now the slope of the (new) secant line AF is not so different from the slope of the tangent line DJ.

In other words, as we make the size of change in production smaller, the size of the residual distance becomes smaller. Therefore, we have the following result. *When a change in production becomes infinitesimally small, the marginal cost equals the slope of the tangent line at the point of production.*

Now we will describe the above process mathematically. Let us use the new diagram in Figure 4.13 so that we can see things clearly.

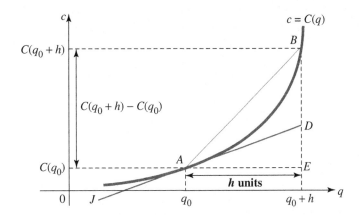

Figure 4.13 Visualising differentiation.

Consider the following situation. Currently you are producing q_0 units of the goods at Point A and so the costs of production are $C(q_0)$. Suppose you increase production *by h units*, and now you are producing $q_0 + h$ units of the goods. At this production level, the total costs are $C(q_0 + h)$. The difference between these two costs is $C(q_0 + h) - C(q_0)$. If we divide this by the change in the level of production h, we obtain the ratio $\frac{C(q_0 + h) - C(q_0)}{h}$. Note that this expression gives the slope of the *secant line AB*.

Now, if we fix q_0 and make h smaller and smaller until it approaches zero (becomes infinitesimally small), then if it exists we denote the limit of this ratio

$$\lim_{h \to 0} \frac{C(q_0 + h) - C(q_0)}{h}$$

by $C'(q_0)$. This expression is read 'C prime q nought'. $C'(q_0)$ is called the **differential coefficient** of the function $C(q)$ at $q = q_0$. If we use q instead of q_0, $C'(q_0)$ becomes $C'(q)$, which is called the **derivative** of the function $C(q)$. We can obtain the derivative of a function from the above definition:

$$C'(q) = \lim_{h \to 0} \frac{C(q + h) - C(q)}{h}. \tag{4.3}$$

When you know the function $C(q)$, the process of obtaining the derivative $C'(q)$ is called **differentiation**. Recall that when a change in production becomes infinitesimally small, the marginal cost equals the slope of the tangent line at the point of production. So, in the context of the cost function, Equation (4.3) is just a mathematical representation of the process of obtaining the marginal cost.

4.5.1 Differentiation rules

Before moving on to depict the marginal cost curve, let us list some rules of differentiation. We use the following notation: a and b are constants, and $f(x)$, $g(x)$, and $h(x)$ are differentiable functions of x.[5] These rules can be derived from the definition of the derivative, but the proofs are omitted.[6] Some practice questions are provided after the list of the rules and you should make sure you are on top of these. It is also strongly recommended that you do the practice questions provided at the end of this chapter (Section 4.8).

Differentiation rules

Rule 1 (The power rule)   If $f(x) = bx^a$, then

$$f'(x) = bax^{a-1}. \tag{4.4}$$

Rule 2 (The sum rule)   If $f(x) = ag(x) \pm bh(x)$, then

$$f'(x) = ag'(x) \pm bh'(x). \tag{4.5}$$

Rule 3 (The product rule)   If $f(x) = g(x)h(x)$, then

$$f'(x) = g'(x)h(x) + g(x)h'(x). \tag{4.6}$$

Rule 4 (The quotient rule)   If $f(x) = \dfrac{g(x)}{h(x)}$, then

$$f'(x) = \frac{g'(x)h(x) - g(x)h'(x)}{[h(x)]^2}. \tag{4.7}$$

Rule 5 (The chain rule)   If $f(x) = g(h(x))$, then

$$f'(x) = g'(h(x))h'(x). \tag{4.8}$$

Rule 6 (Derivative of e)   If $f(x) = e^x$, then

$$f'(x) = e^x. \tag{4.9}$$

Rule 7 (Derivative of logarithm)   If $f(x) = lnx$, then

$$f'(x) = \frac{1}{x}. \tag{4.10}$$

Note that the derivative of a constant is zero. That is, if $f(x) = b$ then $f'(x) = 0$. It makes perfect sense as $f(x) = b$ describes a *horizontal* line that intercepts $(0, b)$ and so its slope (the derivative) is clearly zero regardless of x.

---

5 When we can obtain the derivative of a function, the function is said to be **differentiable**. The right hand side of Equation (4.3) contains a limit. Obviously if the limit does not exist (recall we have seen some examples in Chapter 3), the derivative is undefined. In such cases we say the function is **not differentiable**.

6 Interested readers should consult with some introductory textbooks in quantitative methods, e.g. E. F. Haeussler, Jr., R. S. Paul and R. J. Wood, *Introductory Mathematical Analysis*, 12th edn (Pearson Education, 2008).

Question 1 For the following $f(x)$, obtain $f'(x)$.

(1) $f(x) = 4x^{\frac{1}{2}}$.

(2) $f(x) = 3x^{-1} + 5x^2$.

(3) $f(x) = (3x^2 + 1)(5x - 3)$.

(4) $f(x) = \dfrac{3x^2 + 1}{5x - 3}$.

(5) $f(x) = (3x^2 + 1)^4$.

(6) $f(x) = e^{5x}$.

(7) $f(x) = \ln(5x)$.

Solution

(1) $f(x) = 4x^{\frac{1}{2}}$

$$f'(x) = 4 \cdot \frac{1}{2}x^{\frac{1}{2}-1}$$
$$= 2x^{-\frac{1}{2}}.$$

(2) $f(x) = 3x^{-1} + 5x^2$

$$f'(x) = 3 \cdot (-1)x^{-1-1} + 5 \cdot 2x^{2-1}$$
$$= -3x^{-2} + 10x.$$

(3) $f(x) = (3x^2 + 1)(5x - 3)$

$$f'(x) = (6x + 0)(5x - 3) + (3x^2 + 1)(5 - 0)$$
$$= 6x(5x - 3) + 5(3x^2 + 1)$$
$$= 45x^2 - 18x + 5.$$

(4) $f(x) = \dfrac{3x^2 + 1}{5x - 3}$

$$f'(x) = \frac{6x(5x - 3) - 5(3x^2 + 1)}{(5x - 3)^2}$$
$$= \frac{30x^2 - 6x - 15x^2 - 5}{(5x - 3)^2}$$
$$= \frac{15x^2 - 6x - 5}{(5x - 3)^2}.$$

(5) $f(x) = (3x^2 + 1)^4$

Set $h(x) = 3x^2 + 1$ so $h'(x) = 6x$. Then,

$$f(h) = h^4$$
$$f'(h) = 4h^3.$$

Therefore

$$f'(x) = f'(h) \cdot h'(x)$$
$$= 4h^3 \cdot 6x$$
$$= 24x(3x^2 + 1)^3$$

because we set $h(x) = 3x^2 + 1$.

(6) $f(x) = e^{5x}$

Set $h(x) = 5x$ so $h'(x) = 5$. Then,

$$f(h) = e^h$$
$$f'(h) = e^h.$$

Therefore

$$f'(x) = f'(h) \cdot h'(x)$$
$$= 5e^h$$
$$= 5e^{5x}.$$

(7) $f(x) = \ln(5x)$

Note that $f(x) = \ln 5 + \ln x$ and that $\ln 5$ is a constant.

$$f'(x) = 0 + \frac{1}{x}$$
$$= \frac{1}{x}.$$

Exercise 4.1 Differentiation.

4.5.2 Drawing the *MC* curve

Now let us draw the *MC* curve corresponding to the total cost curve when we allow q to change by an infinitesimally small amount. Look at Figure 4.14. The total cost curve is already drawn in the top part. In the following I demonstrate how we relate the *MC* curve to the *TC* curve step by step.

Step 1. In the top part of Figure 4.14, the *total* cost curve is depicted. As you can see, slopes vary along this curve. We know that the *marginal cost* (for an infinitesimal change in production) is equal to the *slope* of this curve, so it means the *MC* of production varies according to the levels of production.

Step 2. In the bottom part of Figure 4.14, we draw the *MC* curve. The *MC* is shown on the vertical axis. On the horizontal axis we have q corresponding to the qs taken on the top

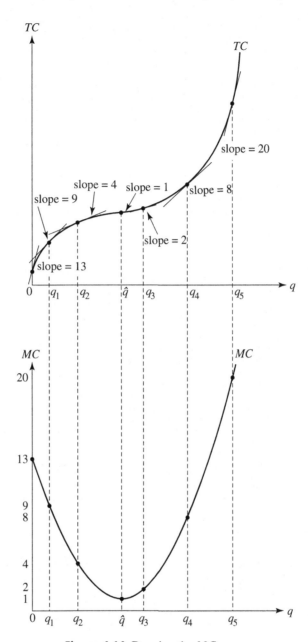

Figure 4.14 Drawing the MC curve.

diagram. In the bottom diagram we try to plot the values of the MC (i.e. the magnitudes of the slopes of the TC curve) for all the levels of production.

Step 3. For example, take $q = 0$ (zero production) and $q = q_1$. You can see that the slope of the TC curve is greater at $q = 0$ than at $q = q_1$. Say these slopes are 13 and 9, respectively. These numbers are plotted as the marginal costs for $q = 0$ and $q = q_1$, respectively, in the bottom diagram.

Step 4. Do the same for $q = q_2$ and $q = \hat{q}$, and say the slopes of the TC curves at these levels of q are 4 and 1, respectively. Plot these numbers in the bottom diagram.

Step 5. Moving from zero production to $q = \hat{q}$, we can observe that the *slope* of the total cost curve becomes smaller (flatter and flatter) and becomes the smallest when the production level is $\hat{q}$. It corresponds to the increasing marginal product of labour. It means that the MC behaves in the same way, i.e. the MC in the bottom diagram decreases until $\hat{q}$.

Step 6. From here the slope of the TC curve, i.e. the MC, starts increasing. For example, take $q = q_3$, $q = q_4$ and $q = q_5$. You can see that the slope of the TC curve becomes greater as q rises. Say these slopes are 2, 8 and 20, respectively. These numbers are plotted as the marginal costs for $q = q_3$, $q = q_4$ and $q = q_5$, respectively, in the bottom diagram. It corresponds to the fact that the diminishing marginal product of labour has kicked in.

Step 7. The above steps explain how the seven dot points on the TC curve in the top diagram correspond to the seven dot points in the lower diagram. For illustrative purposes, only seven levels of production are taken, but we can consider conducting the same operation for all the levels of q. It will result in the MC curve as in the bottom diagram.

We already know that the MC curve is the supply curve as long as the market price is equal to or above the price of shutdown point. Therefore, in order to find a supply curve for a firm, we need to do two things if its cost function is given: (a) differentiate the cost function to obtain the MC; and (b) find the shutdown point. We will go through the process in Section 4.7 but, in the meantime, we shall re-examine the important relationship between the MC, AC and AVC curves we previously discussed, using differentiation.

4.6   The relative positions of *MC*, *AC* and *AVC* revisited

We have already discussed the importance of the relative positions of MC, AC, and AVC curves.

(1) When the marginal cost (MC) is less than the average total cost (AC), then AC is declining. When MC is greater than AC, then AC is increasing.
(2) When the marginal cost (MC) is less than the average variable cost (AVC), then AVC is declining. When MC is greater than AVC, then AVC is increasing.

We have already given intuitive support for these claims, but can we prove them if we allow q to change by an infinitesimally small amount? In the following we will prove the first claim using the technique of differentiation. The second one is left as an additional exercise at the end of the chapter (Section 4.8).

The proof of the first claim is as follows. Denote the average total cost by $AC(q)$ and, by definition, it is equal to $\dfrac{C(q)}{q}$. The slope of the AC curve is given by differentiating $AC(q)$ with respect to q:

$$AC'(q) = \frac{C'(q) \cdot q - C(q)}{q^2}. \tag{4.11}$$

Now, suppose MC is greater than AC. That is:

$$C'(q) > \frac{C(q)}{q}. \tag{4.12}$$

Rearranging this yields:

$$C'(q) \cdot q - C(q) > 0. \tag{4.13}$$

Getting back to Equation (4.11):

$$AC'(q) = \frac{C'(q) \cdot q - C(q)}{q^2}. \tag{4.14}$$

Given Equation (4.13), we know both the numerator and the denominator of the RHS of Equation (4.14) are positive, meaning that the slope of the AC curve, $AC'(q)$, is positive. *Hence AC is increasing.* Recall that we supposed that MC is greater than AC in order to derive this result. Hence, we have shown that, *when MC is greater than AC, then AC is increasing.* When MC is less than AC, you just need to change the direction of inequality and the proof is done.

This claim should imply that when MC and AC are U-shaped, the marginal cost curve cuts the minimum point of the AC curve. In fact, we can demonstrate it. Let us denote q that corresponds to the minimum of AC curve by $\hat{q}$. When $q = \hat{q}$, the slope of AC is zero i.e. $AC'(\hat{q}) = 0$. Therefore,

$$\frac{C'(\hat{q}) \cdot \hat{q} - C(\hat{q})}{\hat{q}^2} = 0. \tag{4.15}$$

For this equation to hold, the numerator of the LHS of (4.15) has to equal zero. It follows:

$$C'(\hat{q}) \cdot \hat{q} - C(\hat{q}) = 0. \tag{4.16}$$

In turn, this implies that the following holds at the minimum of AC curve:

$$C'(\hat{q}) = \frac{C(\hat{q})}{\hat{q}}. \tag{4.17}$$

Let us investigate Equation (4.17) carefully. The LHS is the marginal cost at $\hat{q}$. The RHS is the average cost at $\hat{q}$. This means that the marginal cost curve cuts the minimum of the AC curve.

4.7 Profit maximisation

Now let us show mathematically why the supply curve is identical to a segment of the MC curve. Remember, when we arrived at that conclusion using a numerical example, it was done by investigating a firm's profit maximising behaviour. Hence, we do the same here: we **set up a firm's profit maximisation problem** in a mathematical fashion.

To begin with, denote a firm's profits by π. Since profits are revenue less total costs:

$$\pi = \pi(q) = p \cdot q - C(q). \tag{4.18}$$

While the firm can control (decide) the quantity it supplies (q), since we assume a competitive market, the price p is determined in the market and the firm has no control

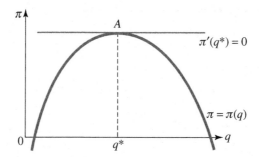

Figure 4.15 The q that maximises $\pi(q)$.

over it. Because p is pre-determined we can consider that the profits are a function of quantity q only, i.e. $\pi = \pi(q) = p \cdot q - C(q)$. Hereafter, let us call $\pi(q)$ the **profit function** in this book.[7]

When the firm attempts to maximise profits and q is the variable under control, we write the **firm's profit maximisation problem** as follows:

$$\max_q \pi(q). \tag{4.19}$$

This expression simply means that our problem is to find the quantity q under which the profit function $\pi(q)$ is maximised. Here our *objective* is to maximise the profit function $\pi(q)$, so $\pi(q)$ is called the **objective function**. You write the objective function to the right of 'max' so everyone knows what you want to maximise. To maximise the objective function, what you *control* (*choose*) is the level of production q, so the variable q is called the **control variable** or the **choice variable**. It is important to write the control variable below 'max' so people know by which means you are maximising your objective.

4.7.1　Solving the maximisation problem in general

For the time being, let us consider finding a maximum of a function *in general*. We will come back to maximising the profit function in Section 4.7.4. We will keep using the same notation, though, to preserve continuity in our discussion. Our problem here is to maximise a function $\pi(q)$ by choosing the level of q (but q and $\pi(q)$ are not really related to quantity and profits, respectively).

Let us start by describing the function $\pi(q)$ diagrammatically, taking q on the horizontal axis and $\pi(q)$ on the vertical axis. *If* it has the shape illustrated as in Figure 4.15, the level of q that maximises the function $\pi(q)$ is obviously q^*.

Notice that at Point A, the tangent line to the function $\pi(q)$ has the slope of *zero*. That is, the differential coefficient of $\pi(q)$ at $q = q^*$, $\pi'(q*)$ is equal to zero. Therefore, if the

---

7 In economics the profit function actually refers to something else. For our purpose, though, it is convenient to have a name for the function $\pi = \pi(q) = pq - C(q)$, and so we shall borrow this terminology. The proper definition of the profit function is a little beyond this book, and you need to wait until you are able to consult some advanced microeconomics textbooks.

shape of the function $\pi(q)$ is as shown in Figure 4.15, we can obtain q that maximises $\pi(q)$ by going through the following procedure.

(1) Differentiating $\pi(q)$ with respect to q;
(2) setting it equal to zero; and
(3) solving for q.

The condition you obtain at Step (2) above is called the **first-order condition** of the maximisation problem. Here are a couple of practice questions.

Question A   Suppose the function you want to maximise is given as $\pi(q) = -\frac{1}{2}q^2 + 70q - 300$. Obtain the q that maximises $\pi(q)$.

Solution   It can be obtained as follows:

(1) $\pi'(q) = -q + 70$.
(2) $\pi'(q) = 0 \Rightarrow -q + 70 = 0$.

The above is the first-order condition.

(3) $q^* = 70$.

Question B   Suppose the function you want to maximise is given as $\pi(q) = \frac{1}{2}q^2 - 70q + 300$. Obtain q that maximises $\pi(q)$.

Solution   Let us follow the same steps:

(1) $\pi'(q) = q - 70$.
(2) $\pi'(q) = 0 \Rightarrow q - 70 = 0$.

The above is the first-order condition.

(3) $q^* = 70$.

Exercise 4.2   First-order condition.

We will find the same q^* in both questions in the above exercise. However, in the second question, what we have actually obtained is the q that *minimises* $\pi(q)$. What went wrong? It is clear if we draw a diagram: $\pi(q) = \frac{1}{2}q^2 - 70q + 300$ is drawn in Figure 4.16. As we can see, its derivative $\pi'(q)$ takes the value zero when the function is minimised at Point B!

This example shows that, to find the maximum of a function, obtaining the first-order condition is not enough. What should we do then? What we need to do is to judge mathematically whether we are looking at the top of the hill (Figure 4.15) or if we are looking at the bottom of the valley (Figure 4.16).

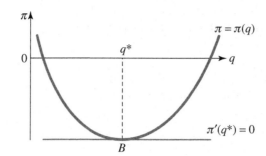

Figure 4.16 The q that minimises $\pi(q)$.

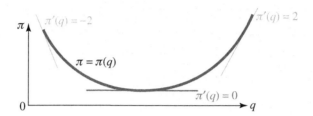

Figure 4.17 $\pi''(q) > 0$: *slope* is increasing.

The mathematical tool that gives us this information is called the **second derivative**. The derivative we have been discussing is called the **first derivative** for the obvious reason: we take the derivative of a function *once*. The second derivative can be obtained by differentiating the first derivative, i.e. differentiating the original function *twice*. For the function $\pi = \pi(q)$, the first derivative is $\pi'(q)$, and we write the second derivative as $\pi''(q)$ (this is read 'pi two prime q').

What is the meaning of the second derivative of a function? Consider a function $\pi = \pi(q)$. Recall that the first derivative shows the *change in $\pi(q)$* due to an infinitesimally small change in q. This is equal to the slope of $\pi(q)$ at the point of our focus. Similarly, the second derivative $\pi''(q)$ shows the *change in the slope* when there is an infinitesimally small change in q. To visualise it, look at Figure 4.17.

We can see that the *slope* of the function in Figure 4.17 is increasing (note the following difference: as q increases the function $\pi(q)$ itself first decreases then starts increasing, but the *slope* of $\pi(q)$ is increasing throughout). In other words, the *change in the slope* is always *positive* for the function in Figure 4.17. As noted, the second derivative shows the change in the slope, so it means $\pi''(q) > 0$. In such a case, we are looking at the bottom of the valley, which we do not want to be doing in finding the q that maximises $\pi(q)$.

We can tell the exact opposite story. Look at Figure 4.18. We can see that the *slope* of the function is decreasing (again note the following difference: as q increases the function $\pi(q)$ itself first increases then starts decreasing, but the *slope* of $\pi(q)$ is decreasing throughout). In other words, the *change in the slope* is always *negative* for the function in Figure 4.18, which implies $\pi''(q) < 0$. In such a case, we are looking at the top of the hill, i.e. which is relevant in finding the q that maximises the function.

Now let us summarise the steps we need to follow in finding the q that maximises $\pi(q)$.

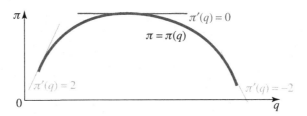

Figure 4.18 $\pi''(q) < 0$: *slope* is decreasing.

(1) Differentiate $\pi(q)$ with respect to q;
(2) set it equal to zero ($\pi'(q) = 0$: first-order condition);
(3) solve for q ($q = q^*$); and
(4) obtain the second derivative $\pi''(q)$ and check that it is *negative* (finding the top of the hill) when $q = q^*$.

The condition we obtain at Step (4) of the above is called the **second-order condition** of the maximisation problem. Now let us redo the previous exercise.

Question A   Suppose the function you want to maximise is given as $\pi(q) = -\dfrac{1}{2}q^2 + 70q - 300$. Obtain the q that maximises $\pi(q)$.

Solution   It can be obtained as follows:

(1) $\pi'(q) = -q + 70$.
(2) $\pi'(q) = 0 \Rightarrow -q + 70 = 0$.

The above is the first-order condition.

(3) $q^* = 70$.
(4) $\pi''(q) = -1 < 0$.

The above is the second-order condition.

The second-order condition shows that the second derivative is negative regardless of the value of q (there is only one hill). Therefore, the value we obtained in (3) is the q that maximises the function (the top of the hill). Hence, $q^* = 70$ is the answer.

Question B   Suppose the function you want to maximise is given as $\pi(q) = \dfrac{1}{2}q^2 - 70q + 300$. Obtain the (q) that maximises $\pi(q)$.

Solution   Following the same steps:

(1) $\pi'(q) = q - 70$.
(2) $\pi'(q) = 0 \Rightarrow q - 70 = 0$.

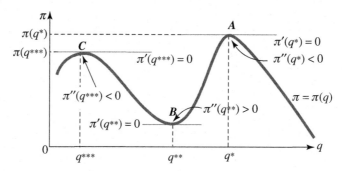

Figure 4.19 Which q is the maximiser?

The above is the first-order condition.

(3) $q^* = 70$.

(4) $\pi''(q) = 1 > 0$.

The above is the second-order condition.

The second-order condition shows that the second derivative is positive regardless of the value of q (there is only one valley). Therefore, the value we obtained in (3) is the q that minimises the function (the bottom of the valley). The second-order condition for the maximisation problem is violated, and hence $q^* = 70$ is not the answer.

Exercise 4.3 Second-order condition.

4.7.2 Maxima and minima

Unfortunately, the story does not end here. Suppose the function $\pi(q)$ has a shape as shown in Figure 4.19.

You can see that there are three values of q under which the derivative $\pi'(q)$ is equal to *zero*. That is, the first-order condition will give us q^*, q^{**} and q^{***}. If we check the second-order condition, it will turn out that $\pi''(q^{**}) > 0$ and we can rule out q^{**}. However, the second derivatives are negative for both q^* and q^{***}, in which case both levels of quantity give us the top of the hill. In this case, we need to compare the actual values of the function under q^* and q^{***}. As we can see from the diagram, $\pi(q^*)$ is greater than $\pi(q^{***})$, so we can conclude that q^* maximises the function. In summary, the steps we need to follow in solving the maximisation problem are as follows.

(1) Differentiate $\pi(q)$ with respect to q.

(2) Set it equal to zero ($\pi'(q) = 0$: first-order condition).

(3) Solve for q ($q = q^*$).

(4) Obtain the second derivative $\pi''(q)$ and check that it is *negative* (finding the top of the hill) when $q = q^*$.

(5) If there are two or more q^*s that satisfy both (3) and (4), calculate $\pi(q^*)$ for each q^* and pick the q^* that corresponds to the greatest $\pi(q^*)$.

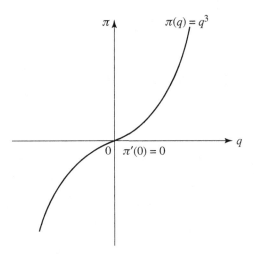

Figure 4.20 A point of inflection.

Let us introduce some terminology here. Points A and C (top of the hill) are called the **local maxima**. Point B (bottom of the valley) is called the **local minimum**. The reason why we use 'local' is because it may be true only locally. That is, the point may not be the maximum or minimum of the entire curve (function). It is true that Point C is a top of a hill. If you look at qs that are close to Point C – in the neighbourhood of the point – there are no higher points. However, $\pi(q)$ takes higher values than that at Point C if you look at qs that are further away from Point C.

The highest point of the entire curve is called the **global maximum**, which occurs in our example when $q = q^*$ at Point A. So Point A is both the local and global maximum.

The lowest point on the entire curve is called the **global minimum**. There is no global minimum in this example (why?).

4.7.3   Some exceptions

If the function is differentiable everywhere, setting the first derivative equal to zero usually gives us either local maxima or local minima. However, there are exceptions. For example, consider $\pi(q) = q^3$. The first derivative is $\pi'(q) = 3q^2$. This is zero only when $q = 0$. But it turns out that $q = 0$ is neither a local maximum nor a local minimum (see Figure 4.20). We shall learn the nature of such a point – point of inflection – in the next chapter, but the lesson for the time being is that when we use the first-order condition (setting the first derivative equal to zero), we do not necessarily obtain a local maximum or a local minimum. Note, the second derivative is $f''(x) = 6x$ and when $x = 0$, $f''(0) = 0$. So, when the *second derivative is zero* at some point, look out; a function *may* not take either a local maximum or a local minimum at that point.[8]

The first-order condition may not be powerful in the case we refer to as the **corner solution**. In Figure 4.21, if we look all values of q, the global maximum happens when

8 A word of caution: even when the second derivative is zero at some point (the first derivative is zero, of course), a function may take a local maximum or a local minimum. To appreciate this point, do the question regarding the point of inflection in Section 5.4 in the next chapter (after reading the relevant section in the next chapter).

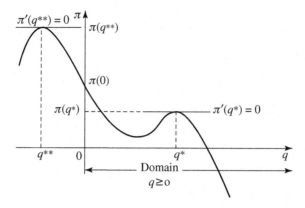

Figure 4.21 Local maximum outside the domain.

$q = q^{**}$. The global maximum value of $\pi(q)$ is $\pi(q^{**})$. However, if the domain of the function is $q \geq 0$ (as in many economic problems), that answer becomes irrelevant. There exists a local maximum q^*, and it is in the domain. However, this local maximum is NOT the global maximum of this function *in the domain*. The global maximum occurs at the boundary, when $q = 0$, as we can see in Figure 4.21. *When the domain is restricted to an interval, we might need to compare the local maximum values of the function with the values at the boundaries.* It is therefore often important to check the vertical intercept of a function in many economic problems (as we tend to focus on non-negative numbers).

In summary, when we solve maximising (minimising) problems, we can usually follow the five steps we previously discussed. However, there are some exceptional cases in which we cannot simply follow them. Therefore *the safest way to ensure that you are doing the right thing is to draw a diagram*, and we will discuss how accurately you can do it – curve sketching – in the next chapter. But to close this section, let us come back to solving the firm's profit maximisation problem we put off solving earlier.

4.7.4 Solving profit maximisation

We start by setting up the profit maximisation problem:

$$\max_q \pi. \tag{4.20}$$

Since the profits are the revenue minus the total costs:

$$\max_q [p \cdot q - C(q)], \tag{4.21}$$

is the problem. We know the first-order condition of the maximisation problem is:

$$p - C'(q) = 0. \tag{4.22}$$

Rearranging this equation gives:

$$p = C'(q). \tag{4.23}$$

What does Equation (4.23) show? This equation is important. The LHS of Equation (4.23) is the market price and the RHS of it is the marginal cost. Yes; we have just shown mathematically that, to maximise the profit, the firm supplies the quantity such that the price equals the marginal cost.

The second-order condition of the maximisation problem is:

$$- C''(q) < 0. \tag{4.24}$$

Rearranging this inequality gives:

$$C''(q) > 0. \tag{4.25}$$

What does Equation (4.25) mean? It tells us that, if the firm is profit maximising by producing a particular quantity q where $p = MC(q)$, then at that q the marginal cost should be increasing. Why? Because if the marginal cost is decreasing at the q where $p = MC(q)$ (the first-order condition is met), then the firm will gain from producing one more unit at that q (the marginal revenue is p and the marginal cost will be less than p), and so the q we are looking at is not a profit maximiser.

To complete the exercise, we need to consider the price below which this firm shuts down. That is, the firm supplies output only if p is greater than or equal to the minimum point of the average variable cost curve (shutdown point). Let us suppose that it happens when $q = \hat{q}$, so the minimum of the AVC is given by $AVC(\hat{q})$.

Then, the quantity supplied is:

$$q = \begin{cases} q^* \text{ such that } p = C'(q^*) & \text{if } p \geq AVC(\hat{q}) \\ 0 & \text{otherwise.} \end{cases}$$

Let us follow this process by using a specific cost function. Try to do the next question by yourself first and then follow the solution. You should also attempt a similar exercise at the end of the chapter.

Question   Consider a firm in a competitive market whose cost function is:

$$c = C(q) = 3q^3 - 18q^2 + 36q + 54,$$

where c is the total cost and q is the quantity of the goods this firm produces. The market price of the goods per unit is denoted by p. Obtain the supply function of this firm.

Solution

The firm's problem is described as follows:

$$\max_q \pi = \max_q [p \cdot q - C(q)].$$

The first-order condition is given as follows:

$$p - C'(q) = 0.$$

Hence

$$p = 9q^2 - 36q + 36$$
$$= 9(q - 2)^2.$$

The second-order condition is given as follows:

$$-C''(q) < 0.$$

It means that

$$18q - 36 > 0 \Rightarrow q > 2.$$

To obtain the supply function, we solve the first-order condition for q:

$$p = 9(q - 2)^2$$

$$q - 2 = \pm\frac{\sqrt{p}}{3}$$

$$q = 2 \pm \frac{\sqrt{p}}{3}.$$

Since $p \geq 0$, $q = 2 - \frac{\sqrt{p}}{3}$ violates the second-order condition. Therefore

$$q = 2 + \frac{\sqrt{p}}{3}.$$

Not all parts of this equation are the supply function. The firm produces only as far as they can recover the variable costs, that is, they produce only when the market price is equal to or greater than the minimum average variable cost (AVC):

$$AVC(q) = \frac{TC(q) - FC}{q}$$

$$= \frac{3q^3 - 18q^2 + 36q}{q}$$

$$= 3q^2 - 18q + 36.$$

The minimum of AVC can be obtained by taking the first derivative of $AVC(q)$ and setting it equal to zero:

$$AVC'(q) = 0$$

$$6q - 18 = 0$$

$$q = 3.$$

This is a minimum because $AVC''(q) = 6 > 0$. The minimum of AVC occurs when $q = 3$ and $AVC(3) = 9$.

Hence, this firm's supply function is:

$$q = \begin{cases} 2 + \frac{\sqrt{p}}{3} & \text{if } p \geq 9 \\ 0 & \text{otherwise.} \end{cases}$$

Exercise 4.4 Profit maximisation.

Table 4.8. Linear cost function.

q	TC	VC	MC	AC	AVC
0	10		N.A.	N.A.	N.A.
1	20				
2	30				
3	40			13.33	
4	50			12.5	
5	60				
6	70			11.67	
7	80			11.43	
8	90			11.25	
9	100			11.11	
10	110				

4.8 Additional exercises

1. **(Marginal and average)** Consider students as they walk into the student union. Suppose the first student is 180 centimetres tall. The second and third are 175 and 170 centimetres tall, respectively. Draw a graph of the marginal and average height of students in the student union, taking height on the vertical axis and number of students on the horizontal axis, in order of their arrival. What do you notice about the relationship between the marginal and the average height? Suppose the fourth student coming into the student union is 180 centimetres tall. What occurs to the average height?

2. **(Marginal and average)** Consider the production technology that is summarised in Table 4.8. What is the magnitude of the fixed cost? Complete the table and plot MC, AC and AVC on the same diagram (some of the numbers for AC have already been calculated: you may round the numbers to two decimal places). Comment on the relationship between their relative positions and the movements of AC and AVC.

3. **(Production decision)** Consider a competitive firm producing a particular good. Verify both algebraically and diagrammatically that a firm will shut down (produce zero) when the price of the good is below its shutdown price.

4. **(Differentiation drills)** Obtain the derivative of $f(x)$.

   (1) $f(x) = -2$.

   (2) $f(x) = x^6$.

   (3) $f(x) = 2x^3 - 3x^2 + 4x$.

   (4) $f(x) = 3 - \frac{2}{3}x^3 + \frac{1}{4}x^2$.

   (5) $f(x) = \frac{1}{12}x^3(4 - x)$.

(6) $f(x) = \frac{1}{2}(x^2 + x)(x^2 - x)$.

(7) $f(x) = (x - 1)(x^2 + x + 1)$.

(8) $f(x) = (x + 2)(x^2 - 2x + 4)$.

(9) $f(x) = (2x^2 + 1)(x^2 - 2x + 3)$.

(10) $f(x) = (2x + 1)(x^2 - x + 1)$.

(11) $f(x) = \frac{1}{x^2}$.

(12) $f(x) = \frac{1}{x^3}$.

(13) $f(x) = \frac{x - 3}{2x^2 + 2}$.

(14) $f(x) = \frac{1}{4x - 3}$.

(15) $f(x) = \frac{1}{x^{\frac{1}{4}}}$.

(16) $f(x) = \sqrt{9 - x^2}$.

(17) $f(x) = \frac{1}{(3x - 2)^2}$.

(18) $f(x) = (2x^2 - 3x + 4)^3$.

(19) $f(x) = \left(\frac{x - 1}{x}\right)^4$.

(20) $f(x) = (4x - x^2)^{\frac{1}{3}}$.

(21) $f(x) = 3e^{-x}$.

(22) $f(x) = 2xe^{-x}$.

(23) $f(x) = -x^2 e^{-2x}$.

(24) $f(x) = \ln(3x + 2)$.

(25) $f(x) = \ln \frac{x - 2}{2x - 3}$.

5. **(The marginal cost and average variable cost)** Prove the following claim mathematically: *when the average variable cost is decreasing (increasing), the marginal cost is less (greater, respectively) than the average variable cost.*

6. **(Marginal and average again)** Suppose we have a linear cost function:

$$C(q) = aq + b,$$

where $a > 0$ and $b > 0$.

(a) Express the marginal cost (MC) in terms of q.

(b) Express the average total cost (AC) in terms of q.

(c) Express the average variable cost (AVC) in terms of q.

(d) Sketch the above three costs on a diagram. Can you find the differences with (and/or the similarities to) the diagram we saw in the text?

7. **(Profit maximisation)** Consider a firm in competitive markets whose cost function is as follows:

$$c = C(q) = 2 + (q - 1)^3,$$

where c and q show the total costs and quantity of the product, respectively.

(a) Obtain the fixed cost (FC).

(b) Express the marginal cost (MC) in terms of q.

(c) Express the average variable cost (AVC) in terms of q.

(d) Sketch MC and AVC on the same diagram. You can restrict the domain to $q \geq 0$.

(e) Denote the price of the product by p. Set up the firm's maximisation problem and obtain its supply function. Explain the first- and second-order conditions. Sketch the supply curve on the diagram.

5

Differential calculus 2

As foreshadowed in the previous chapter, we will learn curve sketching technique in this chapter. Mathematical ideas related to this technique include: maxima and minima, a point of inflection, and curvature (or concavity). The question we did not answer in Chapter 2 – why does the quadratic function have to shape like a parabola? – will also become clear after you learn this technique.

In this chapter, we also introduce the idea of the differential of a function, which is related to the derivative we learnt in the previous chapter. They are similar but different notions and the distinction of them will become important especially in Chapter 6 where we deal with multivariate calculus. We apply these two mathematical ideas to discuss elasticity in the last section of this chapter. The price elasticity of demand will be our particular focus.

Chapter goals By studying this chapter you will

(1) be able to use the differentiation technique to sketch various functions;
(2) be able to explain the difference between the derivative and the differential of a function; and
(3) be able to calculate the price elasticity of demand using differentiation and appreciate the economic information it carries.

5.1 Curve sketching

In the previous chapter, I emphasised the importance of drawing a diagram when we want to find the global maximum or the global minimum of a function. Here, we study the way to sketch a graph of a function that contains sufficient information of it. What we mean by sufficient information will become clear after you have read this section.

Consider a firm in a competitive market whose cost function is as follows:

$$c = C(q) = 2q^3 - 6q^2 + 6q + 8,$$

where the notation is the same as in previous chapters. How can we sketch the graph of this function? Important pieces of information you need to find (in general) are:

(1) intersection(s) of the function with the vertical axis,
(2) the first derivative, i.e. slopes,
(3) the second derivative i.e. curvature (or concavity),

Table 5.1. Information for curve sketching: Steps (1) and (2).

q	$\cdots$	0	$\cdots$	1	$\cdots$
$C'(q)$ (slope)	+	+	+	0	+
$C(q)$	↗	8	↗	10	↗

(4) intersection(s) of the function with the horizontal axis (if needed), and
(5) values of the function at the boundaries (if there are any).

Let us investigate them in turn.

5.1.1 Intersection(s) of the function with the vertical axis

Obtaining this information is straightforward. The value of the function when $q = 0$ is $C(0) = 8$. It shows that the firm's fixed costs are \$8.

5.1.2 The first derivative, i.e. slope

$$C'(q) = 6q^2 - 12q + 6.$$

We can factorise it as follows:

$$C'(q) = 6(q^2 - 2q + 1) = 6(q - 1)^2.$$

This implies the following:

$$C'(q) \begin{cases} = 0 & \text{if } q = 1 \\ > 0 & \text{if } q \neq 1. \end{cases}$$

In other words, we know that the function is increasing (upward sloping, $C'(q) > 0$) everywhere except for the point where $q = 1$. When $q = 1$, the function has zero slope and takes a value $C(1) = 2 - 6 + 6 + 8 = 10$.

The information we have so far can be summarised in Table 5.1 and Figure 5.1. In Figure 5.1, we know that the curve goes through two points, $(0, 8)$ and $(1, 10)$. We also know the slope of the curve is zero at $(1,10)$ but is positive elsewhere. Together it seems $C(q)$ may look like the dashed curve in the figure. To be sure, though, we need to take the second derivative because it provides us with information on curvature (or concavity) of the function.

5.1.3 The second derivative, i.e. curvature (or concavity)

We begin with:

$$C''(q) = 12q - 12.$$

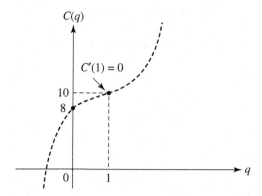

Figure 5.1 Curve sketching: Steps (1) and (2).

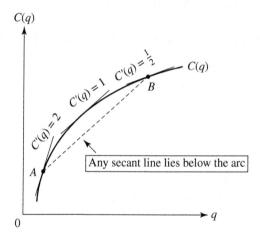

Figure 5.2 $C''(q) < 0$: slope is decreasing; strictly concave function (in this domain).

Factorising this equation yields the following:

$$C''(q) = 12(q - 1).$$

This implies the following:

$$C''(q) \begin{cases} < 0 & \text{if } q < 1 \\ = 0 & \text{if } q = 1 \\ > 0 & \text{if } q > 1. \end{cases}$$

The above information turns out to be valuable in sketching curves. When $q < 1$, $C''(q) < 0$. This means that the *slope of $C(q)$ is decreasing* in this domain ($q < 1$) as in Figure 5.2. In such case, as we can see, any **secant line**, i.e. a line that connects two points of the curve in this domain, lies below the arc made by those two points. For example, in Figure 5.2, the secant line AB lies below the arc $\widehat{AB}$. It is true so long as two points A and B on the curve are picked in this domain.

Table 5.2. Information for curve sketching: Steps (1), (2) and (3).

q	$\cdots$	0	$\cdots$	1	$\cdots$
$C'(q)$ (slope)	$+$	$+$	$+$	0	$+$
$C(q)$	↗	8	↗	10	↗
$C''(q)$ (curvature)	str. concave	str. concave	str. concave	0	str. convex

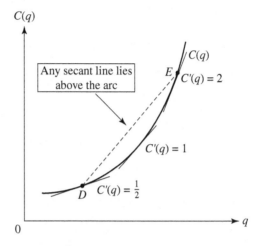

Figure 5.3 $C''(q) > 0$: slope is increasing; strictly convex function (in this domain).

If this is the case, the function is called **strictly concave** (in this domain). Alternatively, we say that $C(q)$ is a **strictly concave function** (in this domain).

On the other hand, $C''(q) > 0$ when $q > 1$. This means that the *slope of $C(q)$ is increasing*, as in Figure 5.3. In such a case, the opposite occurs. As we can see, any secant line lies above the arc if the two points are picked on the curve in this domain. In Figure 5.3, the secant line DE lies above the arc $\overset{\frown}{DE}$. It is true so long as two points D and E on the curve are chosen in this domain.

If this is the case, the function is called **strictly convex** (in this domain). Alternatively, we say that $C(q)$ is a **strictly convex function** (in this domain).

Now let us add these pieces of information to the table we had before. Table 5.2 tells us that the function $C(q)$ should look as shown in Figure 5.4.

Notice that the function is *not* strictly concave *or* strictly convex *for all the domain*.[1] When a function is strictly convex (or concave) everywhere, we can drop the phrase 'in the domain'. Note also that the curvature of the function changes at Point F from strictly concave to strictly convex. The point on which the curvature of a function changes is called a **point of inflection**. It can be the case that the curvature changes from strictly convex to strictly concave. At a point of inflection, it is always the case that the second derivative is zero; in our example $C''(q) = 0$. However, the converse is not necessarily

1 We can say that the function is strictly concave in the domain, $q < 1$. We can also say that the function is strictly convex in the domain, $q > 1$.

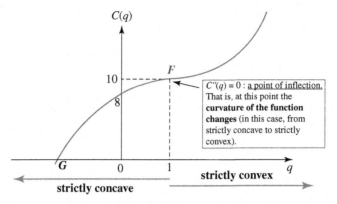

Figure 5.4 Curve sketching: Steps (1), (2) and (3).

true. That is, at the point where the second derivative is zero, the curvature of the function may not change. You should appreciate this relationship by attempting a question related to the point of inflection at the end of the chapter (Section 5.4).

5.1.4 Intersection(s) of the function with the horizontal axis

OK; the next step. We can gather from Figure 5.4 that this curve will cut the horizontal axis once (at Point G). Let us try obtaining that q. To do so, we set $C(q) = 0$:

$$2q^3 - 6q^2 + 6q + 8 = 0.$$

Dividing both sides of this equation by 2 yields:

$$q^3 - 3q^2 + 3q + 4 = 0.$$

The first three terms of the LHS may remind you of something; yes, this equation can be rearranged to:

$$(q^3 - 3q^2 + 3q - 1) + 5 = 0.$$

Rearranging it further gives:

$$5 = -(q^3 - 3q^2 + 3q - 1)$$
$$5 = -(q - 1)^3$$
$$5 = (1 - q)^3$$
$$1 - q = 5^{\frac{1}{3}}$$
$$q = 1 - 5^{\frac{1}{3}}.$$

Without a scientific calculator, this is as far as we can calculate (and so we leave it there). Write this number on the diagram next to Point G. In some cases this step may be important, but as you may have already noticed, in our example this step is redundant in the sense that we do not worry the domain $q < 0$ (it does not make any economic sense).

5.1.5 Obtaining the values of the function at the boundaries (if there are any)

We have already done this final step. The domain in our problem is $q \geq 0$, so the boundary is $q = 0$. When $q = 0$, $C(0) = 8$. It is already written on the diagram, and so we are done.

To make sure you can sketch curves by yourself, try sketching the average cost (AC) curve for the cost function $c = C(q) = 2q^3 - 6q^2 + 6q + 8$. What is the break-even level output? I shall also provide some curve sketching exercises in Section 5.1.7.

5.1.6 Note: concave and strictly concave (convex and strictly convex)

It may be a good time to define what is meant by **concave** and **convex** (without the word "strictly"). We already know what is meant by a strictly concave function. If the second derivative of the function $f(x)$ is negative, i.e. $f''(x) < 0$, then it is strictly concave. Let us now weaken this condition by allowing an equality $(=)$, that is, we make it $f''(x) \leq 0$. In other words, we allow the function $f(x)$ to be either strictly concave $(f''(x) < 0)$ or linear $(f''(x) = 0)$. If a function satisfies $f''(x) \leq 0$, it is called a concave function. Likewise, a convex function is defined by its second derivative satisfying $f''(x) \geq 0$. In a nutshell, we replace strict inequality $(<$ or $>)$ with weak inequality $(\leq$ or $\geq)$ in order to get rid of 'strictly'. By this definition, a linear function is both convex and concave.

5.1.7 Curve sketching exercises

Some curve sketching exercises are provided below. The functions we saw in the previous chapters – a quadratic function, an exponential function, and a logarithmic function – can now be sketched properly using differentiation.

Question A   Sketch $f(x) = -\dfrac{1}{2}x^2 - 8x + 40$ using the curve sketching technique.

Solution   Taking the first and the second derivatives of $f(x)$:

$$f'(x) = -x - 8 \text{ and } f''(x) = -1.$$

Also the vertical intercept is $f(0) = 40$. So we have Table 5.3.

Table 5.3. Information for curve sketching:
$f(x) = -\dfrac{1}{2}x^2 - 8x + 40$.

x	$\cdots$	-8	$\cdots$	0	$\cdots$
$f'(x)$	$+$	0	$-$	$-$	$-$
$f(x)$	$\nearrow$	72	$\searrow$	40	$\searrow$
$f''(x)$			str. concave		

Solving $f(x) = 0$ we get two vertical intercepts $x = -20$ and $x = 4$.

Therefore we can sketch $f(x)$ as in Figure 5.5.

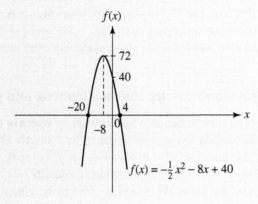

Figure 5.5 Curve sketching: $f(x) = -\dfrac{1}{2}x^2 - 8x + 40$.

Question B   Sketch $f(x) = \dfrac{1}{x}, x \neq 0$ using the curve sketching technique.

Solution   Taking the first and the second derivatives of $f(x)$:

$$f'(x) = -\frac{1}{x^2} \text{ and } f''(x) = \frac{2}{x^3}.$$

Therefore $f'(x) < 0$ (downward sloping everywhere except at $x = 0$).

Also,

$$f''(x) \begin{cases} < 0 & \text{if } x < 0, \\ > 0 & \text{if } x > 0. \end{cases}$$

Now, $f(0)$ and $f'(0)$ are undefined but we know the following:

$$\lim_{x \to 0^+} f(x) = \infty \text{ and } \lim_{x \to 0^+} f'(x) = -\infty.$$

Also, $\lim\limits_{x \to 0^-} f(x) = -\infty$ and $\lim\limits_{x \to 0^+} f'(x) = -\infty$.

Furthermore, $\lim\limits_{x \to \infty} f(x) = 0 = \lim\limits_{x \to -\infty} f(x)$.

Also, $\lim\limits_{x \to \infty} f'(x) = 0 = \lim\limits_{x \to -\infty} f'(x)$.

Taking all these into account, we get Table 5.4.

Table 5.4. Information for curve sketching: $f(x) = \dfrac{1}{x}$.

x	$-\infty$	$\cdots$		0	$\cdots$		∞
$f'(x)$	(0)	$-$	$(-\infty)$		$(-\infty)$	$-$	(0)
$f(x)$	(0)	$\searrow$	$(-\infty)$		(∞)	$\searrow$	(0)
$f''(x)$		str. concave				str. convex	

Therefore we can sketch $f(x)$ as in Figure 5.6.

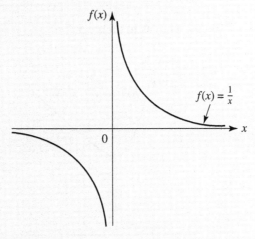

$$f(x) = \frac{1}{x}$$

Figure 5.6 Curve sketching: $f(x) = \dfrac{1}{x}$.

Question C Sketch $f(x) = x + \dfrac{1}{x}$ in the domain $x > 0$ using the curve sketching technique.

Solution Taking the first and the second derivatives of $f(x)$:
$$f'(x) = 1 - \frac{1}{x^2} \text{ and } f''(x) = \frac{2}{x^3}.$$

$$f'(x) \begin{cases} < 0 & \text{if } 0 < x < 1 \\ = 0 & \text{if } x = 1 \\ > 0 & \text{if } x > 1. \end{cases}$$

$f''(x) > 0$ for all $x > 0$.

We know $\lim\limits_{x \to 0^+} f(x) = \infty$.

We also know $\lim\limits_{x \to 0^+} f'(x) = -\infty$.

Taking all these into account we get Table 5.5.

Table 5.5. Information for curve
sketching: $f(x) = x + \dfrac{1}{x}$.

x	0	$\cdots$	1	$\cdots$	∞
$f'(x)$	$(-\infty)$	$-$	0	$+$	(1)
$f(x)$	(∞)	$\searrow$	2	$\nearrow$	
$f''(x)$			str. convex		

Therefore we can sketch $f(x)$ as in Figure 5.7.

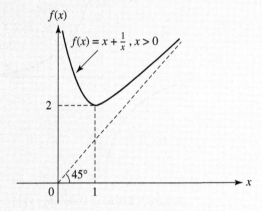

Figure 5.7 Curve sketching: $f(x) = x + \dfrac{1}{x}$.

Note we also used the fact that $\lim\limits_{x\to\infty} f'(x) = 1$ to complete the sketching.

Question D Sketch $f(x) = e^x$ using the curve sketching technique.

Solution Taking the first and the second derivatives of $f(x)$:

$$f'(x) = e^x \text{ and } f''(x) = e^x.$$

Therefore $f'(x) > 0$ and $f''(x) > 0$ for all x.

We also know the following:

$$\lim_{x\to-\infty} f(x) = 0 \text{ and } \lim_{x\to-\infty} f'(x) = 0.$$

Taking all these as well as $f(0) = 1$ into account we get Table 5.6.

Table 5.6. Information for curve sketching: $f(x) = e^x$.

x	$-\infty$	$\cdots$	0	$\cdots$
$f'(x)$	(0)	$+$	1	$+$
$f(x)$	(0)	$\nearrow$	1	$\nearrow$
$f''(x)$		str. convex		

Therefore we can sketch $f(x)$ as in Figure 5.8.

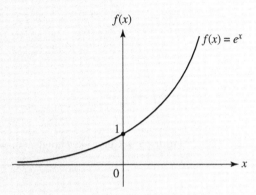

Figure 5.8 Curve sketching: $f(x) = e^x$.

Question E   Sketch $f(x) = \ln x$, $x > 0$, using the curve sketching technique.

Solution   Taking the first and the second derivatives of $f(x)$:

$$f'(x) = \frac{1}{x} \text{ and } f''(x) = -\frac{1}{x^2}.$$

Therefore $f'(x) > 0$ and $f''(x) < 0$ for all $x > 0$.

We also know the following:

$$\lim_{x \to 0^+} f(x) = -\infty \text{ and } \lim_{x \to 0^+} f'(x) = \infty.$$

Note also that the horizontal intercept occurs at $x = 1$.

Taking all these into account we get Table 5.7.

Table 5.7. Information for curve sketching: $f(x) = \ln x$.

x	0	$\cdots$	1	$\cdots$
$f'(x)$	∞	$+$	1	$+$
$f(x)$	$-\infty$	$\nearrow$	0	$\nearrow$
$f''(x)$		str. concave		

Therefore we can sketch $f(x)$ as in Figure 5.9.

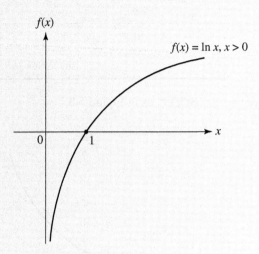

Figure 5.9 Curve sketching: $f(x) = \ln x$.

5.2 The differential

Before we move on to the next section to discuss elasticity, we introduce one more mathematical notion. It is related to the **derivative** of the function, so we start with it. For the cost function $C(q)$, the definition of the derivative is given in Equation (4.3):

$$C'(q) = \lim_{h \to 0} \frac{C(q+h) - C(q)}{h}. \tag{5.1}$$

We know that it shows the slope of the function $C(q)$. Now, use Δq instead of h in the above definition. Recall that Δ is used to show a change in a variable, so Δq means 'a change in q':

$$C'(q) = \lim_{\Delta q \to 0} \frac{C(q + \Delta q) - C(q)}{\Delta q}. \tag{5.2}$$

The numerator of the RHS of this equation is a change in the function $C(q)$ when q changes by Δq. So let us denote this by using Δ as $\Delta C(q)$. Now the definition of the derivative becomes:

$$C'(q) = \lim_{\Delta q \to 0} \frac{\Delta C(q)}{\Delta q}. \tag{5.3}$$

The German mathematician Leibniz used the notation $\dfrac{dC(q)}{dq}$ to express the limit of $\dfrac{\Delta C(q)}{\Delta q}$ when $\Delta q \to 0$. Following this mathematical convention, Equation (5.3) can be

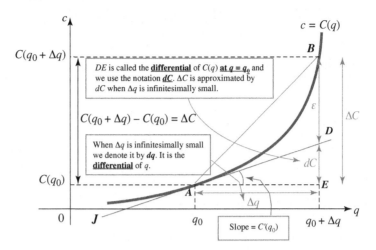

Figure 5.10 Visualising the differential.

written as

$$C'(q) = \frac{dC(q)}{dq}. \tag{5.4}$$

That is, Δ can be replaced by d at the limit where the change in q (Δq) is infinitesimally small. Note that $c = C(q)$, so Equation (5.4) can also be written as the following:

$$C'(q) = \frac{dC(q)}{dq} = \frac{dc}{dq}. \tag{5.5}$$

Hence, $C'(q)$, $\dfrac{dC(q)}{dq}$, and $\dfrac{dc}{dq}$ are all the same for the function $c = C(q)$.

Now, look at Figure 5.10. Look at Point A, where $q = q_0$, and consider a change in q, Δq. The tangent line at this point, DJ, has a slope of $C'(q_0)$. The distance AE is Δq. Therefore, the distance DE can be obtained by multiplying them: $DE = C'(q_0)\Delta q$. The residual distance BD is denoted by a Greek symbol, ε (epsilon). So $\Delta C = C'(q_0)\Delta q + \varepsilon$.

Here is the new idea: $C'(q_0)\Delta q$ is called the **differential** of the function $C(q)$ at $q = q_0$, and it is denoted by dC. It is the distance DE in the diagram. It follows that:

$$dC = C'(q_0)\Delta q. \tag{5.6}$$

Note that ε and $C'(q_0)\Delta q (= dC)$ both become smaller as Δq becomes smaller, but *the former becomes smaller at a faster rate*. To put it another way, when Δq becomes very tiny, ε becomes negligible and hence $\Delta C \approx C'(q_0)\Delta q = dC$. In terms of economics, this means that the change in the total costs ΔC can be approximated by the differential dC at Point A if a change in quantity is very tiny. *A very tiny change in q is described by the notation dq instead of Δq; dq is called the **differential** of q.*

In this case, Equation (5.6) becomes:

$$dC = C'(q_0)dq. \tag{5.7}$$

To make it general, we replace q_0 with q and obtain:

$$dC = C'(q)dq. \tag{5.8}$$

Dividing both sides by dq yields:

$$C'(q) = \frac{dC}{dq}. \tag{5.9}$$

As you can see, the LHS of this equation is the **derivative** of $C(q)$. Hence the important conclusion can be stated as follows: *the derivative of a single-variate function $C(q)$ can be expressed as the **ratio of the differentials** dC and dq*. Whilst this statement is true for single-variate functions such as $c = C(q)$, it is not generally true for multivariate functions, which we will deal with in Chapter 6.

5.3 Elasticity

We have studied the firm's maximisation problem and have seen how differentiation could be used in an economic context. In this section, we focus on an economic notion called **elasticity**. Differentiation turns out to be a powerful tool in examining elasticity as well.

5.3.1 What is elasticity?

Elasticity is a notion that shows the responsiveness of a variable to a change in another variable. Our focus here is the responsiveness of demand. Demand for a certain good appears to respond to three variables in particular.

One is obviously the product's own price. The law of demand tells us that if the own price of the product increases (decreases), demand for that product decreases (increases, respectively). How responsive is demand to a change in the own price? We measure the responsiveness by the **own price elasticity of demand**. Before examining the own price elasticity of demand, though, let us briefly discuss other variables to which demand may respond.

Demand may respond to a change in the prices of other goods. An increase in the price of Head tennis racquets may increase demand for Babolat tennis racquets, whilst an increase in the price of tennis balls and tennis courts may decrease demand for Babolat tennis racquets. Head racquets are called the **substitutes** to Babolat racquets, whereas tennis balls and tennis courts are called **complements** to Babolat racquets. It is difficult to imagine that a change in the price of a stapler influences demand for Babolat racquets: a stapler neither substitutes nor complements Babolat racquets. The responsiveness of demand for a good to a change in the price of another good is measured by the **cross price elasticity of demand**.

Demand is likely to respond to a change in income. If an increase in income leads to an increase in demand for goods, these goods are called **normal goods**. On the other hand, if an increase in income causes a decrease in demand for goods, these goods are called **inferior goods**. The responsiveness of demand to a change in income is measured by the **income elasticity of demand**.

OK; now let us return to discussing the **own price elasticity of demand** (**price elasticity of demand**, hereafter). It shows how responsive demand is to a change in the own price. We usually use a Greek letter η (read eta) for elasticity. The definition of it is as follows:

$$\eta = \left| \frac{\text{proportional change in quantity demanded}}{\text{proportional change in the price}} \right|. \tag{5.10}$$

It is defined as the *absolute value* of a ratio of *proportional changes* in quantity demanded and the price. There are two important things to recognise: (1) we take the absolute value; and (2) we take proportional changes (not just changes) in the price and quantity. Why do we do these? Let us discuss the latter first; the former will be explained later when we actually calculate the elasticity.

Why do we take proportional changes to describe the responsiveness? The reason becomes clear if you think about the following situation. Think about two people: Kris who has 30 cups of coffee a month, and Scott who only takes only one cup of coffee a month. Suppose the price of coffee has decreased by a little and, as a result, Kris and Scott have both increased demand for coffee by one cup: Kris takes 31 cups and Scott takes two. Should we say that both people's demands are equally responsive to the change in price because they both increased demand for coffee by one cup? NO: because for Kris, who has been drinking 30 cups a month, a one-cup increase in coffee is almost nothing, whilst for Scott who has been having only one cup a month, drinking another cup implies doubling the amount of caffeine ingestion. For the same price change, Scott has responded much strongly. The above example shows that it is better to use the proportional change in quantity demanded in order to measure the responsiveness. For the price change, we can tell a similar story.

5.3.2 Elasticity is unit-free

Since we define elasticity by the ratio of the proportional changes, it does not matter which units we use in measuring the price or quantity: this property is called 'unit-free'. It can be seen clearly by using an example. Think about two people: Kris who eats 6(kg) of rice a month, and Scott who eats 6000(g) of rice a month (note that they eat equal amounts of rice). Owing to a decrease in the price of rice, Kris and Scott now eat 9(kg) and 9000(g) of rice, respectively. The change in demand for rice is 3 for Kris and 3000 for Scott. *These changes are the same in the reality, but the numbers are different according to the units we use (kilograms or grams). This means that comparing changes in demand for different goods is difficult because different units are used to count them.*

However, when we calculate the proportional change in the above example, for Kris it is $0.5 \left(\frac{3}{6} \right)$ and for Scott it is $0.5 \left(\frac{3000}{6000} \right)$ as well. In comparing proportional changes, the units we use do not matter. This is same for prices. Comparing changes in the prices across countries is difficult for an obvious reason: currency units are different across countries. But if we take the proportional changes, we need not worry about units. *We can compare the price elasticity of demand across various people, goods, and countries.*

5.3.3   Calculating elasticity

Recall that the definition of the price elasticity of demand is:

$$\eta = \left| \frac{\text{proportional change in quantity demanded}}{\text{proportional change in the price}} \right|. \tag{5.11}$$

We denote the current price and quantity by p_0 and q_0, respectively. Let us also denote very tiny changes in the price and quantity by the differentials dp and dq. Proportional changes in the price and quantity can then be described as $\dfrac{dp}{p_0}$ and $\dfrac{dq}{q_0}$. Hence:

$$\eta_{q_0, p_0} = \left| \frac{\frac{dq}{q_0}}{\frac{dp}{p_0}} \right|. \tag{5.12}$$

Note that elasticity will be different according to the current price and quantity. So we will put a subscript on η to show at which price and quantity we are evaluating elasticity.

Let us rearrange Equation (5.12). Multiply both the numerator and the denominator by $p_0 q_0$. Then it becomes:

$$\eta_{q_0, p_0} = \left| \frac{dq}{dp} \frac{p_0}{q_0} \right|. \tag{5.13}$$

So, in order to obtain the price elasticity of demand, we need two pieces of information. One is the current price and quantity (p_0 and q_0). The other is $\dfrac{dq}{dp}$, which is the ratio of two differentials. We know that this ratio is equal to the differential coefficient $q'(p_0)$ because 'very tiny changes' are the focus.

Suppose Shane's demand for coffee is given by the following function:

$$q = 5 - \frac{1}{2}q. \tag{5.14}$$

The first thing to note is that the differential coefficient $q'(p_0)$ is the same for all p:

$$q'(p) = \frac{dq}{dp} = -\frac{1}{2}. \tag{5.15}$$

It does not depend on the value of p. It is because we have assumed a linear demand function, as in Equation (5.14). Later we will focus upon another type of demand function under which the differential coefficient $q'(p)$ changes according to the value of p. In any case, let us calculate the price elasticity of demand for two particular cases.

Case A $q_A = 4$ and $p_A = 2$.

$$\eta_{q_A, p_A} = \left| \frac{dq}{dp} \frac{p_A}{q_A} \right| = \left| -\frac{1}{2} \frac{2}{4} \right| = \left| -\frac{1}{4} \right| = \frac{1}{4}.$$

Case B $q_B = 1$ and $p_B = 8$.

$$\eta_{q_B, p_B} = \left| \frac{dq}{dp} \frac{p_B}{q_B} \right| = \left| -\frac{1}{2} \frac{8}{1} \right| = |-4| = 4.$$

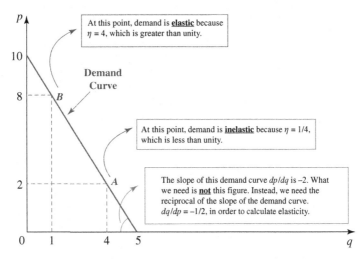

Figure 5.11 Price elasticity of demand.

Now it is clear why we use the absolute value in calculating elasticity. It is simple: because the differential coefficient is generally negative (the law of demand), and the price and quantity are always non-negative, we need to take the absolute to obtain a non-negative number that explains responsiveness of demand.[2]

Here is some terminology you need to remember. In Case A, elasticity is less than unity. At such a point where a proportional change in the price exceeds a proportional change in demand, we say that demand is **inelastic** to a change in the price. In contrast, in Case B, elasticity is greater than unity. At such a point where a proportional change in demand exceeds a proportional change in the price, we say that demand is **elastic** to a change in the price. When the proportional changes are identical, i.e. when elasticity equals unity, we call that demand is **unitary elastic** to a change in the price (at which price and quantity will it occur?).

Figure 5.11 describes the above example. Points *A* and *B* correspond to Cases A and B, respectively. As we can see, *elasticity is generally **not** constant along the demand curve*. Hence, in general, we *cannot* describe the responsiveness of demand as in the following statement: 'This demand curve is elastic (inelastic)'. This is a typical misunderstanding a number of students have. Instead, we should say, '*At Point B (A)*, demand is elastic (inelastic, respectively)'. We need to specify the point of our focus because elasticity changes from a point to another in general.[3]

----

2 As you may have noticed, taking the absolute value in calculating elasticity has no conceptual merit (it is merely a means of obtaining a non-negative number). Indeed, it is usually only at an introductory level of economics that we take the absolute value and, from the intermediate level onwards, the price elasticity is usually left as a negative number.

3 There exist demands whose own price elasticity is constant at all points; we shall see those shortly. There also exist demands whose own price elasticity changes along the curve but are elastic (inelastic) at all points. For these demands, a statement 'The demand is elastic (inelastic)' makes sense and is correct, but if your particular focus is at some consumption point, then you had better say explicitly that 'The demand is elastic (inelastic) at this point'.

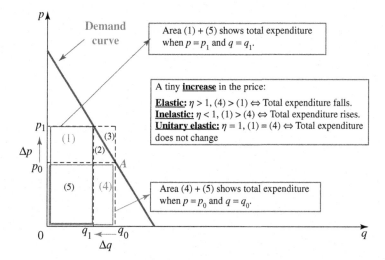

Figure 5.12 Price elasticity and total expenditure.

Another typical misunderstanding concerns the slope of the demand curve. Diagrammatically you might consider the slope of the demand curve to be $\dfrac{dp}{dq}$, because we take the price on the vertical axis. You must note, though, that $\dfrac{dp}{dq}$ is the same as the derivative of the *inverse* supply function. What we need in calculating elasticity is $\dfrac{dq}{dp}$, which is the reciprocal of the slope of the demand curve.

5.3.4 Important economic information we can obtain from elasticity

We have seen that if elasticity is greater (less) than unity at a particular point of a demand curve, the demand is called elastic (inelastic, respectively) at that point. It turns out that elasticity carries important economic information: the direction of the change in total expenditure due to a change in the price. In order to explain the relationship between elasticity and total expenditure in a diagram, we take small changes in the price and quantity. Denote them by Δp and Δq, respectively.

We examine whether Shane's demand is elastic at Point A. At Point A, Shane consumes q_0 observing the price level p_0. Shane's total expenditure for this good is $p_0 q_0$. It is represented by the area $(4) + (5)$ in Figure 5.12.

Say the price has increased by Δp to p_1 and, as a result, Shane's demand has fallen by Δq to q_1. Shane's total expenditure for this good has changed to $p_1 q_1$. It is represented by the area $(1) + (5)$ in the above diagram. The change in total expenditure on this good is $(1) - (4)$. The relationship between a change in total expenditure and sizes of areas can be summarised as follows:

$$\text{Expenditure increases} \Leftrightarrow \text{Area } (1) > \text{Area } (4),$$
$$\text{Expenditure decreases} \Leftrightarrow \text{Area } (1) < \text{Area } (4).$$

Recall that the price elasticity of demand is defined as the absolute value of a ratio of proportional changes in demand and the price. In this case,

$$\eta = \left| \frac{\text{proportional change in quantity demanded}}{\text{proportional change in the price}} \right|$$

$$= \left| \frac{\frac{\Delta q}{q_0}}{\frac{\Delta p}{p_0}} \right|$$

$$= \left| \frac{\Delta q p_0}{\Delta p q_0} \right|$$

$$= \left| \frac{(4)}{(1)+(2)+(3)} \right|.$$

Notice that the area $(2) + (3)$ is equal to $\Delta p \Delta q$. Two variables Δp and Δq themselves are small, and hence the product of these two tiny variables is even smaller and negligible. It follows that elasticity can be written as follows:

$$\eta \approx \left| \frac{(4)}{(1)} \right|.$$

Elastic demand implies that $\eta > 1$, in which case Area (1) < Area (4). It means that total expenditure has fallen when the price has risen by Δp. On the other hand, if total expenditure has increased when the price has risen by a little, we can conclude that demand is inelastic: Area (1) > Area (4), then $\eta < 1$. For unitary elastic demand, Area (4) should equal Area (1) as $\eta = 1$. It implies that total expenditure has not changed by a change in the price.

Intuitively, we can explain the relationship as follows. When the price rises, *if the quantity demanded stayed the same*, total expenditure would unambiguously increase. In reality, for a downward sloping demand schedule, the quantity demanded decreases, but an increase in the price has an effect in increasing total expenditure (for the quantity sold): let us call it the 'price effect'. The 'price effect' is represented by Area (1) in Figure 5.12. On the other hand, when the quantity demanded decreases, *if the price stayed the same*, total expenditure would unambiguously decrease. In reality, a decrease in the quantity demanded is brought about by an increase in the price, but let us call this unambiguous effect in decreasing total expenditure the 'quantity effect'. The 'quantity effect' is represented by Area (4) in the same figure. When the 'quantity effect' dominates the 'price effect', total expenditure decreases. A domination of the 'quantity effect' means that demand is responsive to a change in price. Thus at such a point, we have elastic demand. On the other hand, when the 'price effect' is dominant, total expenditure rises. It occurs when demand does not respond that much to a change in the price, implying demand is inelastic.

As we have discussed, the change in price, elasticity and the change in total expenditure are closely related: if we have information on two of these three things, we can deduce what happens on the other one.

5.3.5 The constant elasticity demand function

For the following demand function, it turns out that the price elasticity of demand is constant:

$$q = Ap^{\varepsilon}. \tag{5.16}$$

Why will the price elasticity be constant for this type of demand function? We will show it in two ways in the following. In passing, in Equation (5.16), ε has to be negative for the law of the demand to hold (why?). (This is an additional exercise.)

Question Obtain the price elasticity of demand for $q = Ap^{\varepsilon}$, where $\varepsilon < 0$.

Solution A

$$q = Ap^{\varepsilon}$$

$$\frac{dq}{dp} = A\varepsilon p^{\varepsilon-1}$$

$$= \varepsilon Ap^{\varepsilon} p^{-1}$$

$$= \varepsilon \frac{q}{p}.$$

Hence, $\dfrac{dq}{dp}$ evaluated at $q = q_0$ and $p = p_0$ is $\varepsilon \dfrac{q_0}{p_0}$.

The price elasticity of demand (at the point where $q = q_0$ and $p = p_0$) is defined as

$$\eta_{q_0,p_0} = \left| \frac{dq}{dp} \frac{p_0}{q_0} \right|,$$

where $\dfrac{dq}{dp}$ is evaluated at $q = q_0$ and $p = p_0$.

Therefore,

$$\eta_{q_0,p_0} = \left| \frac{dq}{dp} \frac{p_0}{q_0} \right| = \left| \varepsilon \frac{q_0}{p_0} \frac{p_0}{q_0} \right| = |\varepsilon|.$$

Exercise 5.1 Constant price elasticity of demand.

We have just shown that, for this demand function, the price elasticity of demand at $q = q_0$ and $p = p_0$ does not depend upon values of the price and quantity: it is a constant $|\varepsilon|$.

The second solution, of course, yields the same result, but contains important techniques that you will frequently encounter in later year units in economics and econometrics.

The trick is taking the logarithm of both sides of the demand function:

$$\ln q = \ln A + \varepsilon \ln p. \tag{5.17}$$

Set $\ln A = B$. Then Equation (5.17) becomes:

$$\ln q = B + \varepsilon \ln p. \tag{5.18}$$

The demand function in a form of Equation (5.18) is called the **log-linear demand function**. It is because, in Equation (5.18), the RHS is a linear function of $\ln p$. When the LHS is a logarithm, which is the case here ($\ln q$), the function is sometimes called a **log-log function**, rather casually. Equation (5.18) is merely a **log transformation** of Equation (5.16) (i.e. taking the logarithms of both sides of Equation (5.16)), and hence both the equations represent the same demand behaviour. Hence the previous question can be rephrased as the following.

Question   Obtain the price elasticity of demand for $\ln q = B + \varepsilon \ln p$, where $\varepsilon < 0$.

Solution B

Differentiating $\ln q$ with respect to $\ln p$ yields:

$$\frac{d \ln q}{d \ln p} = \varepsilon. \tag{5.19}$$

In the meantime, note that $\dfrac{d \ln q}{dq} = \dfrac{1}{q}$ and $\dfrac{d \ln p}{dp} = \dfrac{1}{p}$. These imply that $d \ln q = \dfrac{dq}{q}$ and $d \ln p = \dfrac{dp}{p}$.

Equation (5.19) can therefore be written as:

$$\frac{\frac{dq}{q}}{\frac{dp}{p}} = \varepsilon. \tag{5.20}$$

The absolute value of the LHS of Equation (5.20) is the definition of the price elasticity of demand:

$$\eta = \left| \frac{\frac{dq}{q}}{\frac{dp}{p}} \right| = |\varepsilon|.$$

Exercise 5.2   Constant price elasticity of demand (after the log transformation).

This solution is important. It demonstrates that *elasticity can be shown as the ratio of two differentials of the logarithms*. It explains why elasticity is constant along the demand curve if the demand function is log-log. If you encounter the log-log function in the future – presumably when you study econometrics – you should always recall the above solution.

5.3.6   The second law of the demand

The responsiveness of demand to a change in price is unlikely to be constant over time. In fact, it is likely to increase over time. Why? Consider the following example. Suppose

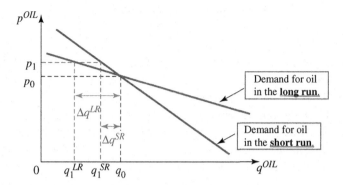

Figure 5.13 Elasticity increases over time: the second law of the demand.

the price of oil increased (the major increases occurred twice in the 1970s; which are known as the 1973 oil crisis and the 1979 energy crisis). How would the demand for oil be affected? An increase in the price of oil would be transmitted to an increase in the price of petroleum, and it would bring about reduced mileage driven in motor vehicles. It would also be likely that temperature and duration of oil heating would be reduced. These changes in consumer behaviour have therefore lowered the quantity of oil demanded. It is represented in Figure 5.13 as the movement along the *short-run* demand schedule. The price of oil has increased from p_0 to p_1 and demand for oil has responded by Δq^{SR} (from q_0 to q_1^{SR}).

These effects are likely to be bigger in the long run. In the long run, smaller cars with more efficient engines will become available, and people will start driving them instead of driving less efficient cars that consume a lot of petroleum. As for heating, people tend to swap from rather expensive oil heating to cheaper heating (electric, gas, etc.).

In general, consumers prefer changing their consumption patterns gradually. Even if they preferred changing it quickly, supply may not keep up with it. As a result, demand tends to change more responsively to a change in the price in a longer run. This demand behaviour is called the **second law of the demand**. The change in the long run is represented by the movement along the *long-run* demand schedule. Following the increase in the price of oil from p_0 to p_1, the quantity of oil demanded responded by Δq^{LR} (from q_0 to q_1^{LR}).

5.4 Additional exercises

1. **(Curve sketching)** Sketch the graph of the following functions (in the specified domain). Does any x correspond to a local maximum, a local minimum or a point of inflection? Does a global maximum or a global minimum exist in each of the functions?

   (1) $f(x) = \dfrac{4x + 3}{x^2 + 1}, x \in (-\infty, \infty)$.

   (2) $f(x) = x \ln x$, $x \in (0, \infty)$.

   (3) $f(x) = (x - 1)^3 (x - 6)^2$, $x \in (-\infty, \infty)$.

   (4) $f(x) = 100 - e^{-x^2}$, $x \in (-\infty, \infty)$.

2. **(Point of inflection)** Sketch $f(x) = x^3$ as well as $g(x) = x^4$. Obtain any x that satisfies $f''(x) = 0$. Do they correspond to a point of inflection?

3. **(Profit maximisation)** Consider a firm in competitive markets whose cost function is as follows:

$$c = C(q) = 3q^3 - 18q^2 + 36q + 54,$$

where c and q show the total costs and quantity of the product, respectively. Note that the set up is the same as Exercise 4.4 in Chapter 4.

   (a) Denoting the price of the product by p, write down the profit function in terms of q.

   (b) Sketch the profit function when $p = 1$.

   (c) Sketch the profit function when $p = 3$.

   (d) According to your graphs, what are the profit maximising levels of output in parts (b) and (c)? Check if your answers are consistent with the solution in Exercise 4.4 in Chapter 4.

4. **(The differential)** Consider a firm in competitive markets whose cost function is as follows:

$$c = C(q) = 3 + (q - 1)^3,$$

where c and q show the total costs and quantity of the product, respectively.

   (a) Obtain the fixed cost (FC).

   (b) (b) Express the marginal cost (MC) in terms of q.

   (c) Suppose currently this firm is producing at $q = 4$. Obtain the marginal cost of production using your result from part (b).

   (d) What is the extra cost to produce the fifth unit? In other words, what is the actual difference between $C(5)$ and $C(4)$?

   (e) Compare your results in parts (c) and (d). Are they identical? If so, why? If not, explain why not.

5. **(Elasticity)** Suppose the market demand for coffee is given as $p = \dfrac{1}{q + 1}$.

   (a) Restricting the domain to $q \geq 0$, carefully sketch the market demand curve, taking price on the vertical axis.

   (b) When $q = 10$, by what percentage will the demand for coffee decrease if there is an increase of 1 per cent in the price of coffee?

   (c) True, false or uncertain? 'The demand for coffee is always elastic in this problem.'

6. (**Elasticity and total revenue**) Estimates of the own price elasticity of demand for bottles of water in the Tokyo Cricket Ground (TCG) is less than unity at the current price. With the help of a diagram (you may suppose a linear demand), comment carefully on the veracity (true, false or uncertain?) of the following statement. 'The TCG will collect less revenue from selling bottles of water by marginally lowering the price.'

6 Multivariate calculus

In Chapter 4, our focus was the firm that maximises its profits. We set up the profit maximisation problem for a firm in a competitive market, and derived its supply function. In doing so, we obtained the first- and second-order conditions, which involved obtaining the first and second derivatives of the profit function, respectively.

In turn, this chapter deals with the consumer's problem. Similar mathematical techniques to those we used in examining the firm's profit maximisation problem will be introduced. The main difference is that, here, we will control two variables instead of one. Recall that, in the firm's maximisation problem, the quantity produced (q) is the only variable that the firm could control, and hence it required differentiating the profit function with respect to one variable (q). In this chapter, we deal with two goods on which a consumer can spend his/her limited income. How should the consumer allocate his/her income to the consumption of each of the goods?

Our fundamental assumption about consumers' behaviour is that they choose a combination of goods they consume so as to maximise their satisfaction. We express the degree of satisfaction by using the term 'utility', whose unit of measurement is a 'util'. We consider a consumer who makes a decision on how much of which goods he/she consumes so as to maximise his/her utility. Our main objective in this chapter is to find the bundle of goods that maximises a consumer's utility, when he/she has a limited amount of income. This problem is known as the constrained optimisation, because he/she faces a constraint in maximising his/her utility. In this particular problem, the constraint is called the budget constraint. We will first discuss a simpler version of this problem, the unconstrained optimisation with two variables, and discuss how we can find the local maximum and the local minimum. Then, three methods of solving the consumer's utility maximisation problem will be explained. The method that has no particular name will be covered first, because it contains a lot of economic intuition and because it is diagrammatically appealing. The second method is called the substitution method, and you will see that our problem will be reduced to the single-variate problem we studied in Chapter 4. The third method is frequently used in various economic applications and is called the Lagrange multiplier method. Unsurprisingly, these methods yield the same result.

Chapter goals By studying this chapter you will

(1) be able to partially differentiate the utility function to calculate the marginal utility of a particular good;

(2) be able to visualise how the utility function relates to indifference curves as well as marginal utilities;

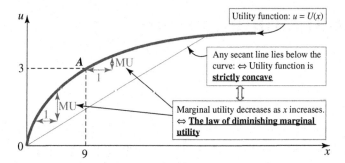

Figure 6.1 Utility function (for one good).

(3) be able to explain the economic meaning of the marginal rate of substitution and calculate it using the implicit differentiation;

(4) be able to solve the unconstrained optimisation problem;

(5) be able to solve the solve the utility maximisation problem using three different methods; and

(6) be able to explain how the individual demand schedule is derived from the consumer's utility maximising behaviour.

6.1 The utility function

6.1.1 The utility function for one good

The one-good case is simple. Consider a good that is beneficial for you (goods that are bad for you – for example, pollution – are sometimes called 'bads' in economics, in passing). In this case, the more you consume that good, the more utility (satisfaction) you obtain. In economics, the **utility function** is used to show the degree of satisfaction a person obtains from consuming a bundle of goods. The utility function shows numerical values of utility a person obtains by consuming a bundle of goods.

Let us draw the utility function. We have the level of utility (u) on the vertical axis and quantity of the good (x) on the horizontal axis. The more you consume, the higher the utility, so the curve is upward sloping. Note that we are just abstracting from the reality and discussing levels of consumption that are relevant. For many goods, if you consume too much (having 100 pints of beer), your utility may start decreasing, but we don't consider the levels of consumption as such. In any case, the utility function $u = U(x)$ is illustrated in Figure 6.1.

On the diagram in the figure, a person consumes 9 units of the good (at Point A). The graph indicates that the level of utility he/she obtains from that consumption is 3 (utils). Consider that a person consumes one more unit of the good. The additional utility this person obtains from this unit is called the **marginal utility**. For example, if utility increases from 3 to 3.1, then the marginal utility is 0.1.

6.1 The utility function

When we consider an infinitesimally small change in x (imagine that the utility function is a smooth curve), the marginal utility equals the slope of the line that is tangent to the utility function at the point of consumption. It is the same argument as in Chapter 4 where we discussed the cost function and the marginal cost. The slope of the utility function is obtained by taking the first derivative of the utility function, which is $U'(x)$. The function is always upward sloping, so $U'(x) > 0$ for all $x > 0$.

Look at the diagram. I have deliberately drawn the graph so that the marginal utility decreases as quantity consumed increases. It means that the previous unit of consumption gives you larger satisfaction than the current unit. Imagine that you very much want to drink beer. The first pint is precious, and you appreciate it a lot. You may appreciate the second pint, but perhaps not as much as the first one. The third pint still gives you some satisfaction because you like beer, but not as much as the previous pint. This pattern displayed by the marginal utility is called the **law of diminishing marginal utility**.

Mathematically, the law of diminishing marginal utility simply implies that the slope of the utility function $U'(x)$ decreases as x increases. It means that the second derivative $U''(x)$ is negative for all $x > 0$. In turn, $U''(x) < 0$ implies that the utility function $U(x)$ is **strictly concave**. You can see this because any secant line of the utility function lies under the curve. Let us use some numbers to consolidate these ideas.

Question Obtain the utility and marginal utility if a person is consuming 25 units of a good ($x = 25$) and his/her utility function is given as $u = U(x) = \sqrt{x}$. Check that the law of diminishing marginal utility holds if $x > 0$.

Solution $U(x) = \sqrt{x}$ so $U'(x) = \dfrac{1}{2\sqrt{x}}$.

$$U(25) = \sqrt{25} = 5.$$

$$U'(25) = \frac{1}{2\sqrt{25}}$$

$$= \frac{1}{2 \cdot 5}$$

$$= \frac{1}{10}.$$

Finally, $U''(x) = -\dfrac{1}{4x\sqrt{x}}$. This expression is negative for all $x > 0$.

Exercise 6.1 The law of diminishing marginal utility.

6.1.2 The two-good case

Now we focus on an individual who consumes two goods. This individual's objective is to find a bundle of the two goods that maximises his/her utility. To begin with, we introduce some notation. We consider Good 1 and Good 2 and denote the levels of consumption by

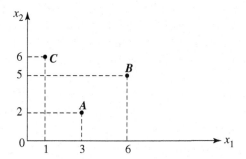

Figure 6.2 Consumption bundles.

x_1 and x_2. The bundle this consumer chooses will be denoted by a combination of the two goods, (x_1, x_2).

We know that an individual consumes either zero or a positive amount of each good. That is, $x_1 \geq 0$ and $x_2 \geq 0$. It implies that all the possible combinations of the two goods can be described on the first quadrant (including the points on the adjacent axes) of the coordinate plane, where x_1 and x_2 are taken on the horizontal and vertical axes, respectively.

In Figure 6.2, three consumption bundles are indicated (Points A, B and C). For example, on Point A, this person consumes 3 units of Good 1 and 2 units of Good 2.

For all the possible consumption bundles, a person is supposed to have 'taste'. For instance, if both goods give positive utility (i.e. if they are not the 'bads'), this person will rank Point B ahead of Point A (why?). However, for this person, the choice between Point A and Point C is rather difficult. On Point A this person consumes more units of Good 1 than on Point C, but on Point C he/she consumes more units of Good 2 than on Point A. We will assume that this person can rank these two bundles, i.e. can tell which one is better (or can tell they are equally desirable). The ranking is really up to this consumer's taste over the two goods.

The taste over the consumption of the goods is called **preferences** in economics. In the following, we show that a person's preferences can be represented by the utility function. If we denote a bundle of goods and utility by (x_1, x_2) and u, respectively, the utility function is written as follows:

$$u = U(x_1, x_2). \tag{6.1}$$

This function simply means that utility that a person obtains depends on the amounts of Good 1 and Good 2 that he/she consumes. Think about two bundles $(\tilde{x}_1, \tilde{x}_2)$ and $(\hat{x}_1, \hat{x}_2)$. Let us denote the levels of utility that correspond to these bundles by $\tilde{u}$ and $\hat{u}$, respectively. Then using the utility function, we can write:

$$\tilde{u} = U(\tilde{x}_1, \tilde{x}_2) \text{ and } \hat{u} = U(\hat{x}_1, \hat{x}_2).$$

If we compare $\tilde{u}$ and $\hat{u}$, and if $\tilde{u} > \hat{u}$, we say that a consumer (strictly) **prefers** Bundle $(\tilde{x}_1, \tilde{x}_2)$ to Bundle $(\hat{x}_1, \hat{x}_2)$, and vice versa. When $\tilde{u} = \hat{u}$, we say that a consumer is **indifferent** between Bundle $(\tilde{x}_1, \tilde{x}_2)$ and Bundle $(\hat{x}_1, \hat{x}_2)$. The function U represents this person's preferences this way.

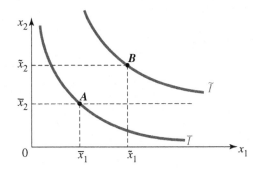

Figure 6.3 Indifference curves.

6.2 Indifference curves

Let us consider the situation where a consumer is choosing a particular consumption bundle $(\bar{x}_1, \bar{x}_2)$ and is obtaining utility $\bar{u}$. Now let us look for other consumption bundles that might give the same utility level $\bar{u}$.

Suppose consumption of both Good 1 and Good 2 provides a person with positive utility. It means that if consumption on Good 1 falls, to keep the utility level constant at $\bar{u}$, consumption on Good 2 has to rise. Likewise, even if consumption on Good 2 falls, if consumption on Good 1 rises by some appropriate amount, a person can keep his/her utility level constant at $\bar{u}$. Therefore, the set of consumption bundles that provides a person with the utility level $\bar{u}$ will be expressed as a downward sloping curve $\bar{I}$ that cuts Point A, $(\bar{x}_1, \bar{x}_2)$, as in Figure 6.3.

All the consumption bundles on Curve $\bar{I}$ give the same utility level $\bar{u}$ to the consumer, and hence for this consumer all the points on Curve $\bar{I}$ are indifferent. For this reason, Curve $\bar{I}$ is called the **indifference curve**.

An indefinite number of indifference curves exists. For example, Curve $\tilde{I}$ illustrated in Figure 6.3 gives the same utility as the consumption bundle $(\tilde{x}_1, \tilde{x}_2)$ at Point B. We have postulated that consumption of both Good 1 and Good 2 provides a person with positive utility. Under this assumption, an indifference curve that lies further to the top-right than another corresponds to the higher level of utility. A diagram that illustrates a collection of indifference curves is called an **indifference map**.

6.3 The marginal utility for the two-good case

We have discussed the marginal utility for the one-good case. For the two-good case, it is not as simple. We are looking at two goods now, and there is an important thing for you to remember for the rest of the discussion. When we talk about the marginal utility of one good, we *keep the level of consumption of the other good intact*.

Let us again consider the situation where a consumer is choosing a particular consumption bundle $(\bar{x}_1, \bar{x}_2)$ and is obtaining utility $\bar{u}$. We keep $\bar{x}_2$ intact and consider a change

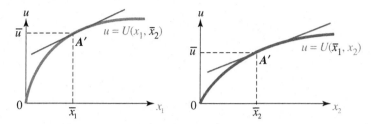

Figure 6.4 Marginal utility of Good 1 and Good 2.

in the consumption of Good 1 only. That is, we are concerned only about points on the dotted line horizontal to the x_1-axis that goes through Point A in Figure 6.3.

In Figure 6.4, two diagrams are depicted. The left one shows that a consumer's utility increases as x_1 rises, holding $x_2 = \bar{x}_2$. Here, the **marginal utility of Good 1** is defined as an incremental change in utility when the Good 1 consumption increases by an infinitesimally small amount, *holding the Good 2 consumption constant*. It is the slope of the curve $u = U(x_1, \bar{x}_2)$ at the level of x_1 in question. It is normally assumed that the marginal utility of Good 1 declines as the Good 1 consumption x_1 rises (the law of diminishing marginal utility), as illustrated in the figure.

We introduce a new mathematical notion here, to express the slope of this curve, i.e. the marginal utility of one good holding the other constant. Consider a small change in x_1, Δx_1. Then the slope of the curve $u = U(x_1, \bar{x}_2)$ can be expressed as

$$\lim_{\Delta x_1 \to 0} \frac{U(x_1 + \Delta x_1, \bar{x}_2) - U(x_1, \bar{x}_2)}{\Delta x_1}. \tag{6.2}$$

We call this expression the **partial derivative** of the function $U(x_1, x_2)$ **with respect to** x_1 (when $x_2 = \bar{x}_2$). We use either $\left.\dfrac{\partial u}{\partial x_1}\right|_{x_2=\bar{x}_2}$, $\dfrac{\partial U(x_1, \bar{x}_2)}{\partial x_1}$, $\left.\dfrac{\partial U}{\partial x_1}\right|_{x_2=\bar{x}_2}$ or $U_1(x_1, \bar{x}_2)$ to show the partial derivative of $U(x_1, x_2)$ with respect to x_1 (when $x_2 = \bar{x}_2$). That is:

$$\lim_{\Delta x_1 \to 0} \frac{U(x_1 + \Delta x_1, \bar{x}_2) - U(x_1, \bar{x}_2)}{\Delta x_1} = U_1(x_1, \bar{x}_2) \tag{6.3}$$

$$= \frac{\partial U(x_1, \bar{x}_2)}{\partial x_1}$$

$$= \left.\frac{\partial U}{\partial x_1}\right|_{x_2=\bar{x}_2}$$

$$= \left.\frac{\partial u}{\partial x_1}\right|_{x_2=\bar{x}_2}.$$

The process of obtaining the partial derivative with respect to x_1 is called the **partial differentiation** with respect to x_1.

Likewise, the partial derivative of $u = U(x_1, x_2)$ with respect to x_2 (when $x_1 = \bar{x}_1$) is:

$$\lim_{\Delta x_2 \to 0} \frac{U(\bar{x}_1, x_2 + \Delta x_2) - U(\bar{x}_1, x_2)}{\Delta x_2} = U_2(\bar{x}_1, x_2) \qquad (6.4)$$

$$= \frac{\partial U(\bar{x}_1, x_2)}{\partial x_2}$$

$$= \frac{\partial U}{\partial x_2}\bigg|_{x_1 = \bar{x}_1}$$

$$= \frac{\partial u}{\partial x_2}\bigg|_{x_1 = \bar{x}_1}.$$

Let's go through some problems to consolidate the ideas.

Question   Obtain the partial derivative of the function $u = U(x_1, x_2) = \sqrt{x_1}\sqrt{x_2}$ with respect to x_1 and x_2, when $x_1 = 25$, $x_2 = 100$. How do they change if $x_2 = 1$?

Solution   The trick to obtaining the partial derivative is to view a variable that is not the focus as a constant, and to take the derivative with respect to the focussed variable. For instance, for the partial derivative with respect to x_1, we view x_2 as a constant, and differentiate the function with respect to x_1:

$$\frac{\partial U(x_1, x_2)}{\partial x_1} = \sqrt{x_2}\frac{d\sqrt{x_1}}{dx} = \sqrt{x_2}\frac{1}{2\sqrt{x_1}} = \frac{\sqrt{x_2}}{2\sqrt{x_1}}.$$

Evaluating this at $x_1 = 25$, $x_2 = 100$ gives:

$$\frac{\partial U(x_1, x_2)}{\partial x_1}\bigg|_{x_1 = 25, x_2 = 100} = \frac{\sqrt{100}}{2\sqrt{25}} = \frac{10}{2 \cdot 5} = 1.$$

If $x_1 = 25$, $x_2 = 1$:

$$\frac{\partial U(x_1, x_2)}{\partial x_1}\bigg|_{x_1 = 25, x_2 = 1} = \frac{\sqrt{1}}{2\sqrt{25}} = \frac{1}{2 \cdot 5} = \frac{1}{10}.$$

The partial derivative has gone down from 1 to $\frac{1}{10}$. Roughly speaking, it means that the 26th unit of x_1 when $x_2 = 100$ gives an additional utility of 1, whereas when $x_2 = 1$, the additional utility is only $\frac{1}{10}$. We can infer that the consumer enjoys an extra unit of x_1 more when he/she has more x_2.

What about the partial derivative with respect to x_2?

$$\frac{\partial U(x_1, x_2)}{\partial x_2} = \sqrt{x_1}\frac{d\sqrt{x_2}}{dx_2} = \sqrt{x_1}\frac{1}{2\sqrt{x_2}} = \frac{\sqrt{x_1}}{2\sqrt{x_2}}.$$

Evaluating this at $x_1 = 25$, $x_2 = 100$ gives:

$$\left.\frac{\partial U(x_1, x_2)}{\partial x_2}\right|_{x_1=25, x_2=100} = \frac{\sqrt{25}}{2\sqrt{100}} = \frac{5}{2 \cdot 10} = \frac{1}{4}.$$

If $x_1 = 25$, $x_2 = 1$:

$$\left.\frac{\partial U(x_1, x_2)}{\partial x_2}\right|_{x_1=25, x_2=1} = \frac{\sqrt{25}}{2\sqrt{1}} = \frac{5}{2 \cdot 1} = \frac{5}{2}.$$

The partial derivative has gone up from $\frac{1}{4}$ to $\frac{5}{2}$. Roughly speaking, it means that the 101st unit of x_2 when $x_1 = 25$ gives an additional utility of $\frac{1}{4}$, whereas the additional utility from the second unit of x_2 is much higher. We can infer that the law of diminishing marginal utility holds for x_2.

Exercise 6.2 The partial derivatives and the marginal utility.

An important thing to notice in this example is that the partial derivative with respect to a certain variable is a function not only of the variable itself but also of the other variable. That is, the marginal utility of a good depends upon both Good 1 consumption and Good 2 consumption.

6.3.1 The relationship between indifference curves and the utility function

In Figure 6.5, the utility function $u = U(x_1, x_2)$ is depicted. As we can see, it is shown in three-dimensional (3D) space because the relationship between three variables x_1, x_2 and u is the focus. The utility function is shown as a three-dimensional object, which looks like a mountain (with no summit).

Let me explain the diagram. Imagine that a person chooses a consumption bundle $(\bar{x}_1, \bar{x}_2)$ at Point A on the x_1x_2-plane. The level of utility that he/she obtains is shown by the distance AA', which is $\bar{u}$ (in the context of the mountain, the utility level is measured by the altitude). A contour (labelled $\bar{H}$) that passes Point A' is drawn on the diagram. Any points on this contour give the person the same utility $\bar{u}$ because the contour is made by cutting the mountain *horizontally* (to the x_1x_2-plane) at Point A'. The indifference curve can be obtained by projecting the contour to the x_1x_2-plane. The two-dimensional version of this diagram is Figure 6.3. We can easily work out that an indifference curve that lies further to the top-right than another corresponds to a higher level of utility.

6.3.2 The relationship between the marginal utility and the utility function

We have discussed previously that the marginal utility of one good can be obtained by taking the partial derivative of the utility function with respect to that good. What does it mean diagrammatically in relation to the utility function? Recall that, in obtaining the partial derivative with respect to one good, we hold the consumption of the other good

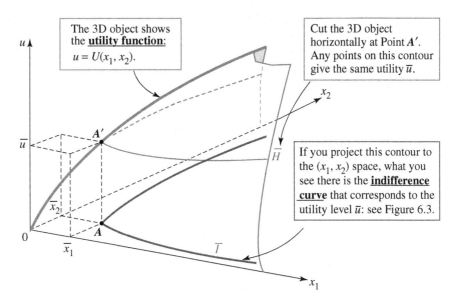

Figure 6.5 The utility function and indifference curves.

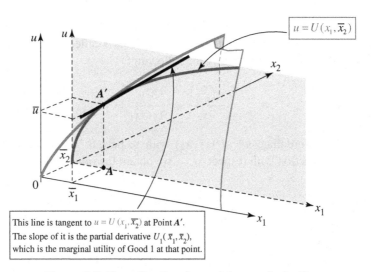

Figure 6.6 The utility function and the marginal utility.

constant. It motivates us to cut the 3D object at $x_2 = \bar{x}_2$ *vertically* to the (x_1, x_2)-space. A surface will appear on the 3D object (see the shaded surface in Figure 6.6).

The edge of this surface shows the curve $u = U(x_1, \bar{x}_2)$. It shows how utility changes according to the level of x_1 holding x_2 constant at $\bar{x}_2$. Therefore, the slope of this curve shows the marginal utility of Good 1. What we have drawn on this surface is the same as what we drew in Figure 6.4 (the one on the left).

6.3.3 The second-order partial derivatives

We can think about cutting the utility function vertically at different x_2s, and in that case the partial derivative of $u = U(x_1, x_2)$ with respect to x_1 can be written simply as $\frac{\partial u}{\partial x_1}$. We call this partial derivative the **first-order partial derivative**, since we partially differentiate u with respect to one of the arguments only once. We might consider further differentiating it with respect to the same argument, x_1, and as you might guess, it will show the curvature (concavity) of the function $u = U(x_1, x_2)$ (in the direction of x_1). We define the **second-order partial derivative** of $u = U(x_1, x_2)$ with respect to x_1 as the following:

$$\frac{\partial \left(\frac{\partial u}{\partial x_1} \right)}{\partial x_1} = \frac{\partial^2 u}{\partial x_1^2} = U_{11}(x_1, x_2). \tag{6.5}$$

Likewise, the second-order partial derivative of $u = U(x_1, x_2)$ with respect to x_2 is:

$$\frac{\partial \left(\frac{\partial u}{\partial x_2} \right)}{\partial x_2} = \frac{\partial^2 u}{\partial x_2^2} = U_{22}(x_1, x_2). \tag{6.6}$$

We can actually differentiate the first-order partial derivative with respect to another argument. In $u = U(x_1, x_2)$, we can first differentiate it with respect to x_1 and obtain $\frac{\partial u}{\partial x_1}$, and then differentiate that with respect to x_2. This is called the (second-order) **cross-partial derivative** and we denote it by the following:

$$\frac{\partial \left(\frac{\partial u}{\partial x_1} \right)}{\partial x_2} = \frac{\partial^2 u}{\partial x_2 \partial x_1} = U_{12}(x_1, x_2). \tag{6.7}$$

If we differentiate $u = U(x_1, x_2)$ with respect to x_2 first and then differentiate the resulting function with respect to x_1, we obtain the other cross-partial derivative:

$$\frac{\partial \left(\frac{\partial u}{\partial x_2} \right)}{\partial x_1} = \frac{\partial^2 u}{\partial x_1 \partial x_2} = U_{21}(x_1, x_2). \tag{6.8}$$

When both $U_1(x_1, x_2)$ and $U_2(x_1, x_2)$ are continuously differentiable, it is known that these cross-partial derivatives are identical.[1] It is called **Young's Theorem**: when $U_1(x_1, x_2)$ and $U_2(x_1, x_2)$ are continuously differentiable,

$$U_{12}(x_1, x_2) = U_{21}(x_1, x_2). \tag{6.9}$$

This implies that it does not matter which way you calculate the cross-partial derivatives. Here's an exercise.

---

[1] We say that a function is continuously differentiable when (i) all the partial derivatives exist; and (ii) they are continuous.

Question　Consider $u = U(x_1, x_2) = x_1^2 + x_1 x_2 + x_2^2$. Obtain the second-order partial derivatives and cross-partial derivatives. Verify that Young's Theorem holds.

Solution

$$U_1(x_1, x_2) = 2x_1 + x_2,$$
$$U_2(x_1, x_2) = 2x_2 + x_1.$$

Hence,

$$U_{11}(x_1, x_2) = 2,$$
$$U_{22}(x_1, x_2) = 2,$$

and

$$U_{12}(x_1, x_2) = 1,$$
$$U_{21}(x_1, x_2) = 1.$$

Therefore,

$$U_{12}(x_1, x_2) = U_{21}(x_1, x_2).$$

Exercise 6.3　The second-order partial derivatives and cross-partial derivatives.

6.4　The marginal rate of substitution

In Figure 6.7, an indifference curve $\bar{I}$ is depicted. Let us focus on Point A where a person consumes $(\bar{x}_1, \bar{x}_2)$. Suppose that we take one unit of Good 1 away from this person. It will lower his/her utility. However, this person would be able to retain his/her utility if we gave him/her an appropriate amount of Good 2, Δx_2. In other words, if you were this consumer, you would be willing to substitute Δx_2 for one unit of Good 1 (because it would keep your utility level the same). For this reason, we call Δx_2 the **marginal rate of substitution of Good 1 for Good 2**. Put it another way, the marginal rate of substitution of Good 1 for Good 2 shows how much the consumer values the last unit of Good 1 in terms of Good 2. Hereafter, we will just call it the marginal rate of substitution, and denote it by MRS_{12}.

Now think about an infinitesimally small change in Good 1. Then, the marginal rate of substitution can be shown by the *absolute value of the slope of the indifference curve* at the point of consumption.

The important thing to note here is that MRS_{12} changes along the indifference curve. If the indifference curve is shaped as illustrated on the diagram in Figure 6.7, the marginal rate of substitution decreases as consumption on Good 1 increases. The marginal rate of substitution at Point B is less than that at Point A. It makes sense because at Point B this person consumes Good 1 more than at Point A, so MRS_{12} that shows the value of (the last unit of) Good 1 in terms of Good 2 should be lower. In economics, this property on MRS_{12} is called the **law of the diminishing marginal rate of substitution**. In mathematics, we

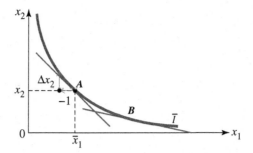

Figure 6.7 The marginal rate of substitution.

say that the indifference curve is **strictly convex** *to the origin*. That is, if the indifference curve is decreasing, and also, if it is strictly convex, the law of the diminishing MRS holds.

6.4.1 The relationship between the marginal utility and the marginal rate of substitution

There is an important relationship between the marginal utility and the marginal rate of substitution. As we have seen, the marginal rate of substitution (MRS_{12}) is the amount of Good 2 required to just compensate for an infinitesimally small decrease in Good 1. When Good 1 decreases by an infinitesimally small amount, holding Good 2 consumption constant, the level of utility of a consumer decreases by $\dfrac{\partial U}{\partial x_1}$.

A one-unit increase in Good 2 increases the level of utility of a consumer by $\dfrac{\partial U}{\partial x_2}$, and hence in order to increase the level of utility by one, Good 2 should increase by $\dfrac{1}{\partial U/\partial x_2}$ units. It follows that, in order to compensate for an infinitesimally small decrease in Good 1, Good 2 should increase by $\dfrac{\partial U/\partial x_1}{\partial U/\partial x_2}$ units.

We have established an important relationship between the marginal utility and the marginal rate of substitution:

$$MRS_{12} = \frac{\partial U/\partial x_1}{\partial U/\partial x_2}. \tag{6.10}$$

This equation implies that the marginal rate of substitution of Good 1 for Good 2 is equal to the ratio of the marginal utility of Good 1 and the marginal utility of Good 2.

Question　Assume a utility function $u = U(x_1, x_2) = \sqrt{x_1} \cdot x_2$. What is the level of utility when $x_1 = 25$, $x_2 = 1$? Calculate the marginal utility of Good 1 and Good 2 when $x_1 = 25$, $x_2 = 1$. What is the marginal rate of substitution of Good 1 for Good 2 at that point? Does the law of diminishing marginal utility hold?

Solution

We have

$$u = U(25, 1) = \sqrt{25} \cdot 1 = 5 \times 1 = 5,$$

$$\frac{\partial U(x_1, x_2)}{\partial x_1} = x_2 \frac{d\sqrt{x_1}}{dx} = x_2 \frac{1}{2\sqrt{x_1}} = \frac{x_2}{2\sqrt{x_1}},$$

$$\frac{\partial^2 U(x_1, x_2)}{\partial x_1^2} = -\frac{x_2}{4x_1\sqrt{x_1}}.$$

The law of diminishing marginal utility of Good 1 holds because $U_{11} < 0$, for all $x_1 > 0$ and $x_2 > 0$.

Now evaluating the marginal utility of Good 1 at $x_1 = 25$ and $x_2 = 1$ gives:

$$\left.\frac{\partial U(x_1, x_2)}{\partial x_1}\right|_{x_1=25, x_2=1} = \frac{1}{2\sqrt{25}} = \frac{1}{2 \cdot 5} = \frac{1}{10},$$

$$\frac{\partial U(x_1, x_2)}{\partial x_2} = \sqrt{x_1}\frac{dx_2}{dx_2} = \sqrt{x_1}.$$

The marginal utility of Good 2 does not depend on the Good 2 consumption, so it is obvious that the law of diminishing marginal utility of Good 2 does not hold.

Evaluating the marginal utility of Good 2 at $x_1 = 25$ and $x_2 = 1$ gives:

$$\left.\frac{\partial U(x_1, x_2)}{\partial x_2}\right|_{x_1=25, x_2=1} = \sqrt{25} = 5,$$

$$MRS_{12} = \frac{\partial U/\partial x_1}{\partial U/\partial x_2} = \frac{x_2/2\sqrt{x_1}}{\sqrt{x_1}} = \frac{x_2}{2x_1}.$$

Evaluating MRS at $x_1 = 25$ and $x_2 = 1$ gives:

$$MRS_{12} = \frac{1}{50}.$$

Exercise 6.4 The marginal rate of substitution and the marginal utility.

6.5 Total differentiation and implicit differentiation

In the previous section, we derived the relationship between the marginal rate of substitution and the marginal utility, as in Equation (6.10). Here we will derive the same relationship by using a different mathematical technique. This section also deals with some more new mathematical notions that we will use later in solving the consumer's utility maximisation problem.

6.5.1 Total differential and total differentiation

Recall that, in Chapter 4, we defined the *differential* of a single-variate function $C(q)$ as the following:

$$dC = C'(q)dq.$$

It means the effect of a tiny change in q upon C is given by the product of the derivative of the function $C'(q)$ and the differential dq.

A similar idea for a multivariate function $u = U(x_1, x_2)$ can be expressed: if we have a very tiny change in x_1, which we denote by dx_1, the consequent change in the value of u is given by:

$$du = \frac{\partial U(x_1, x_2)}{\partial x_1} dx_1. \tag{6.11}$$

Note that we use the partial derivative with respect to x_1, $\dfrac{\partial U(x_1, x_2)}{\partial x_1}$. Equation (6.11), if it *held*, would be written as:

$$\frac{du}{dx_1} = U_1, \tag{6.12}$$

which relates to our statement at the end of Section 5.2: the derivative (in this case, the partial derivative on the RHS) of a function can be expressed as the ratio of the differentials. In Equation (6.12), the partial derivative U_1 is expressed as the ratio of the differentials du and dx_1. However, Equation (6.11) (or (6.12)) will not generally hold. That is, the ratio of the differentials, du and dx_1, and the partial derivative U_1 are different, with some exceptions. I show why it is the case in the following.

Since there are two arguments to the function $u = U(x_1, x_2)$, in addition to a change in x_1, we need to consider a small change in x_2. Let us denote this change in x_2 as dx_2 (the differential of x_2). Multiplying this differential by $\dfrac{\partial U(x_1, x_2)}{\partial x_2}$ gives us the effect of the change in x_2 on u, and together with the effect of the change in x_1 on u, we obtain the total effect on u:

$$du = \frac{\partial U(x_1, x_2)}{\partial x_1} dx_1 + \frac{\partial U(x_1, x_2)}{\partial x_2} dx_2. \tag{6.13}$$

We call du in Equation (6.13) the **total differential** of the function $u = U(x_1, x_2)$. It is the sum of the marginal changes in all the arguments of the function, multiplied by the corresponding partial derivatives. The technique of taking the total differential of a function is called **total differentiation**.

Now let us divide both sides of Equation (6.13) by dx_1:

$$\frac{du}{dx_1} = \frac{\partial U(x_1, x_2)}{\partial x_1} + \frac{\partial U(x_1, x_2)}{\partial x_2} \frac{dx_2}{dx_1}. \tag{6.14}$$

The LHS of Equation (6.14) is called the **total derivative** of the function $u = U(x_1, x_2)$ with respect to x_1. It is the ratio of the two differentials du and dx_1. As we can see, it equals the RHS of Equation (6.14), which consists of two terms. The first term is the

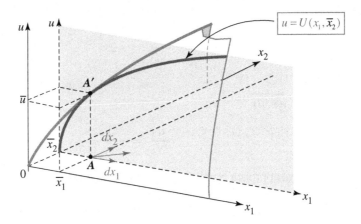

Figure 6.8 The total derivative.

partial derivative of u with respect to x_1, $\dfrac{\partial U(x_1, x_2)}{\partial x_1}$, and the second is $\dfrac{\partial U(x_1, x_2)}{\partial x_2} \dfrac{dx_2}{dx_1}$.

What this equation says is important. It says that the effect of a tiny change in x_1 upon u can be decomposed into two things. The first term shows the 'direct effect' of a tiny change in x_1 upon u (because when we take the partial derivative, $\dfrac{\partial U(x_1, x_2)}{\partial x_1}$, we are holding x_2 constant), whereas the second term shows an "indirect effect" of a tiny change in x_1 upon u through a change in x_2. Therefore, so long as the indirect effect is not zero, the total derivative, i.e. the ratio of the differentials, and the partial derivative are different.

Let us see intuitively what we have done. For this purpose I will use Equation (6.13) and Figure 6.8 (which is essentially the same as Figure 6.6).

The (total) differential du measures the change in the level of utility (or the change in the altitude of where you are standing on the 3D object), as a consequence of changing consumption by an infinitesimally small amount in *any* direction. That is, here, we are no longer constrained to move only in the direction of x_1 or in the direction of x_2. For example, we can move somewhere in between the directions of x_1 and x_2.

6.5.2   Implicit differentiation

Total differentiation is very useful: it can be used to differentiate single-variate functions, which would be rather cumbersome to handle in the usual way. For example, to calculate $\dfrac{dy}{dx}$ for an implicit function:

$$y^2 + x = 0, \tag{6.15}$$

we can write this as:

$$x = -y^2. \tag{6.16}$$

Hence:

$$\frac{dx}{dy} = -2y. \tag{6.17}$$

Since $\dfrac{dy}{dx} = \dfrac{1}{dx/dy}$,

$$\frac{dy}{dx} = -\frac{1}{2y}. \tag{6.18}$$

An alternative approach is called **implicit differentiation**. It involves applying the total differentiation to the implicit function and goes as follows. First, we regard $y^2 + x$ as a function of x and y, which we express by using the following notation:

$$f = F(x, y) = y^2 + x = 0. \tag{6.19}$$

Taking the total differentials (recall Equation (6.13)) gives the following:

$$df = \frac{\partial F(x, y)}{\partial x} dx + \frac{\partial F(x, y)}{\partial y} dy. \tag{6.20}$$

In this equation, df has to be zero because f always equals zero (remember, df is a tiny movement in f. If $f = 0$ always hold, then df has to be zero). Therefore:

$$0 = \frac{\partial F(x, y)}{\partial x} dx + \frac{\partial F(x, y)}{\partial y} dy. \tag{6.21}$$

This expression boils down to:

$$\frac{dy}{dx} = -\frac{\frac{\partial F(x,y)}{\partial x}}{\frac{\partial F(x,y)}{\partial y}} = -\frac{1}{2y}. \tag{6.22}$$

which is the same as what we have got in Equation (6.18).

Now, think about the indifference curve corresponding to a certain level of utility, $\bar{u}$, that is:

$$u = U(x_1, x_2) = \bar{u}. \tag{6.23}$$

Suppose we have tiny changes in x_1 and x_2 along this indifference curve (meaning that we are not moving off the curve). Since we consider changes along the same indifference curve, $u = \bar{u}$, and so $du = 0$:

$$du = \frac{\partial U(x_1, x_2)}{\partial x_1} dx_1 + \frac{\partial U(x_1, x_2)}{\partial x_2} dx_2 = 0. \tag{6.24}$$

This expression boils down to:

$$-\frac{dx_2}{dx_1} = \frac{\partial U/\partial x_1}{\partial U/\partial x_2}. \tag{6.25}$$

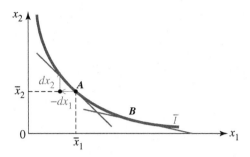

Figure 6.9 Obtaining *MRS* by using implicit differentiation.

Using the fact that the marginal rate of substitution (MRS_{12}) is the absolute value of the slope of the indifference curve at the point of consumption (see Figure 6.9), we can conclude that:

$$MRS_{12} = \frac{\partial U / \partial x_1}{\partial U / \partial x_2}. \tag{6.26}$$

Now let us go through a question on the implicit differentiation to consolidate the understanding.

Question   Consider $x^2 - y^2 = 6$. Obtain $\dfrac{dy}{dx}$.

Solution   Let f be the following:

$$f = F(x, y) = x^2 - y^2 = 6.$$

Taking the total differentials (recall Equation (6.13)) gives the following:

$$df = \frac{\partial F(x, y)}{\partial x} dx + \frac{\partial F(x, y)}{\partial y} dy.$$

In this equation, df has to be zero because f always equals 6. Therefore:

$$0 = \frac{\partial F(x, y)}{\partial x} dx + \frac{\partial F(x, y)}{\partial y} dy.$$

This expression boils down to:

$$\frac{dy}{dx} = -\frac{\frac{\partial F(x, y)}{\partial x}}{\frac{\partial F(x, y)}{\partial y}} = -\frac{2x}{(-2y)} = \frac{x}{y}.$$

Exercise 6.5   Implicit differentiation.

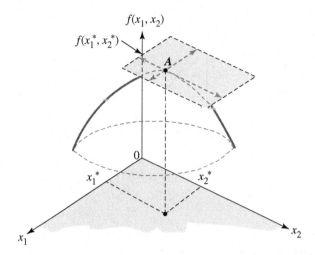

Figure 6.10 Local maximum.

6.6　Maxima and minima revisited

In Chapter 4, we discussed how we should go about solving the maximisation (minimisation) problem for a single-variate function. What are the procedures if the function is bi-variate? Recalling that we used the first and second derivatives in Chapter 4, some of you may think about using the first- and second-order partial derivatives in the same way. It's great if you think like that, but the problem turns out to be much more complicated.

Forget about the utility maximisation problem for a while, and consider finding the maximum/minimum of a general function, $f(x_1, x_2)$. This problem is referred to as the **unconstrained optimisation problem** because you can choose *any* (x_1, x_2) to maximise/minimise the function; that is, you are not constrained to choose from particular combinations of (x_1, x_2). In contrast, in the utility maximisation problem, which we come back to later, you can't choose any (x_1, x_2) because you have a limited budget. For now, however, you are allowed to choose any combination of (x_1, x_2).

Look at Figure 6.10. As you can see, the maximum of the function is achieved at Point A, and (x_1^*, x_2^*) is the optimal combination of x_1 and x_2. Let us think about the mathematical properties at Point A. What has to be true at Point A?

Firstly, it has to be the case that if we draw a plane (the shaded parallelogram) that is tangent to the function, it has to be parallel to the (x_1, x_2) plane (also shaded). This is analogous to the single-variable case where we could draw a horizontal line at the maximum. In the mathematics context, it means the following.

Allow x_1 and x_2 to move simultaneously by an infinitesimally small amount from Point A (both directions as the arrows suggest on the diagram). It corresponds to taking the total differential of the function:

$$df = \frac{\partial f(x_1, x_2)}{\partial x_1} dx_1 + \frac{\partial f(x_1, x_2)}{\partial x_2} dx_2, \tag{6.27}$$

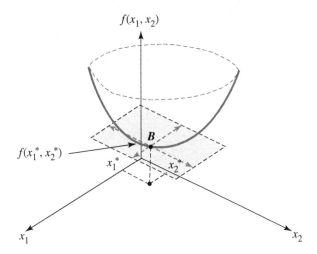

Figure 6.11 Local minimum.

where dx_1 and dx_2 correspond to the changes in x_1 and x_2. For Point A to be the local maximum, the total differential df must be zero, for any small movements dx_1 and dx_2 (because it is on the top; not going up or down). It follows that *both* the partial derivatives in Equation (6.27) must be zero.

However, as we can guess, this property is not enough. As in the one-variable case, we can find the exact opposite case, where we find the local minimum of a function by using the same condition. That situation is depicted in Figure 6.11, where Point B is the local minimum of the function.

In any case, we find one of the conditions for the local maximum/minimum of a bi-variate function:

$$\frac{\partial f(x_1, x_2)}{\partial x_1} = \frac{\partial f(x_1, x_2)}{\partial x_2} = 0. \tag{6.28}$$

At the local maximum/minimum, the above set of equations has to hold. It constitutes the **first-order conditions** for the local maximum/minimum. Now, go back to Figure 6.10, where the local maximum is depicted. The second thing that has to be true at Point A is that the function is at the local maximum *in both directions* x_1 *and* x_2. It is the same as saying that both of the second-order partial derivatives of the function are negative:

$$\frac{\partial^2 f(x_1, x_2)}{\partial x_1^2} < 0, \quad \frac{\partial^2 f(x_1, x_2)}{\partial x_2^2} < 0. \tag{6.29}$$

Likewise, in Figure 6.11, the opposite has to hold at the local minimum, Point B:

$$\frac{\partial^2 f(x_1, x_2)}{\partial x_1^2} > 0, \quad \frac{\partial^2 f(x_1, x_2)}{\partial x_2^2} > 0. \tag{6.30}$$

They are *parts* of the second-order conditions for the local maximum and local minimum, respectively.

In passing, I have depicted in Figure 6.12 a special case, where the first-order conditions are met but, for the second-order conditions (those so far covered), one of the partial

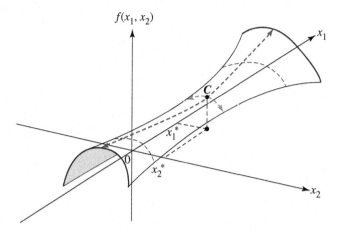

Figure 6.12 A saddle point.

derivatives is positive, and the other is negative. Point C corresponds to such a case, where it is the local minimum in the direction of x_1, but is the local maximum in the direction of x_2. Mathematically,

$$\frac{\partial^2 f(x_1, x_2)}{\partial x_1^2} > 0, \quad \frac{\partial^2 f(x_1, x_2)}{\partial x_2^2} < 0. \tag{6.31}$$

Such a point is referred to as a **saddle point**, for obvious reasons.

Let us return to the second-order conditions for the local minimum, i.e. (6.30). I have said that they are parts of the conditions. Indeed, we can find a counter-example in which these conditions are satisfied at a point, yet the point is neither a local maximum nor a local minimum. I will demonstrate this case in the following.

Consider the following function:

$$y = f(x_1, x_2) = x_1^2 + 10x_1x_2 + x_2^2. \tag{6.32}$$

The first-order conditions are:

$$\frac{\partial f(x_1, x_2)}{\partial x_1} = 2x_1 + 10x_2 = 0, \tag{6.33}$$

$$\frac{\partial f(x_1, x_2)}{\partial x_2} = 10x_1 + 2x_2 = 0. \tag{6.34}$$

The only combination of x_1 and x_2 that simultaneously satisfies Equations (6.33) and (6.34) is $(x_1^*, x_2^*) = (0, 0)$. To check whether this point is the local maximum, local minimum or a saddle point, we investigate the second-order conditions:

$$\frac{\partial^2 f(x_1, x_2)}{\partial x_1^2} = 2 > 0, \quad \frac{\partial^2 f(x_1, x_2)}{\partial x_2^2} = 2 > 0. \tag{6.35}$$

Equation (6.35) implies that $(x_1^*, x_2^*) = (0, 0)$ is the local minimum (see (6.30)), and the value of the function at that point is $y = f(0, 0) = 0$. However, consider a real number a and take a point $(x_1, x_2) = (-a, a)$. Substituting this point into Equation (6.32) yields the following:

$$f(-a, a) = a^2 - 10a^2 + a^2 = -8a^2. \tag{6.36}$$

Note that $\lim_{a \to 0} f(-a, a) = 0$, which means $f(-a, a)$ approaches 0 as a becomes closer to zero. But, more importantly, $f(-a, a)$ approaches 0 from *negative values*. Looking at it from the other way, it implies that a movement from $(0, 0)$ to $(-a, a)$ will lower the value of the function, which suffices in showing that $(0, 0)$ is not the local minimum. It is not a local maximum either, in passing (try using (a, a) instead of $(-a, a)$ to verify this claim).

It turns out that, for the point we find using the first- and second-order conditions (that have been introduced so far) to be either the local maximum or the local minimum, the following relationship has to be satisfied at the point in question:

$$\frac{\partial^2 f(x_1, x_2)}{\partial x_1^2} \cdot \frac{\partial^2 f(x_1, x_2)}{\partial x_2^2} > \left[\frac{\partial^2 f(x_1, x_2)}{\partial x_2 \partial x_1} \right]^2, \tag{6.37}$$

or, more concisely,

$$f_{11} \cdot f_{22} > f_{12}^2. \tag{6.38}$$

This expression completes the **second-order conditions**. The derivation of this condition will not be given here, to maintain the flow of our discussion. If you are interested in the derivation, see Appendix A. In the meantime, we will just check that this condition is not met for the problem we just investigated. For $f(x_1, x_2) = x_1^2 + 10x_1 x_2 + x_2^2$:

$$\frac{\partial^2 f(x_1, x_2)}{\partial x_2 \partial x_1} = 10. \tag{6.39}$$

The RHS of (6.37) is 100, whereas the LHS is 4. Hence (6.37) (or (6.38)) is violated.

Question (The profit maximisation problem with two inputs)   Think about applying what we have learnt to the profit maximisation problem. Although we maintain the assumption of the competitive input and output markets, the setup here is slightly different from that in Chapter 4. That is, we have *two* inputs of production, instead of one. Denoting the level of production by q, the production function of the firm can be expressed as follows:

$$q = f(K, L), \tag{6.40}$$

where L is labour and K is the number of robots. Since there are two inputs the firm want to choose the optimal K and L, not just the output, q. In the case where K does not exist (as in Chapter 4), controlling L meant the same as controlling q. But here, the firm can control K as well as L, and different combinations of K and L might result in producing the same amount of q. In that case, the firm would want to choose the most efficient combination of K and L to produce that amount. Hence, we consider the firm that tries maximising the profits by choosing the amount of both robots (K) and labour (L). Let us denote the price of the good, a robot and labour by $p > 0, r > 0$, and $w > 0$, respectively. Then the profits of the firm can be expressed as:

$$\pi(K, L) = pf(K, L) - rK - wL. \tag{6.41}$$

Notice that $\pi(K, L)$ is expressed as a function of K and L: but not $\pi(q)$ as it was in Chapter 4. Also we are assuming that the fixed cost of production is zero. Now we can mathematically represent the profit maximisation problem as follows:

$$\underset{K,L}{Max}\, \pi(K, L). \tag{6.42}$$

Now, the **question** is the following: if the production function is given as (6.43) and inputs prices are given as $r = 2$ and $w = 1$, solve the profit maximisation problem and obtain the amounts of the inputs that the firm hires:

$$f(K, L) = K^{\frac{1}{3}} L^{\frac{1}{3}}. \tag{6.43}$$

Solution

$$\underset{K,L}{Max}\, \pi(K, L) = \underset{K,L}{Max}\, [pf(K, L) - 2K - L].$$

The first-order conditions are:

$$p\frac{\partial f(K, L)}{\partial K} = 2,$$

$$p\frac{\partial f(K, L)}{\partial L} = 1.$$

These equations imply the following:

$$\frac{1}{3}pK^{-\frac{2}{3}}L^{\frac{1}{3}} = 2,$$

$$\frac{1}{3}pK^{\frac{1}{3}}L^{-\frac{2}{3}} = 1.$$

Solving the above for K and L, the input combination that satisfies the first-order conditions is,

$$(K^*, L^*) = \left(\frac{p^3}{108}, \frac{p^3}{54} \right).$$

To check this combination is the true local (and global) maximum, we check the second-order conditions:

$$\frac{\partial^2 \pi}{\partial K^2} < 0,$$

$$\frac{\partial^2 \pi}{\partial L^2} < 0,$$

$$\frac{\partial^2 \pi}{\partial K^2} \cdot \frac{\partial^2 \pi}{\partial L^2} - \left[\frac{\partial^2 \pi}{\partial L \partial K} \right]^2 > 0.$$

Calculating the LHS of these, we have:

$$\frac{\partial^2 \pi}{\partial K^2} = -\frac{2}{9}pK^{-\frac{5}{3}}L^{\frac{1}{3}},$$

$$\frac{\partial^2 \pi}{\partial L^2} = -\frac{2}{9}pK^{\frac{1}{3}}L^{-\frac{5}{3}},$$

$$\frac{\partial^2 \pi}{\partial K^2} \cdot \frac{\partial^2 \pi}{\partial L^2} - \left[\frac{\partial^2 \pi}{\partial L \partial K}\right]^2 = \frac{1}{9}pK^{-\frac{2}{3}}L^{-\frac{2}{3}}.$$

Therefore, given $p > 0$, the second-order conditions are satisfied for any $K > 0$ and $L > 0$ (and so of course they are satisfied at the point of concern $(K^*, L^*) = \left(\frac{p^3}{108}, \frac{p^3}{54}\right)$):

$$-\frac{2}{9}pK^{-\frac{5}{3}}L^{\frac{1}{3}} < 0, \ \forall K > 0, L > 0,$$

$$-\frac{2}{9}pK^{\frac{1}{3}}L^{-\frac{5}{3}} < 0, \ \forall K > 0, L > 0,$$

$$\frac{1}{9}pK^{-\frac{2}{3}}L^{-\frac{2}{3}} > 0, \ \forall K > 0, L > 0.$$

The maximised profits are:

$$\pi(K^*, L^*) = pf(K^*, L^*) - 2K^* - L^*$$

$$= p\left[\left(\frac{p^3}{108}\right)^{\frac{1}{3}}\left(\frac{p^3}{54}\right)^{\frac{1}{3}}\right] - 2\frac{p^3}{108} - \frac{p^3}{54}$$

$$= \frac{1}{18}p^3 - \frac{1}{27}p^3$$

$$= \frac{1}{54}p^3.$$

Exercise 6.6 The profit maximisation with two inputs.

6.7 The utility maximisation problem: constrained optimisation

Now we go back to solving the consumer's utility maximisation problem. This problem is different from the maximisation problem we investigated in the previous section, in the sense that here the consumer will face the constraint: as we know, our budget is limited. Here we will discuss how a consumer makes his/her consumption decisions based on his/her preferences (represented by his/her utility function), given his/her limited income. Because we are looking at a situation where a consumer's utility maximisation

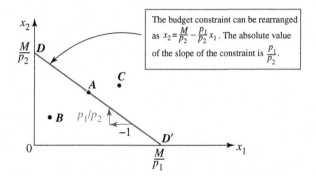

Figure 6.13 The budget constraint.

behaviour is *constrained* by his/her limited income, the problem is called the **constrained optimisation**. If there were only one good, the problem would be simple. A person will use all of his/her income for that good. Our focus is the consumer's behaviour when there are two goods.[2]

We continue denoting Good 1 consumption and Good 2 consumption by x_1 and x_2, respectively. We introduce some new notation. We denote the prices of Good 1 and Good 2 by $p_1 > 0$ and $p_2 > 0$, respectively. The income level is denoted by $M > 0$. We assume that the consumer is a price taker so he/she cannot influence p_1 or p_2.

The consumer's total expenditure $p_1 x_1 + p_2 x_2$ has to be within his/her income. He/she need not use up all his/her income, but suppose that he/she does not save and spends all his/her income on the two goods. Then x_1 and x_2 have to satisfy the following relationship, which is called the consumer's **budget constraint**:

$$p_1 x_1 + p_2 x_2 = M. \tag{6.44}$$

The segment DD' in Figure 6.13 shows the budget constraint. If the person does not consume Good 1 at all, he/she consumes $\dfrac{M}{p_2}$ units of Good 2 (Point D). On the other hand, if he/she does not consume Good 2 at all, he/she consumes $\dfrac{M}{p_1}$ units of Good 1 (Point D'). All possible combinations of x_1 and x_2 are on the segment DD'. For this reason, the line connecting Points D and D' is called the **budget line**.

Point A is on the budget line, satisfying the budget constraint (Equation (6.44)). Point B is inside the budget line, meaning that this bundle is **feasible**, but not all income is used. All points outside the budget line, such as Point C, correspond to combinations of x_1 and x_2 that are **infeasible**.

How does a consumer whose preferences are represented by the utility function $u = U(x_1, x_2)$ choose the optimal consumption bundle (x_1^*, x_2^*)? He/she cannot choose the

---

2 The mathematical techniques we will learn for the two-good case can be applied to the cases with more than two goods as well. It suffices to have two goods to illustrate the trade-off a consumer faces – to consume more of one good, he/she needs to give up some of the other – when his/her income is limited. Looking at the two-good case also allows us to interpret important ideas diagrammatically.

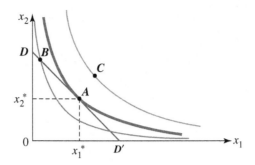

Figure 6.14 Utility maximisation occurs at Point A.

bundle freely, i.e. it has to be on the budget line DD' in Figure 6.13. Hence the consumer will choose the bundle (x_1^*, x_2^*) that is on the budget line, to maximise his/her utility.

More mathematically (formally), the consumer's utility maximisation problem is written as follows: the consumer maximises $u = U(x_1, x_2)$ *subject to* the budget constraint $p_1 x_1 + p_2 x_2 = M$:

$$\underset{x_1, x_2}{Max}\ U(x_1, x_2)$$
$$\text{s.t. } p_1 x_1 + p_2 x_2 = M. \tag{6.45}$$

Equation (6.45) is the formal representation of the consumer's **utility maximisation problem**, where 's.t.' stands for 'subject to'. From here, our focus is how we go about solving this problem. First, we take an intuitive approach and discuss what should be true, and then we apply different methods to solving the same problem. Unsurprisingly, these methods give the same result.

Look at Figure 6.14. The budget line is given by DD'. Which point on the budget line will the consumer choose? Consider Point B. At Point B, the budget line and the indifference curve *intersect*. It is on the budget line, but will not maximise the consumer's utility. Why? Because there exists Point A, which is also on the budget line, and is on the indifference curve that corresponds to a higher level of utility (it is just a diagrammatical explanation; we will provide an economic explanation shortly).

At Point A, the indifference curve is *tangent* to the budget line. Does any point exist on the budget line that gives higher utility to the consumer than this point? No, there doesn't. Point C is on the indifference curve that gives higher utility than Point A, but is outside the budget line: such points are infeasible. Therefore, this consumer will choose the utility maximising bundle (x_1^*, x_2^*) at Point A.

We have checked that the consumer chooses the point where the indifference curve is tangent to the budget line. We know that the absolute value of the slope of the budget line is $\frac{p_1}{p_2}$. We also know that the absolute value of the slope of the indifference curve is the marginal rate of substitution MRS_{12}. Therefore, the consumer chooses the point where:

$$MRS_{12} = \frac{p_1}{p_2}. \tag{6.46}$$

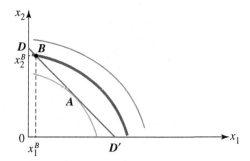

Figure 6.15 Utility maximisation does NOT occur at Point A.

Note that this equation can be written as follows using the fact that $MRS_{12} = \dfrac{\partial U/\partial x_1}{\partial U/\partial x_2}$:

$$\frac{\partial U/\partial x_1}{\partial U/\partial x_2} = \frac{p_1}{p_2}. \tag{6.47}$$

What is the economic intuition behind this equation? Let us call Good 1 and Good 2 hamburger and meat pie, respectively. Suppose that the price per hamburger and the price per meat pie are the same at \$2, so the price ratio is 1. Look at Point B on the diagram in Figure 6.14. At this point, MRS_{12} is greater than 1 (the slope of indifference curve is steeper), say 2. It means that for the consumer, one hamburger is valued equivalent to two meat pies. Put it another way, the consumer's utility will be unchanged if he/she gives up two meat pies and obtains one hamburger. There is an opportunity for this consumer to get higher utility: this consumer can sell two meat pies and obtain \$4; use \$2 out of \$4 to buy one hamburger, which will maintain the original level of utility; and he/she still has \$2 in his/her pocket (this \$2 can be used to buy either a hamburger or a meat pie, which makes this consumer's utility higher than the original level).

As shown above, if the marginal rate of substitution is different from the price ratio (e.g. at Point B), the consumer can always find another bundle of goods that gives him/her the higher level of utility. If the consumer is maximising his/her utility, it has to be the case that Equation (6.46) holds.

Before you are persuaded by the argument, don't forget the following. The above argument is valid only if the indifference curves are strictly convex to the origin. It means that the indifference curve (1) is always downward sloping; and (2) is strictly convex. In other words, we can use this method only if the law of diminishing marginal rate of substitution holds. Figure 6.15 illustrates the situation where the marginal rate of substitution is increasing (so the indifference curves are strictly concave towards the origin). In this is the case, finding the bundle that satisfies Equation (6.46) does not lead the consumer to maximise his/her utility. In Figure 6.15, Point A corresponds to that point, but it is obvious that Bundle B corresponds to higher utility. Since Bundle B is on the budget line, we showed that Point A is not optimal (in fact, it will minimise this consumer's utility). Checking the curvature of indifference curves is equivalent to checking whether the second-order condition is satisfied.

Let us try the next question to consolidate our understanding.

Question Consider an agent who consumes Good 1 and Good 2. We denote the amount of those goods by x_1 and x_2, respectively. The utility function of this agent is given by $u = U(x_1, x_2) = x_1^{\frac{1}{2}} x_2^{\frac{1}{2}}$. This agent has an income of 12 and does not save. If the prices of the two goods are $p_1 = 2$ and $p_2 = 1$, respectively, what is the bundle of goods this agent chooses to consume?

Solution The first step is to check if the indifference curves are strictly convex towards the origin.

$$u = x_1^{\frac{1}{2}} x_2^{\frac{1}{2}}.$$

Solving for x_2 we have:

$$x_2 = \frac{u^2}{x_1}.$$

It shows the indifference curve for a certain utility level, u. So let us denote it by the following:

$$I(x_1) = \frac{u^2}{x_1}.$$

Note that $u > 0$ for all $x_1 > 0$ and $x_2 > 0$. For any utility level $u > 0$, the indifference curve is convex towards the origin because it is decreasing in x_1 and strictly convex in x_1. That is, $\forall x_1 > 0$:

$$I'(x_1) = -\frac{u^2}{x_1^2} < 0,$$

$$I''(x_1) = \frac{2u^2}{x_1^3} > 0.$$

Since indifference curves are convex towards the origin, we can use the method we have just learnt. Let's write down the marginal utility of two goods first:

$$\frac{\partial U}{\partial x_1} = \frac{\sqrt{x_2}}{2\sqrt{x_1}},$$

$$\frac{\partial U}{\partial x_2} = \frac{\sqrt{x_1}}{2\sqrt{x_2}}.$$

Then we can obtain the marginal rate of substitution:

$$MRS_{12} = \frac{\partial U/\partial x_1}{\partial U/\partial x_2} = \frac{\sqrt{x_2}/2\sqrt{x_1}}{\sqrt{x_1}/2\sqrt{x_2}} = \frac{x_2}{x_1}.$$

The utility maximising consumer will choose the bundle where the marginal rate of substitution and the price ratio are equal:

$$MRS_{12} = \frac{p_1}{p_2} \Leftrightarrow \frac{x_2}{x_1} = \frac{p_1}{p_2} = 2,$$

which collapses to

$$x_2 = 2x_1.$$

The budget constraint this consumer faces is: $2x_1 + x_2 = 12$. Solving the following system of equations gives us the solution:

$$\begin{cases} x_2 = 2x_1 \\ 2x_1 + x_2 = 12 \end{cases} \Rightarrow \begin{cases} x_1^* = 3 \\ x_2^* = 6. \end{cases}$$

Exercise 6.7 Solving the utility maximisation problem using $MRS_{12} = \frac{p_1}{p_2}$.

It turns out that we can solve the above problem by using different methods. In the following section, we will study the substitution method, which reduces the two-variable problem into a one-variable problem. Hence, it has a flavour of the optimisation problem we discussed in Chapter 4.

6.8 The substitution method

Let us try solving the same problem as in the previous exercise, but by using a different method. Consider a price taking consumer who spends his/her income only on Good 1 and Good 2. We denote these goods by x_1 and x_2, respectively. The utility function of this person is given by $u = U(x_1, x_2) = x_1^{\frac{1}{2}} x_2^{\frac{1}{2}}$. The person has an income of 12 and does not save. If the prices of Good 1 and Good 2 are $p_1 = 2$ and $p_2 = 1$, respectively, what is the bundle of the goods he/she chooses to consume?

The first step in this method is to write down the budget constraint:

$$2x_1 + x_2 = 12. \tag{6.48}$$

Secondly, we solve this equation for one of the variables; here let's take x_2:

$$x_2 = 12 - 2x_1. \tag{6.49}$$

Thirdly, substitute x_2 into the utility function $U(x_1, x_2) = x_1^{\frac{1}{2}} x_2^{\frac{1}{2}}$:

$$U(x_1) = x_1^{\frac{1}{2}} (12 - 2x_1)^{\frac{1}{2}}. \tag{6.50}$$

Now the maximisation problem involves only one variable x_1, so we can use the same technique we used for the profit maximisation problem in Chapter 4:

$$\underset{x_1}{Max} \left[x_1^{\frac{1}{2}} (12 - 2x_1)^{\frac{1}{2}} \right]. \tag{6.51}$$

The first-order condition is:

$$\frac{\sqrt{12 - 2x_1}}{2\sqrt{x_1}} - \frac{\sqrt{x_1}}{\sqrt{12 - 2x_1}} = 0. \tag{6.52}$$

Solving this equation we get $x_1 = 3$, and substituting $x_1 = 3$ into the budget constraint yields $x_2 = 6$.

Hence the first-order condition suggests the following solution:

$$\begin{cases} x_1^* = 3 \\ x_2^* = 6. \end{cases} \tag{6.53}$$

But what we have found may be a local minimum. We need to check the second-order condition as we did in the profit maximisation problem. As we know, the second-order condition for a local maximum is:

$$U''(x_1^*) < 0. \tag{6.54}$$

The second-order partial derivative of (6.50) is, after tedious calculation,

$$U''(x_1) = -\frac{36}{(12x_1 - 2x_1^2)^{\frac{3}{2}}}. \tag{6.55}$$

Hence, when $x_1 = x_1^* = 3$:

$$U''(3) = -\frac{\sqrt{2}}{3} < 0. \tag{6.56}$$

The second-order condition for a local maximum is satisfied. In fact, $U''(x_1) < 0$ for all $x_1 \in (0, 6)$ (note x_1 cannot be greater than 6 because of the budget), so $x_1^* = 3$ is a local maximum as well as a global maximum. So we conclude that the bundle $(x_1^*, x_2^*) = (3, 6)$ is the utility maximiser.

This method is called the **substitution method** because we substitute the budget constraint into the utility function (the function we want to maximise) in the beginning. The substitution method may be appealing to you since it reduces a bi-variate problem into a seemingly simple single-variate problem. However, the downside is computation: it is usually tedious.

Question Choose (x_1, x_2) to maximise $y = x_1 x_2$ subject to the constraint $4x_1 + x_2 = 4$. Use the substitution method.

Solution First we solve the constraint for x_2:

$$x_2 = 4 - 4x_1.$$

Substituting it into the objective function, we get:

$$y = f(x_1) = x_1(4 - 4x_1).$$

The first-order condition for a local maximum is:

$$f'(x_1) = 4 - 8x_1 = 0.$$

Here $x_1 = \frac{1}{2}$ satisfies the condition. The second-order condition for a local maximum is:

$$f''(x_1) < 0.$$

This inequality is satisfied for $x_1 = \dfrac{1}{2}$ as well as for all x_1 (because $f''(x_1) = -8$ whatever x_1 is), hence it is a local and global maximum. Therefore, $x_1^* = \dfrac{1}{2}$. Substituting this back to the constraint gives $x_2^* = 2$.

Exercise 6.8 Solving the utility maximisation problem by using the substitution method.

6.9 The Lagrange multiplier method

Now we will look at the **Lagrange multiplier method**, which is used in a wide range of economic applications. Unfortunately, though, it is simply beyond the scope of this book to discuss *why* this method works, and so I shall resort to a cook-book approach. For the target audience of this book, just becoming familiar with the method and becoming able to solve constrained optimisation problems by using this method will be sufficient, at least for the moment.[3]

We go through solving the same problem as in the previous two sections. Consider a price taking individual who consumes Good 1 and Good 2. We denote the amount of those goods by x_1 and x_2, respectively. The utility function of this agent is given by $U(x_1, x_2) = x_1^{\frac{1}{2}} x_2^{\frac{1}{2}}$. This individual has \$12 and does not save. If the prices of Good 1 and Good 2 are $p_1 = 2$ and $p_2 = 1$, respectively, what is the bundle of the goods he/she chooses?

We know the budget constraint can be written as $2x_1 + x_2 = 12$ but, in employing the Lagrange multiplier method, we want to express the constraint in the way that the whole expression equals zero. That is:

$$g(x_1, x_2) = 2x_1 + x_2 - 12 = 0. \tag{6.57}$$

Note that, for a reason that will become clear later, we have denoted $2x_1 + x_2 - 12$ (which has to be zero all the time) by $g(x_1, x_2)$, a function of two variables.

Now let us introduce a new function, which is called the **Lagrangian**:

$$L = U(x_1, x_2) - \lambda g(x_1, x_2). \tag{6.58}$$

The Lagrangian consists of two parts. The first part is the utility function we want to maximise: we have learnt that this is called the objective function. From the objective function, we subtract the second part, which is the product of λ (a Greek letter, lambda) and the budget constraint. This new variable λ is called the **Lagrange multiplier**. Substituting the utility function and the budget constraint into Equation (6.58) yields the following:

$$L = x_1^{\frac{1}{2}} x_2^{\frac{1}{2}} - \lambda(2x_1 + x_2 - 12). \tag{6.59}$$

---

3 If you would like to further your study in economics, though, I strongly recommend that you consult a more advanced book in quantitative methods and learn why this method works. For example, see K. Sydsaeter and P. Hammond, *Essential Mathematics for Economic Analysis*, 3rd edn (Prentice Hall, 2008).

Now our problem is to maximise this Lagrangian by controlling the three variables, x_1, x_2 and λ.[4] It is an unconstrained optimisation problem and the first-order conditions consist of the following three equations:

$$\frac{\partial L}{\partial x_1} = 0, \tag{6.60}$$

$$\frac{\partial L}{\partial x_2} = 0, \tag{6.61}$$

$$\frac{\partial L}{\partial \lambda} = 0. \tag{6.62}$$

They can be written respectively as:

$$\frac{1}{2}\left(\frac{x_2}{x_1}\right)^{\frac{1}{2}} - 2\lambda = 0, \tag{6.63}$$

$$\frac{1}{2}\left(\frac{x_1}{x_2}\right)^{\frac{1}{2}} - \lambda = 0, \tag{6.64}$$

$$2x_1 + x_2 - 12 = 0. \tag{6.65}$$

Note that Equation (6.65) is the same as the budget constraint (6.57). From Equations (6.63) and (6.64) we can eliminate λ and obtain the following:

$$x_2 = 2x_1. \tag{6.66}$$

Substituting it into Equation (6.65), we can obtain that $x_1^* = 3$ and $x_2^* = 6$. Substituting them into Equation (6.63) gives $\lambda^* = \dfrac{\sqrt{2}}{4}$.[5]

As in the previous two methods, we need to discuss the second-order condition. Unfortunately, there is no good diagrammatical explanation to convey the intuition for this condition. Here, we will just state the condition for a maximum:

$$2 \cdot \frac{\partial^2 L}{\partial x_2 \partial x_1} \cdot \frac{\partial g(x_1, x_2)}{\partial x_1} \cdot \frac{\partial g(x_1, x_2)}{\partial x_2} > \frac{\partial^2 L}{\partial x_1^2} \cdot \left[\frac{\partial g(x_1, x_2)}{\partial x_2}\right]^2 + \frac{\partial^2 L}{\partial x_2^2} \cdot \left[\frac{\partial g(x_1, x_2)}{\partial x_1}\right]^2 \tag{6.67}$$

or, more concisely,

$$2 \cdot L_{12} \cdot g_1 \cdot g_2 > L_{11} \cdot g_2^2 + L_{22} \cdot g_1^2. \tag{6.68}$$

For a minimum, we just need to reverse the direction of the above inequality.

. . . .

4 Careful readers may have realised that I converted the original constrained optimisation problem to a new unconstrained optimisation problem that involves the Lagrangian multiplier. As mentioned earlier, it is beyond the scope of this book to discuss why the solutions to the two problems coincide.

5 The λ^* we obtained here is called the **marginal utility of income**. It says that an infinitesimal increase in the consumer's income will increase the (maximised) utility by $\frac{\sqrt{2}}{4}$ utils. Unfortunately, it is again outside the scope of this book to demonstrate why λ^* represents the marginal utility of income (interested readers should consult with the reference in footnote 3 of this chapter), but it is a useful result to know in any case.

Question Verify that the second-order condition is met for the above problem.

Solution Let us write down the information that is necessary to calculate the LHS and the RHS of Equation (6.67):

$$\frac{\partial^2 L}{\partial x_2 \partial x_1} = \frac{1}{4}\left(\frac{1}{x_1 x_2}\right)^{\frac{1}{2}},$$

$$\frac{\partial g(x_1, x_2)}{\partial x_1} = 2,$$

$$\frac{\partial g(x_1, x_2)}{\partial x_2} = 1,$$

$$\frac{\partial^2 L}{\partial x_1^2} = -\frac{1}{4x_1}\left(\frac{x_2}{x_1}\right)^{\frac{1}{2}},$$

$$\frac{\partial^2 L}{\partial x_2^2} = -\frac{1}{4x_2}\left(\frac{x_1}{x_2}\right)^{\frac{1}{2}}.$$

If we show that the difference between the LHS and the RHS of (6.67) is positive, then we have done the job:

$$\text{LHS} - \text{RHS} = \left(\frac{1}{x_1 x_2}\right)^{\frac{1}{2}} - \left[-\frac{1}{4x_1}\left(\frac{x_2}{x_1}\right)^{\frac{1}{2}} - \frac{1}{x_2}\left(\frac{x_1}{x_2}\right)^{\frac{1}{2}}\right]$$

$$= \left(\frac{1}{x_1 x_2}\right)^{\frac{1}{2}} + \frac{1}{4x_1}\left(\frac{x_2}{x_1}\right)^{\frac{1}{2}} + \frac{1}{x_2}\left(\frac{x_1}{x_2}\right)^{\frac{1}{2}}.$$

This expression is positive for all $x_1 > 0$ and $x_2 > 0$.

Exercise 6.9 The second-order condition for the Lagrange multiplier method.

Question Choose (x_1, x_2) to maximise $y = x_1 x_2$ subject to the constraint $4x_1 + x_2 = 4$. Use the Lagrange multiplier method.

Solution First, we set up the Lagrangian, where the constraint is $g(x_1, x_2) = 4x_1 + x_2 - 4 = 0$:

$$L = x_1 x_2 - \lambda(4x_1 + x_2 - 4).$$

The first-order conditions are:

$$x_2 - 4\lambda = 0,$$

$$x_1 - \lambda = 0,$$

$$4x_1 + x_2 - 4 = 0.$$

We can eliminate λ by using the first two equations:

$$x_2 = 4x_1.$$

Substituting x_2 into the third equation yields:

$$8x_1 = 4.$$

Hence, $(x_1^*, x_2^*, \lambda^*) = \left(\dfrac{1}{2}, 2, \dfrac{1}{2}\right)$ satisfies these condition.

To check the second-order condition, we list the necessary pieces of information:

$$\frac{\partial^2 L}{\partial x_2 \partial x_1} = 1,$$

$$\frac{\partial g(x_1, x_2)}{\partial x_1} = 4,$$

$$\frac{\partial g(x_1, x_2)}{\partial x_2} = 1,$$

$$\frac{\partial^2 L}{\partial x_1^2} = 0,$$

$$\frac{\partial^2 L}{\partial x_2^2} = 0.$$

Hence the RHS of Equation (6.67) is zero. The LHS is always 8, so (6.67) always holds, and $(x_1^*, x_2^*) = \left(\dfrac{1}{2}, 2\right)$ is therefore a global maximum.

Exercise 6.10 The substitution method and the Lagrange multiplier method.

6.10   The individual demand function

To conclude this chapter, I'd like to talk a bit about the individual demand function. Recall the consumer's utility maximisation problem we discussed in the previous three sections. A price taking individual whose preferences are represented by the utility function $U(x) = x_1^{\frac{1}{2}} x_2^{\frac{1}{2}}$ allocates \$12 to buying only two goods, Good 1 and Good 2. We figured out that when $p_1 = 2$ and $p_2 = 1$, the bundle of the goods he/she chooses is $(x_1^*, x_2^*) = (3, 6)$.

Let us put this question slightly differently. Fix Good 2's price $p_2 = 1$ and the consumer's income $M = 12$. We already know that, when $p_1 = 2$, the consumer's demand for Good 1 is $x_1 = 3$, but how does it change when p_1 takes other values? To answer this question, I will consider the following maximisation problem:

$$\underset{x_1, x_2}{Max}\ U(x_1, x_2)$$

$$\text{s.t. } p_1 x_1 + x_2 = 12, \tag{6.69}$$

where $U(x) = x_1^{\frac{1}{2}} x_2^{\frac{1}{2}}$.

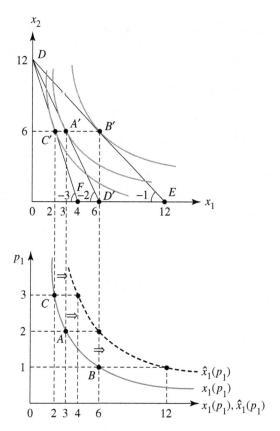

Figure 6.16 The individual demand schedule.

I will leave this problem as an exercise for you, but the utility maximising x_1 will be $x_1^* = \dfrac{6}{p_1}$. Note that it is consistent with our previous analysis. That is, when $p_1 = 2$ we can get $x_1^* = 3$. For other prices, we get different values of x_1^*. For example, when $p_1 = 1$, $x_1^* = 4$; and when $p_1 = 3$, $x_1^* = 2$. Since x_1^* varies as p_1 changes, let us express it as a function of p_1:

$$x_1^* = x_1(p_1) = \frac{6}{p_1}. \tag{6.70}$$

This function is called the **individual demand function** for Good 1. It shows a consumer's demand for Good 1 in terms of its price, *given prices of other goods (in this case, the price of Good 2) and his/her income.*

The graph of the individual demand function for Good 1 is illustrated in the bottom diagram in Figure 6.16. By applying the curve sketching technique you learnt in Chapter 5, you ought be able to sketch the graph of this function, taking $x_1(p_1)$ on the horizontal axis and p_1 on the vertical axis. Three combinations of the price and the quantity demanded are shown in the figure: Points A, B and C. These points correspond to Points A', B' and C', respectively, on the top diagram in the same figure.

In the top diagram, x_1 and x_2 are taken on the axes, the x_1-axis is common to both diagrams in that figure. The line that goes through D and D' shows the budget line when

$p = 2$. Because the price of Good 2 is equal to unity, (the absolute value of) the slope of the budget line represents the price of Good 1, p_1. The consumer chooses Point A' to maximise his/her utility and the quantity of x_1 demanded is hence $x^* = 3$. When the price of Good 1 goes down to $p_1 = 1$, then the budget line pivots around Point D to the right to DE. Now the slope of the budget line is equal to unity, and the utility maximising bundle is Point B' where $x^* = 4$. In contrast, the budget line pivots around Point D to the left to DF when the price of Good 1 goes up to $p_1 = 3$. The corresponding quantity of Good 1 demanded at this price is $x^* = 2$ (Point C').

Likewise, if you pivot the budget line around Point D (meaning you are changing p_1, but holding both p_2 and M constant), you can figure out the quantity of Good 1 this consumer will demand *for each and every* $p_1 > 0$ (other than those we already looked at), given $p_2 = 1$ and $M = 12$. The graph of $x_1(p_1)$ is the collection of the $(p_1, x(p_1))$ obtained through this procedure.

Now consider another exercise: how will the individual demand function for Good 1 change if the consumer's income is $M = 24$? The utility maximisation problem for this consumer when $M = 24$ is expressed as:

$$\underset{x_1, x_2}{Max}\ U(x_1, x_2) \tag{6.71}$$
$$\text{s.t. } p_1 x_1 + x_2 = 24,$$

where $U(x) = x_1^{\frac{1}{2}} x_2^{\frac{1}{2}}$.

Again I will leave this problem for you to solve, but you should find the solution to be:

$$\hat{x}_1(p_1) = \frac{12}{p_1}. \tag{6.72}$$

In the bottom diagram of Figure 6.16, $\hat{x}_1(p_1)$ is illustrated as a dashed schedule. You can see that the individual demand schedule for Good 1 has *shifted to the right* when the consumer's income has *risen*. In other words, the quantity of Good 1 demanded by this consumer is greater for each and every price of Good 1 when he/she has more income. Check that this exercise conforms to the comparative static analysis we studied in Section 2.10.

Now we are almost done with uncovering what is behind the demand and supply analysis. In this chapter, we have derived the individual demand function by solving a consumer's utility maximisation problem. Recall also that in Chapter 4 we derived the individual firm's supply function by solving its profit maximisation problem. The (market) demand function we used in Section 2.10 as well as in Chapter 1 can be obtained by aggregating all the consumers' individual demand functions. Likewise, the (market) supply function is the sum of all the firms' supply functions. One of the topics we will cover in the next chapter is the aggregation of these individual schedules.

In any case, hopefully by now you realise that the demand and supply schedules we looked at in Section 2.10 as well as in Chapter 1 did not come from nowhere. On the contrary, the utility maximisation by each of the consumers in the market and the profit maximisation by each of the producers in the market give rise to these schedules, respectively.

6.11 | Additional exercises

1. **(Marginal utility with one good)** Pat consumes only one good; this is called rice. The level of utility Pat obtains by rice consumption is shown by the following utility function: $u = U(x) = \frac{1}{4}x^2$, where u is the level of utility and x is the amount of rice (kg).

   (a) Carefully sketch Pat's utility function. Restrict the domain to $x \geq 0$.

   (b) What is the marginal utility of rice when Pat consumes 10 kg of rice?

   (c) What is the marginal utility of rice when Pat consumes 40 kg of rice?

   (d) Does the law of the diminishing marginal utility hold if $x > 0$? What does it imply in terms of the curvature of the utility function?

2. **(Marginal utility with two goods)** Imagine a person whose eating behaviour is rather extreme, that is, he eats only two things, rice and miso-soup. Denote the consumption of these two goods by x_R and x_M, respectively. The person's utility level is given by the following: $u = U(x_R, x_M) = x_R^2 x_M$. Answer the following questions.

   (a) Suppose the utility level this consumer obtains is 16. Under this situation, express x_M in terms of x_R.

   (b) Sketch on the (x_R, x_M) coordinate plane the curve you obtained in part (a), using the curve sketching technique. Briefly explain what it shows.

   (c) Obtain the marginal utility of each of the two goods. What is the marginal utility of rice when this person chooses $(x_R, x_M) = (2, 1)$?

   (d) How does your answer to part (c) change if the person chooses $(x_R, x_M) = (4, 1)$? Explain carefully the comparison of the two situations.

3. **(The marginal rate of substitution)** Consider the situation described in Question 2. Obtain the marginal rate of substitution of rice for miso-soup (MRS_{RM}) for the person, and evaluate it at $(x_R, x_M) = (4, 1)$. It turns out that, in the market to which the person has access, rice and miso-soup are traded one-to-one. That is, one unit of rice can buy one unit of miso-soup. Assuming that the consumer has no left-over income when that bundle is chosen, comment on the veracity of the following statement: 'The bundle cannot be utility maximising for this consumer'.

4. **(Total differentiation)** For each equation, use the total differential to approximate the change in y when there are changes in x and z as specified.

   (1) $y = x^3 + 3x - \frac{1}{2}z^2 - 2xz$, where $x = 1$, $z = 2$, $\Delta x = -2$, $\Delta z = -1$.

   (2) $y = \ln x^2 - 4x^3 + xz$, where $x = 1$, $z = 2$, $\Delta x = 1$, $\Delta z = -1$.

   (3) $y = xz + e^{\frac{2}{3}}$, where $x = 0$, $z = 3$, $\Delta x = 1$, $\Delta z = -1$.

5. **(Maxima and minima)** For each of the following functions, find a set of (u, v) that satisfies the first-order conditions for a local maximum/minimum. Check whether each of the (u, v) you have found corresponds to a local maximum, a local minimum,

or a saddle point. One of the second-order conditions for a local maximum/minimum is $g_{11} \cdot g_{22} > (g_{12})^2$.

(1) $g(u, v) = 160u + 60v - 3u^2 - 2v^2 - 4uv$.

(2) $g(u, v) = uv - u^2 - v^2$.

(3) $g(u, v) = \dfrac{1}{3}u^3 + \dfrac{1}{3}v^3 - uv$.

(4) $g(u, v) = e^{u+v} + e^{u-v} - 2u$.

6. (The substitution method) Answer the following problems.

(1) Maximise $y = 6x_1 + 3x_1x_2$ subject to $x_1 + x_2 = 10$, using the substitution method.

(2) Maximise $y = -x_1\sqrt{x_2}$ subject to $2x_1 + x_2 = 12$, using the substitution method.

(3) Maximise $y = 2x_1 + x_2^2$ subject to $x_1^2 + x_2^2 = 4$, using the substitution method.

7. (Consumer's utility maximisation problem) Harry consumes only two goods, apples and bananas. Denote his consumption of these two goods by A and B, respectively. A utility maximiser, Harry's utility level is given by the following utility function: $u = U(A, B) = A^{\frac{1}{3}}B^{\frac{2}{3}}$. In the market, apples and bananas are both sold at $1 per unit, so $p_A = 1$ and $p_B = 1$. Harry's income is $300 and he does not save. Solve Harry's utility maximisation problem using the substitution method. Make sure that you check the second-order condition for a maximum.

8. (Consumer's utility maximisation problem) Solve the utility maximisation problems described by Equation (6.69) and (6.71) using the Lagrange multiplier method.

7 Integral calculus

Our main aim in this chapter is to study the welfare effects of taxation. The government levies tax on various goods, and we would like to evaluate how our well-being might be affected by the taxation. To this end, we ought to discuss a notions called consumer surplus and producer surplus. They measure consumers' and producers' well-being in terms of dollars.

As will become clear in the following sections, measuring consumer surplus or producer surplus involves calculating the area in between the demand and supply schedules. As long as both curves are linear, there is no problem because we all know how to calculate the area of a triangle. However, if one (or both) of the demand and supply schedules is (are) non-linear, we need to introduce a certain mathematical technique that allows us to calculate the area in question. This technique is called **integral calculus**. We begin by studying this technique in the following two sections, which will be followed by its application to finance where I introduce more elaborate techniques called integration by substitution and integration by parts.

We then discuss the demand and supply analysis from a different point of view. More specifically, we will give a different interpretation to the demand and supply schedules we discussed in Chapter 1. It will be the basis of explaining the notion of surplus. We will also study how to aggregate an individual demand (supply) schedules to obtain the market demand (supply, respectively) schedule. I then demonstrate how we can incorporate taxation into the demand and supply analysis. It will be shown that taxation lowers the total surplus in the market. This loss shows the inefficiency in the market and is called the deadweight loss of taxation.

Chapter goals By studying this chapter you will

(1) be able to calculate an anti-derivative of a function (where possible);
(2) be able to calculate the area of an area under a curve (where possible);
(3) be able to explain consumer surplus and producer surplus;
(4) be able to carry out demand and supply analysis in the presence of taxation; and
(5) be able to integrate demand and supply functions to calculate the deadweight loss of taxation.

7.1 An anti-derivative and the indefinite integral

Consider a function $f(x) = 4x$ and a function $F(x) = 2x^2 + 6$. If we differentiate $F(x) = 2x^2 + 6$ with respect to x, we get $4x$, that is $\dfrac{dF(x)}{dx} = f(x)$ or $F'(x) = f(x)$.

7.1 An anti-derivative and the indefinite integral

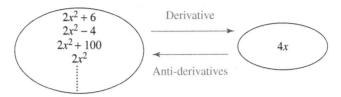

Figure 7.1 The derivative and anti-derivatives.

When such a relationship holds between two functions, $F(x)$ is called an **anti-derivative** of $f(x)$.

You may notice that there are many anti-derivatives of $f(x) = 4x$. For example, aside from $F(x) = 2x^2 + 6$, $2x^2 - 4$, $2x^2 + 100$, $2x^2$, (and so on) are all anti-derivatives of $f(x) = 4x$ (see Figure 7.1).

As we can see, the anti-derivatives of a function differ only by a constant. It is because the derivative of any constant is zero. If we denote a constant by C, then all anti-derivatives of $4x$ can be written as $2x^2 + C$ (C can be 6, -4, 100, 0, or whatever constant).

Therefore, $2x^2 + C$ is the general representation of anti-derivatives of $4x$. In mathematics, we denote the relationship as follows:

$$\int 4x\,dx = 2x^2 + C. \tag{7.1}$$

The LHS is 'the **indefinite integral** of $4x$ with respect to x'. The symbol $\int$ is called the **integral sign**, and $4x$ and C are called the **integrand** and the **constant of integration**, respectively. Do not forget to place dx after the integrand, which shows the variable of the focus: in this case, x is the **variable of integration**.

More generally, if any anti-derivative of a function $f(x)$ is $F(x)$, then:

$$\int f(x)\,dx = F(x) + C, \tag{7.2}$$

where C is a constant. When we know $f(x)$, to integrate simply means the process of finding $\int f(x)\,dx$.

7.1.1 Integration rules (the indefinite integral)

Let me list some rules of the indefinite integral in the following. We use the following notation: k and n are constants, and $f(x)$, $g(x)$ are anti-differentiable functions of x. You are expected to be able to apply these rules to solve problems. Some examples are provided after the list of the rules.

Rule 1

$$\int kx^n dx = k \int x^n dx = \frac{kx^{n+1}}{n+1} + C. \qquad (7.3)$$

Rule 2

$$\int \frac{1}{x} dx = \ln |x| + C. \qquad (7.4)$$

Rule 3

$$\int e^x dx = e^x + C. \qquad (7.5)$$

Rule 4

$$\int [f(x) \pm g(x)] dx = \int f(x) dx \pm \int g(x) dx. \qquad (7.6)$$

Question Obtain the following indefinite integrals.

(1) $\int x \, dx.$

(2) $\int 4 \, dx.$

(3) $\int [4x - 3x^2] dx.$

Solution

(1)

$$\int x \, dx = \frac{1}{2} x^2 + C.$$

(2)

$$\int 4 \, dx = 4x + C.$$

(3)

$$\int [4x - 3x^2] dx = \int 4x \, dx - \int 3x^2 \, dx$$

$$= 4 \int x \, dx - 3 \int x^2 \, dx$$

$$= 4 \left(\frac{1}{2} x^2 + C_1 \right) - 3 \left(\frac{1}{3} x^3 + C_2 \right)$$

$$= 2x^2 - x^3 + 4C_1 - 3C_2$$

$$= -x^3 + 2x^2 + C,$$

where $C = 4C_1 - 3C_2$.

Exercise 7.1 Indefinite integral.

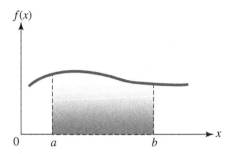

Figure 7.2 The definite integral.

The fundamental theorem of integral calculus

Consider a function $f(x)$. Suppose $f(x)$ is continuous and $f(x) \geq 0$ on the interval from $x = a$ to $x = b$, where $a < b$ as in Figure 7.2.

We denote the area of the region below the function and above the x-axis from $x = a$ to $x = b$ by the following formula:

$$\int_a^b f(x)dx. \tag{7.7}$$

The above is called the **definite integral** (as opposed to the indefinite integral) of $f(x)$ on the **interval** from $x = a$ to $x = b$. The numbers a and b are called **limits of integration**, where in this case a is the **lower limit** and b is the **upper limit**. As in the indefinite integral, $f(x)$ is called the **integrand** and x is the **variable of integration** (note that dx is placed after $f(x)$).

If $f(x)$ is continuous on the interval from $x = a$ to $x = b$ and $F(x)$ is any anti-derivative of $f(x)$ on that interval, it is known that the following relationship holds:

$$\int_a^b f(x)dx = F(b) - F(a). \tag{7.8}$$

This relationship in (7.8) is known as the **fundamental theorem of integral calculus**.[1] To find $\int_a^b f(x)dx$, we need (1) to find an anti-derivative of $f(x)$, which is $F(x)$; (2) to find $F(b)$ and $F(a)$; and (3) to subtract the latter from the former. If $f(x)$ is non-negative ($f(x) \geq 0$) on the interval from $x = a$ to $x = b$, by following these three steps, we can obtain the area of the region below the function and above the x-axis from $x = a$ to $x = b$.

Usually, $F(b) - F(a)$ is expressed by the notation $[F(x)]_a^b$. That is:

$$F(b) - F(a) = [F(x)]_a^b. \tag{7.9}$$

Now I list some rules of the definite integral and then give some numerical examples. Notation is the same as in the previous rules.

---

[1] We do not delve into the discussion of this theorem in this book. Interested readers should consult some introductory textbooks in quantitative methods, e.g. Haeussler, Jr. *et al.*, *Introductory Mathematical Analysis*.

Rule 5

$$\int_a^b kf(x)dx = k \int_a^b f(x)dx. \qquad (7.10)$$

Rule 6

$$\int_a^b [f(x) \pm g(x)]dx = \int_a^b f(x)dx \pm \int_a^b g(x)dx. \qquad (7.11)$$

Rule 7

$$\int_a^b f(x)dx = \int_a^c f(x)dx + \int_c^b f(x)dx. \qquad (7.12)$$

Question A　Obtain the area of the region bounded by the curve $f(x) = \sqrt{x}$, the x-axis, and the line $x = 1$.

Solution　It is always useful to draw a diagram so that we can visualise what we are doing.

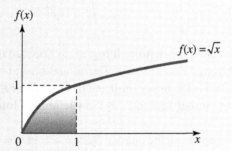

We want to calculate the area of the shaded region. We need to calculate the definite integral of $f(x) = \sqrt{x}$ on the interval from 0 to 1:

$$S = \int_0^1 \sqrt{x}dx.$$

An anti-derivative of $f(x) = \sqrt{x}$ is $F(x) = \frac{2}{3}x^{\frac{3}{2}}$. Therefore, from the fundamental theorem of integral calculus, we have:

$$S = \int_0^1 \sqrt{x}dx$$

$$= \left[\frac{2}{3}x^{\frac{3}{2}} \right]_0^1$$

$$= \frac{2}{3} - 0$$

$$= \frac{2}{3}.$$

Question B　Obtain the area of the region bounded by the curve $f(x) = \sqrt{x}$, the y-axis, and the line $y = 1$.

Solution 1   Do not be tricked by the question. It appears similar to the previous question but the area we want is different from the previous one. What we want to obtain now is the area of the following shaded region.

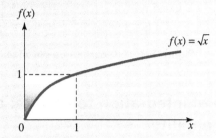

We already know that the area of the region bounded by the curve $f(x) = \sqrt{x}$, the x-axis, and the line $x = 1$ is $\dfrac{2}{3}$ (Question A). We also know that the area of the square with a side equal to 1 is unity. So, obviously, the area of the shaded region is $1 - \dfrac{2}{3} = \dfrac{1}{3}$. Although the area can be obtained this way, for the future purpose, it is important to study an alternative solution.

Solution 2 (important alternative solution)   Let us denote $f(x)$ by y. Then, we can rearrange the function as follows (by taking the square): $y^2 = x$. And then, *flip* the diagram so that it looks like the following:

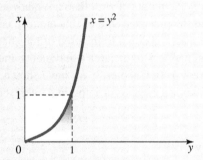

What we need to do is to obtain the definite integral of $x = y^2$ on the interval from $y = 0$ to $y = 1$, but note that the variable of integration is y, not x.

$$
\begin{aligned}
S &= \int_0^1 y^2 dy \\
&= \left[\frac{1}{3} y^3 \right]_0^1 \\
&= \frac{1}{3} - 0 \\
&= \frac{1}{3}.
\end{aligned}
$$

Of course, we have got the same result.

Exercise 7.2   Calculating the area of the region under a curve

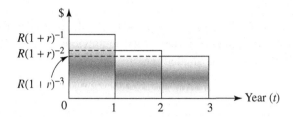

Figure 7.3 The present value of an ordinary annuity.

7.3 Application of integration to finance: the present value of a continuous annuity

Recall the mathematics of finance that we studied in Chapter 3. One of the notions we studied is an ordinary annuity. An ordinary annuity is regular payments (or repayments) made at the end of each period. The present value of an annuity is the sum of the present values of all the payments (or repayments). We know how to obtain it if the periodic rate r and the amount of each payment R are given.

Now, we introduce a special case of this annuity, which is called a **continuous annuity**. Payments are now made *continuously* over the time from $t = 0$ to $t = T$. How can we calculate the present value of this annuity when interest is compounded continuously at a nominal rate r (we did not do this in Chapter 3)?

To see this problem, let us consider a discrete case first, and consider there are three periods. When the three payments of R dollars are made at the end of each year, and the periodic rate is r, then the present value of this annuity is: $A = R(1 + r)^{-1} + R(1 + r)^{-2} + R(1 + r)^{-3}$. Note that A is equal to the area of the shaded region in Figure 7.3.

Now think what happens to the area if payments and compounding occur continuously until the end of Year 3. In Chapter 3, we have shown that the compound amount R of a principal of P dollars after t years at a nominal interest rate r compounded continuously is:

$$R = Pe^{rt}. \tag{7.13}$$

Solving for P we get:

$$P = Re^{-rt}. \tag{7.14}$$

Therefore, under continuous compounding at a nominal interest rate r, the present value P (for the payment R made in t) is given by $P = Re^{-rt}$. Let us draw this present value function in Figure 7.4.

Now I think you can guess the region that represents the present value of a continuous annuity. Yes: it is the region under the present value function and above the t-axis on the interval from 0 to 3, which is shown in Figure 7.5.

We know how to obtain the area of the shaded region. It is equivalent to the definite integral of $P = Re^{-rt}$ on the interval from 0 to 3. That is:

$$A = \int_0^3 Re^{-rt}dt. \tag{7.15}$$

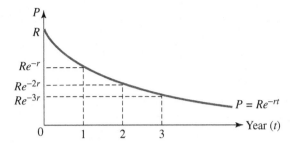

Figure 7.4 The present value of continuous payments.

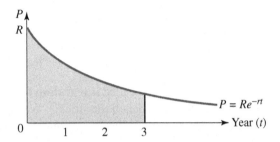

Figure 7.5 The present value of a continuous annuity.

In order to obtain A, we need to know how to obtain the definite integral of e^{-rt} with respect to t. This is not straightforward, but there is a simple trick: let $-rt$ be some other variable, say s, that is, we set $-rt = s$. Why? Because we know how to obtain the definite integral of e^s with respect to s (because we know an anti-derivative of e^s is e^s). So let us substitute $-rt = s$ into (7.15) (R is a constant so it can be put outside the integral; see Equation (7.10)):

$$A = R \int_{t=0}^{t=3} e^s \, dt. \tag{7.16}$$

Now, look at the definite integral. The integrand is a function of s but the variable of integration is t. Also the upper and the lower limits of integration are both given in terms of t. So we need to convert both the variable of integration and limits of integration into s. How can we convert them? It can be simply done by going back to the trick, '$-rt = s$'. When $t = 0$, $s = 0$. When $t = 3$, $s = -3r$. Use these as the lower and the upper limits of integration, respectively:

$$A = R \int_{s=0}^{s=-3r} e^s \, dt. \tag{7.17}$$

Now both the integrand and the limits of integration are in terms of s, but we still have the variable of integration in terms of t, and this needs to be corrected. Again we go back to the trick equation, which can be rearranged as $t = -\frac{1}{r}s$. Totally differentiating this equation yields:

$$dt = -\frac{1}{r}ds. \tag{7.18}$$

Now, substitute Equation (7.18) into Equation (7.17) to get the following (r is a constant so it can be put outside the integral):

$$A = -\frac{R}{r}\int_0^{-3r} e^s\,ds. \tag{7.19}$$

Therefore (recalling that the anti-derivative of e^s is e^s):

$$A = -\frac{R}{r}\left[e^s\right]_0^{-3r}$$

$$= -\frac{R}{r}\left(e^{-3r} - 1\right).$$

The technique described above is called **integration by substitution**. We substituted s for $-rt$ in the beginning (which I called the 'trick'). We should not forget the following point: we also need to convert both the limits of integration and the variable of integration to the variable substituted.

Here's an example.

Question   Consider a continuous annuity of $1000 for 10 years. Find the present value of this continuous annuity at a nominal rate of 10 per cent.

Solution

$$A = \int_0^{10} 1000 e^{-0.1t}\,dt$$

$$= 1000 \int_{s=0}^{s=-1} e^s\,dt$$

$$= -10\,000 \left[e^s\right]_0^{-1}$$

$$= -10\,000 \left[e^{-1} - 1\right]$$

$$= 10\,000 \left(1 - \frac{1}{e}\right).$$

Exercise 7.3   Calculating the present value of a continuous annuity.

7.3.1   Integration by parts

In the above analysis, continuous payments are constant to be R. What if continuous payments are not constant, say they keep increasing over time? Instead of assuming the payment of R at time t, let us assume that the payment at time t is Rt. Then the present value of a continuous annuity over three years is:

$$A = \int_0^3 Rte^{-rt}dt. \tag{7.20}$$

This definite integral can be solved by applying the rule called **integration by parts**:

$$\int_a^b f'(t)g(t)dt = [f(t)g(t)]_a^b - \int_a^b f(t)g'(t)dt. \tag{7.21}$$

You need not remember this rule because it is derived readily by integrating the both sides of Equation (4.6) in Chapter 4, which is the product rule of differentiation:

$$\frac{d}{dx}[f(x)g(x)] = f'(x)g(x) + f(x)g'(x)$$

$$\int \frac{d}{dx}[f(x)g(x)]\,dx = \int f'(x)g(x)dx + \int f(x)g'(x)dx$$

$$f(x)g(x) = \int f'(x)g(x)dx + \int f(x)g'(x)dx$$

$$\int f'(x)g(x)dx = f(x)g(x) - \int f(x)g'(x)dx.$$

It can be applied to the definite integral as shown in Equation (7.21). Anyway, try going through a couple of questions.

Question A Obtain $\int_1^3 \ln t\,dt$.

Solution Set $f(t) = t$ and $g(t) = \ln t$. Then $f'(t) = 1$ and $g'(t) = \dfrac{1}{t}$.

$$\int_1^3 \ln t\,dt = \int_1^3 1 \cdot \ln t\,dt$$

$$= [t \ln t]_1^3 - \int_1^3 t\frac{1}{t}dt$$

$$= [t \ln t]_1^3 - \int_1^3 dt$$

$$= [t \ln t]_1^3 - [t]_1^3$$

$$= (3 \ln 3 - \ln 1) - (3 - 1)$$

$$= 3 \ln 3 - 2.$$

Question B Obtain $\int_0^1 te^t dt$.

Solution　Set $f(t) = e^t$ and $g(t) = t$. Then $f'(t) = e^x$ and $g'(t) = 1$.

$$\int_0^1 te^t dt = \int_0^1 e^t t \, dt$$

$$= [e^t t]_0^1 - \int_0^1 (e^t \cdot 1) \, dt$$

$$= (e - 0) - [e^t]_0^1$$

$$= e - (e - 1)$$

$$= 1.$$

Exercise 7.4　Integration by parts.

Now let us use integration by parts to obtain the continuous annuity of the increasing payments we have discussed (Equation (7.20)).

Question　Obtain $A = \int_0^3 Rte^{-rt} dt$.

Solution　First, we use integration by substitution. Let $-rt = s$ hence $t = -\dfrac{1}{r}s$ and $dt = -\dfrac{1}{r} ds$. Substituting these into the equation above, we obtain (also notice the changes in the limits of integration):

$$A = R \int_0^{-3r} \left(-\frac{1}{r}s \right) e^s \left(-\frac{ds}{r} \right)$$

$$= \frac{R}{r^2} \int_0^{-3r} se^s ds.$$

Now we use integration by parts. Set $f(s) = e^s$ and $g(s) = s$. Then $f'(s) = e^s$ and $g'(s) = 1$.

$$A = \frac{R}{r^2} \int_0^{-3r} se^s ds$$

$$= \frac{R}{r^2} \left\{ [se^s]_0^{-3r} - \int_0^{-3r} e^s ds \right\}$$

$$= \frac{R}{r^2} \left\{ -3re^{-3r} - [e^s]_0^{-3r} \right\}$$

$$= \frac{R}{r^2} \left[-3re^{-3r} - (e^{-3r} - 1) \right]$$

$$= \frac{R}{r^2} \left[1 - e^{-3r} (3r + 1) \right].$$

Exercise 7.5　Integration by parts.

For example, if a nominal rate is 10 per cent ($i = 0.1$), then the present value of this annuity is:

$$A = 100R \left[1 - 1.3e^{-0.3} \right].$$

Now that we have studied all the basic integration techniques, let us move on to the main topic of this chapter: examining the effect of taxation.

7.4 Demand and supply analysis revisited

7.4.1 The individual supply and market supply

In Chapter 4, we looked at a particular firm's profit maximising problem and saw what the supply schedule of the firm looks like. We have shown that the short-run supply schedule of an individual firm in a competitive market is identical to its marginal cost curve (above the shutdown price). The market supply schedule we discussed in Chapter 1 can be obtained by summing up individual firms' supply schedules for each and every price. Adding the individual supplies of the firms mathematically can be tricky at times, and to see why, let us look at the simplest case where there are two firms who sell apples in the competitive market. But remember, although there are only two firms, we still maintain the assumption of the competitive market; that is, these two firms take the price as given (if you are not comfortable with the assumption, then you can consider that there are two groups of firms).

Firm A's supply schedule of apples $q^A \geq 0$ is given by the following demand function:

$$q^A = -1 + 2p, \tag{7.22}$$

where $p > 0$ is the price of apples.

Likewise, Firm B's supply schedule of apples $q^B \geq 0$ is:

$$q^B = -6 + 3p. \tag{7.23}$$

Shall we add these two supplies and obtain the market supply q? We obtain

$$q = q^A + q^B = -7 + 5p. \tag{7.24}$$

Is this correct? In fact, there's something wrong going on. . . . Look at Figure 7.6, in which three diagrams are drawn side by side. On the first diagram, Firm A's supply schedule is depicted. It says that the firm does not supply any apples if the price is below $\frac{1}{2}$. The middle diagram shows Firm B's supply schedule, which tells us that it does not supply any apple if unless the price is above 2 (it suggests Firm B is employing an inferior production technology). In any case, the market supply schedule is depicted on the third diagram. An important thing to note first is that the aggregate supply of apples for the prices below 2 is identical to Firm A's individual supply (of course, because Firm B supplies no apples). When the price is above 2, then Firm B starts supplying according to Equation (7.23). For example, when $p = 3$, Firm A supplies $q^A = 5$ and Firm B supplies $q^B = 3$, and hence the market supply is $q = q^A + q^B = 8$ when $p = 3$. Diagrammatically, we added individual supplies horizontally at that price. If you go through the same procedure –

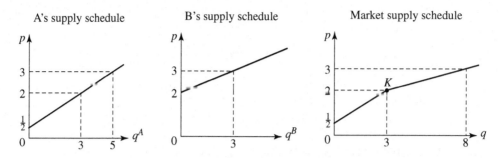

Figure 7.6 Adding supply schedules (horizontally).

adding individual supplies – for each and every price, you will obtain the market supply schedule.

Then, the slope of the market supply schedule when $p > 2$ will be flatter than it is when $p < 2$, because Firm B's (positive) supply is added horizontally on to Firm A's supply. So the market supply schedule should have a "kink" at Point K when $p = 2$. Given our analysis using the diagrams, it is now quite obvious that Equation (7.24) does not represent the market supply schedule because it is a linear function that has no kink.

Now let us discuss how we go about obtaining the market supply schedule algebraically. Recall that neither firm's supply function is defined if $p < \dfrac{1}{2}$. That is, both firms' supply will be negative (but it has to be non-negative). What it means is that, if $p < \dfrac{1}{2}$, neither firm supplies and hence the market supply is zero.

If $\dfrac{1}{2} \le p < 2$, the market supply consists of Firm A's supply only, which implies:

$$q = -1 + 2p \text{ if } \frac{1}{2} \le p < 2. \tag{7.25}$$

If $p \ge 2$, the market supply consists of supplies of both Firms A and B, therefore,

$$q = -7 + 5p \text{ if } p \ge 2. \tag{7.26}$$

We can summarise the above as the following:

$$q = \begin{cases} 0 & \text{if } p < \frac{1}{2}, \\ -1 + 2p & \text{if } \frac{1}{2} \le p < 2, \\ -7 + 5p & \text{if } p \ge 2. \end{cases} \tag{7.27}$$

This case-defined function is the kinked market supply schedule depicted on the third diagram in Figure 7.6. It is tempting to add two individual supply functions (7.22) and (7.23) to get Equation (7.24), because it is a straightforward procedure. However, by examining Equation (7.24) and the diagrams in Figure 7.6 together, we have realised that something has gone wrong. This example tells us that, when we examine economic problems, we should always take a mathematical result carefully and think if it really makes sense. It also makes us realise the importance of visualising our results using diagrams.

7.4.2 The vertical interpretation of the supply schedule

Perhaps you are used to interpreting the supply schedule in the following way: it shows the quantity of the good supplied when the price is given. Namely, starting on the vertical axis with a particular price, we go *horizontally* to the right until we hit the supply schedule, and then go downwards to find the quantity of the good supplied. Both the individual and market supply schedules can be read this way. For example, in Figure 7.6, when $p = 3$, Firms A and B supplies $q^A = 5$ and $q^B = 3$, respectively, and the market supply is $q = 8$. Some textbooks call it the **horizontal interpretation** of the market supply schedule. Indeed, I explained the market supply schedule this way in Chapter 1.

Some textbooks also emphasise a different way of interpreting the supply schedule, which is called the **vertical interpretation**. For this interpretation, we start with a particular quantity supplied (by an individual firm or by the market), and go *vertically* until we hit the corresponding supply schedule. As discussed many times previously, the short-run supply schedule of an individual firm in a competitive market is identical to its marginal cost schedule (above the shutdown price). So the height of the supply schedule represents the incremental cost of further supplying an infinitesimally small amount of this good. To put it another way, the height of the supply schedule represents the **marginal cost** of supplying the good.

Let us look at an example. In the above story of the apple market, the two firms' supply schedules and market supply schedules are represented by Equations (7.22), (7.23) and (7.27), respectively. Suppose there is no apple supplied in the market, $q = 0$. Then the first bit of an apple should be supplied by Firm A who has a lower marginal cost, and the marginal cost of supplying the next apple for Firm A is $\$\frac{1}{2}$. By looking at the third diagram, you can see that when $q = 0$ the cost of supplying the next apple *to the market* is $\$\frac{1}{2}$, because Firm A will be the supplier of it. When the quantity of apples supplied in the market is $q = 8$, then both firms are supplying with $q^A = 5$ and $q^B = 3$. By looking at the third diagram, we know that the cost of supplying the *next* apple to the market is $3, i.e. $MC(8) = 3$. It is the same as both firms' marginal cost when $q^A = 5$ and $q^B = 3$, which shows that either of these two firms can be the supplier of that next apple.

7.4.3 Producer surplus

Given the vertical interpretation of the supply schedule, it is straightforward to understand the surplus that accrues to the suppliers. Figure 7.7 replicates Figure 7.6, except that some regions are shaded and that they are now labelled as marginal cost schedules. Suppose the price of an apple is $p = 3$, so $q^A = 5$, $q^B = 3$ and $q = 8$.

Now look at the diagram for Firm A: $p = 3$ is what Firm A receives per apple sold whereas the height of Firm A's marginal cost schedule shows how much it costs for it to produce another bit of an apple. So the vertical difference between the horizontal line $p = 3$ and the marginal cost schedule can be considered to be the *surplus* Firm A makes by selling 5 apples. By the same token, the surplus Firm B makes by selling 3 apples is

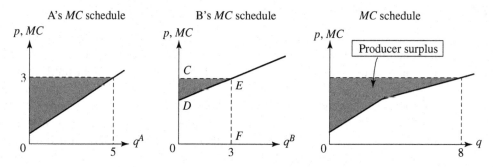

Figure 7.7 Producer surplus.

represented by the shaded region, Area CDE, on the second diagram in the same figure. In total, two firms will make surplus represented by the shaded region in the third diagram (verify it by yourselves). It is the surplus that producers as a whole make, and for that reason, the region below the price above the market supply schedule is called the **producer surplus**.

As explained above, if the market price of apples is given as $p = 3$, Firm B's surplus is defined as Area CDE. We can also see from the middle diagram in Figure 7.7 that it is the difference between Firm B's total revenue (Area $OCEF$) and Area $ODEF$. Note that Firm B's supply schedule is its marginal cost schedule, which we denote by $C_B'(q)$, where $C_B(q)$ is Firm B's cost function. Using the fundamental theorem of integral calculus, we can obtain Area $ODEF$:

$$ODEF = \int_0^3 C_B'(q)dq$$

$$= [C_B(q)]_0^3$$

$$= C_B(3) - C_B(0).$$

$C_B(3)$ is Firm B's total costs of producing 3 apples and $C_B(0)$ is the fixed cost, so Area $ODEF$ represents Firm B's *total variable cost* of producing 3 apples. In general, therefore, when Firm B produces q_B^* given p^*, if we denote its surplus by PS_B:

$$PS_B = \underbrace{p^*q_B^*}_{\text{Revenue}} - \underbrace{\left[C_B(q_B^*) - C_B(0)\right]}_{\text{Total variable cost}}. \tag{7.28}$$

If we ignore the fixed cost $C_B(0)$, Firm B's surplus (PS_B) is equal to its profits from the producing and selling q^* apples. The producer surplus on the third diagram of Figure 7.7 therefore is equal to the sum of the profits of the all sellers (in this case, Firms A and B) if both firms' fixed costs are zero.

So far, we have postulated only two apple sellers in the competitive market, but if it consists of *a number of* different sellers, then you can imagine that the market supply schedule has no kinks (like Point K in Figure 7.6) and becomes a smooth schedule as in Figure 7.8. Producer surplus is the shaded region on the diagram.

Now, let me give you a numerical example.

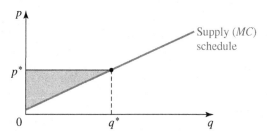

Figure 7.8 Producer surplus when the market supply schedule is smooth.

Question   The market supply of apples is found to be the following: $q = 4p - 4$, where q and p are quantity and the price of apples, respectively. The market price of apples is $2. Obtain the producer surplus in the apple market.

Solution 1   When the price is 2, 4 apples are supplied. Solving the supply function for p gives the inverse supply function as follows:

$$p = \frac{1}{4}q + 1.$$

Diagrammatically, the situation can be described as the following.

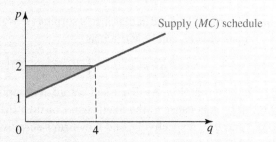

This problem is straightforward. Since the supply curve is linear, the producer surplus is a triangle (where base $= 1$ and height $= 4$, or the other way round). The producer surplus is 2.

Let us use the integration technique to obtain the same area. (If the supply curve is non-linear, you need to use it. Most of the time this is the case, so we might as well practise it now.)

Solution 2   The total revenue is 8 ($p^* = 2$ and $q^* = 4$). The area under the supply curve is obtained by calculating the definite integral of the inverse supply function on the interval from 0 to 4:

$$\int_0^4 \left(\frac{1}{4}q + 1\right) dq = \left[\frac{1}{8}q^2 + q\right]_0^4$$
$$= 2 + 4$$
$$= 6.$$

Hence:

$$PS = 8 - 6 = 2.$$

Solution 3 (quicker alternative solution)   We can obtain the producer surplus by calculating the definite integral of the supply function on the interval from 1 to 2 (notice that the variable of integration is p):

$$PS = \int_1^2 (4p - 4)\, dp$$
$$= \left[2p^2 - 4p \right]_1^2$$
$$= (8 - 8) - (2 - 4)$$
$$= 0 - (-2)$$
$$= 2.$$

Exercise 7.6   Obtaining the producer surplus.

7.4.4   The change in producer surplus

As we discussed previously, a particular firm's surplus (PS^*), when the price and quantity are p^* and q^*, respectively, can be written as

$$PS^* = p^* q^* - \left[C(q^*) - C(0) \right], \tag{7.29}$$

where $C(q)$ is its cost function. As discussed before, it is approximately equal to the firm's profits, but is different because of the fixed cost. Consider that the price and quantity have changed to p^{**} and q^{**}, respectively, and now firm's surplus changes to (PS^{**}), which is expressed as follows:

$$PS^{**} = p^{**} q^{**} - \left[C(q^{**}) - C(0) \right]. \tag{7.30}$$

The difference is:

$$PS^{**} - PS^* = p^{**} q^{**} - \left[C(q^{**}) - C(0) \right] - \left[p^* q^* - \left(C(q^*) - C(0) \right) \right]$$
$$= p^{**} q^{**} - C(q^{**}) - \left[p^* q^* - C(q^*) \right]$$
$$= \pi(q^{**}) - \pi(q^*). \tag{7.31}$$

So, we can state the following. A firm's surplus per se does not exactly represent its profits (because of the fixed cost), but the change in the surplus exactly represents the change in the profits (because the fixed cost cancels out). It is true at the market level. That is, the producer surplus per se does not measure the profits of the firms' in the market, but the change in producer surplus exactly measures the change in the profits the firms in the market raise. Hence, using the change in producer surplus to measure the change in producers' welfare is indeed relevant. The shaded region in Figure 7.9 shows the change in producer surplus when the price of the product changes from p^* to p^{**}.

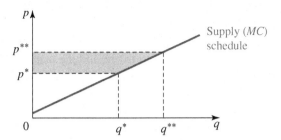

Figure 7.9 The change in producer surplus.

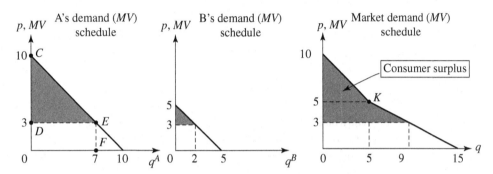

Figure 7.10 Individual and market demand schedules.

7.4.5 The vertical interpretation of the demand schedule

Now we turn to discuss the demand side. Suppose there are only two consumers in the apple market.

Consumer A's demand for apples $q^A \geq 0$ is given by the following demand function:

$$q^A = 10 - p, \tag{7.32}$$

where $p > 0$ is the price of apples. Likewise, Consumer B's demand for apples $q^B \geq 0$ is:

$$q^B = 5 - p. \tag{7.33}$$

If we add the two consumers' demands for apples horizontally, it gives us the market demand schedule for apples. Figure 7.10 describes three demand schedules. The first two are for Consumer A and Consumer B, respectively, and the third one is the market demand schedule. As you can see, the market demand schedule has a kink at Point K. We already discussed how the aggregation of individual schedules can be done algebraically – in the context of obtaining the market supply schedule – so I will leave that task for you as an exercise.

Recall that we can interpret supply schedules in two different ways. We can interpret demand schedules in horizontal and vertical ways as well. The horizontal interpretation of the demand schedule is this: the schedule shows the quantity of the good demanded when the price is given. Namely, starting on the vertical axis with a particular price, we go *horizontally* to the right until we hit the demand schedule, and then go downwards to find the quantity of the good demanded. Both the individual and market demand schedules can be interpreted this way. For example, in Figure 7.10, when $p = 3$, Consumers A and B demand $q^A = 7$ and $q^B = 2$, respectively, and the market demand is $q = 9$. It is the way I explained the market demand schedule in Chapter 1, and perhaps you are comfortable with interpreting it this way.

To explain the vertical interpretation, though, we need to introduce a new idea. Suppose Consumer A has no apple at present, i.e. $q^A = 0$. What is the maximum amount of money he/she is willing to give up to get the first bite of an apple? We know the consumer is unwilling to pay more than $10 for the first bite because the demand is zero if the price is above $10. When the price of an apple is, say, $5, he/she will buy 5 apples so he must be willing to sacrifice at least $5 per apple for the first bite. Following this logic, you can deduce that the amount of money he/she is willing to give up for the very first bite of an apple is exactly $10 per apple, which is the height of his/her demand schedule at $q^A = 0$. The height of Consumer A's demand schedule becomes smaller as his/her apple consumption q^A increases, showing that the maximum amount of money he/she wishes to sacrifice decreases as his/her apple consumption increases. For example, at $q^A = 5$, i.e. he/she has already had 5 apples, he/she is willing to pay $5 per apple to have the next bite. In other word, his/her *valuation* of that bite of an apple is $5.

In any case, the preceding discussion implies that the height of consumer's demand schedule shows his/her **marginal willingness to pay (*MWTP*)** or **marginal valuation (*MV*)** of the good in question. The notion is applicable to the market demand schedule. The height of the market demand schedule shows the marginal valuation of the good in question for the market participants. Interpreting the demand schedule this way is the key to understanding the surplus consumers make by buying goods in the market.[2]

To consolidate the understanding, let us use some numbers to describe the idea. Consider Figure 7.10, and suppose the price an apple is $p = 3$ and hence the quantity of apples demanded in the market is $q = 9$. Note that Consumers A and B buy $q^A = 7$ and $q^B = 2$, respectively. By looking at the third diagram in the figure, we know that the marginal valuation of an apple for the market participants is $3 per apple, i.e. $MV(9) = 3$. There are two market participants, so for each of them, the value of this next bite must be $3 per apple. If you look at two consumers' marginal valuations when $q^A = 7$ and $q^B = 2$, they are indeed equal to $3 per apple, i.e. each of them is willing to pay a maximum of $3 per apple to have the next bite of an apple.

7.4.6   Consumer surplus

Now the difference between what the consumer is willing to pay (marginal valuation) and what he/she actually has to pay (market price) can be considered as that consumer's

---

2 Strictly speaking, only under certain circumstances are these two interpretations consistent with each other. The demand schedule derived following the horizontal interpretation is called the **Marshallian** (or **uncompensated**) **demand schedule** whereas the one that is derived by the vertical interpretation is called the **Hicksian** (or **compensated**) **demand schedule**. We will just assume that these two schedules are identical in this book, but interested readers can consult textbooks in intermediate microeconomics to study this further.

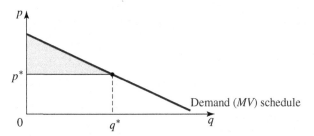

Figure 7.11 Consumer surplus.

surplus. For example, when the price of an apple is $p = 3$, Consumer A chooses $q^A = 7$. What he has to pay to get 7 apples is $21, which is represented by the area $ODEF$ on the first diagram in Figure 7.10. In contrast, in total, he/she willing to pay the dollar amount represented by the area under his/her MV schedule, $OCEF$. That is the sum of his/her marginal valuation over $q^A = 0$ to $q^A = 7$ and is called the **total valuation (TV)** (or **total willingness to pay (TWTP)**). The difference is the surplus for this consumer and it is represented by the area of the shaded region, CDE. Similarly the shaded region on the second diagram shows the surplus for Consumer B.

The shaded region in the market diagram shows the sum of the surplus of the two consumers. It is the area below the MV schedule (the market demand schedule) above the price. Because it represents the surplus created by the consumers in the market, it is called the **consumer surplus**. If there are a number of consumers in the apple market, the market demand schedule becomes smooth without any kink, as shown in Figure 7.11.

Now we know what the consumer surplus is and how it is represented on the diagram. The next step is to obtain the area of the consumer surplus when the demand function is given. Two questions are given in the following: one deals with the linear demand whereas the other deals with the non-linear demand.

Question A   The market demand for apples is found to be the following: $q = 10 - p$, where q and p are quantity and the price of apples, respectively. The market price of apples is $4. Obtain the consumer surplus.

Solution   When the price is 4, 6 apples are demanded. We can show this diagrammatically.

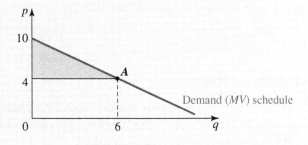

Calculating the area of the triangle gives the consumer surplus:

$$6 \times 6 \times \frac{1}{2} = \$18.$$

Note We measure welfare in terms of money. That is, the unit we use for surplus is 'dollar' (because we multiply 'apple' by '$ per apple').

Question B The market demand for apples is found to be the following: $q = 10 - p^2$, where q and p are quantity and the price of apples, respectively. The market price of apples is $2. Obtain the consumer surplus.

Solution When the price is 2, 6 apples are demanded. Diagrammatically, the situation can be described as follows.

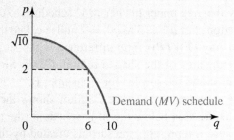

We can obtain the consumer surplus by calculating the definite integral of the demand function on the interval from 2 to $\sqrt{10}$ (notice that the variable of integration is p):

$$CS = \int_{2}^{\sqrt{10}} \left[10 - p^2\right] dp$$

$$= \left[10p - \frac{1}{3}p^3\right]_{2}^{\sqrt{10}}$$

$$= 10\sqrt{10} - \frac{10}{3}\sqrt{10} - 20 + \frac{8}{3}$$

$$= \frac{20}{3}\sqrt{10} - \frac{52}{3}$$

$$= \frac{4}{3}\left(5\sqrt{10} - 13\right).$$

Exercise 7.7 Calculating the consumer surplus.

7.4.7 Total economic surplus

Now let us put the consumer surplus and the producer surplus together. In Figure 7.12, market demand and market supply schedules for apples are drawn. The market equilibrium occurs at Point A, where demand equals supply.

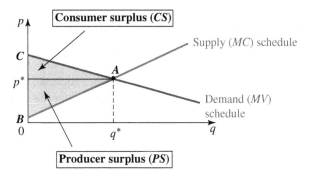

Figure 7.12 Total surplus.

At equilibrium, the market price is p^* and q^* units of apples are traded. Under this situation, the consumer surplus is CAp^* and the producer surplus is Bp^*A. So in total, if the market operates, it will create a surplus that is equal to the sum of the consumer surplus and the producer surplus, ABC. We call this the **total economics surplus** and we use it as the measure of welfare.

Question The market demand schedule for apples is found to be the following: $q = 8 - p^2$, where q and p are quantity and the price of apples, respectively. The market supply schedule of apples is given as follows: $q = 4p - 4$. Obtain the equilibrium market price of apples and the total economic surplus created in this market.

Solution Let us obtain the market price first. At equilibrium, demand equals supply:

$$8 - p^2 = 4p - 4$$
$$p^2 + 4p - 12 = 0$$
$$(p + 6)(p - 2) = 0$$
$$p = -6, 2.$$

The market price has to be non-negative, so $p^* = 2$.

When the market price is 2, quantity of apples traded is 4. The market diagram can be drawn as follows.

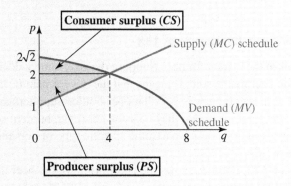

The producer surplus is easy to calculate because the supply curve is linear:

$$PS = 2.$$

To calculate the consumer surplus, we calculate the definite integral of the demand function $q = 8 - p^2$ on the interval from 2 to $2\sqrt{2}$ (notice that the variable of integration is p):

$$CS = \int_{2}^{2\sqrt{2}} \left(8 - p^2\right) dp$$

$$= \left[8p - \frac{1}{3}p^3\right]_{2}^{2\sqrt{2}}$$

$$= \left(16\sqrt{2} - \frac{16}{3}\sqrt{2}\right) - \left(16 - \frac{8}{3}\right)$$

$$= \frac{32}{3}\sqrt{2} - \frac{40}{3}.$$

Therefore, the total economic surplus W is:

$$W = CS + PS$$

$$= \frac{32}{3}\sqrt{2} - \frac{40}{3} + 2$$

$$= \frac{32}{3}\sqrt{2} - \frac{34}{3}$$

$$= \frac{2}{3}\left(16\sqrt{2} - 17\right).$$

Exercise 7.8 Obtaining the total welfare.

7.5 The deadweight loss of taxation

Previously we have seen the total economic surplus created in the competitive market, where the equilibrium price is determined at the point where demand equals supply. In this section, we will see what occurs to the total economic surplus in the presence of taxation.

7.5.1 The economic incidence of tax

Let us look at the market for beer. Suppose the government decides to introduce a **production tax** on beer that is sold. It means that the government taxes the producers (suppliers) of beer. Let us say the tax is T dollars per bottle. Suppliers are **legally liable** to pay the tax, but it does not mean that they bear the entire tax burden: some burden will be passed on to the consumers unless we assume specific type of demand and/or supply schedules. Let us see why.

In Figure 7.13, Point E shows the equilibrium of the beer market without the tax. The equilibrium price of beer per bottle is p^* and q^* bottles are traded. To illustrate the story

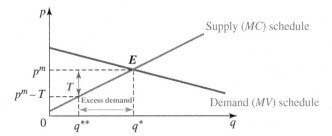

Figure 7.13 There will be an excess demand if suppliers bear the entire tax burden.

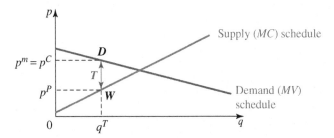

Figure 7.14 The economic incidence of a production tax.

clearly, let us introduce another idea called the **shelf price**, p^m. The shelf (or market) price is the price that is written on the tag of the beer, so it shows the dollar amount that the buyer actually hands over to the seller. When there is no tax, the shelf price is equal to p^*, so you might wonder why we need p^m for this discussion, but it will become clear why I introduced it.

Now let us think what occurs when the production tax of T is levied. Remember that beer suppliers will produce so long as the price *they receive* exceeds their marginal cost of production. So, when the production tax is present, they produce so long as $(p^m - T)$ exceeds the marginal cost of production.

Suppose that the suppliers bear the entire tax burden, that is, the shelf price stays the same at $p^* = p^m$. It means consumers pay the same price even after the introduction of this tax, and so they bear no tax burden. Then, the quantity of beer demanded will stay the same at q^* (of course, because they are facing the same price as before), whereas the suppliers choose quantity q^{**} (where $p^m - T = MC(q^{**})$). There will be an *excess demand* for beer (distance $q^{**}q^*$). It means that the shelf price has got to rise. The simple intuition is: when suppliers are taxed, the market supply falls, which drives up the shelf price.

Now we know that the shelf price must rise, but by how much? Let us think about it by using a diagram. Since the new shelf price has to clear the beer market, it has to be determined at the level p^m illustrated in Figure 7.14.

Because consumers are not legally liable to pay the tax, p^m is all they have to pay per bottle of beer: we call this the **consumer price** p^C. As we can observe, p^C is higher than the original price p^*. It means that although consumers are not legally liable to pay the

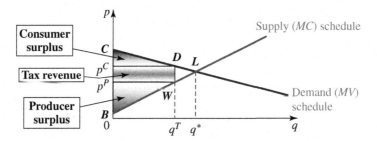

Figure 7.15 The deadweight loss (*DWL*) of taxation.

tax, they bear part of the tax burden. Demand for beer is q^T when the consumer price is p^C (Point D where $p^C = MV(q^T)$).

Suppliers of beer, when they sell beer, receive p^m per bottle from the consumer, but they have to pay T dollars per bottle to the government. Hence, what they receive per bottle after paying the tax is $p^P = p^m - T$: we call this price the **producer price**. When the producer price is p^P, the supply of beer is q^T (point W, where $p^P = MC(q^T)$). The beer market clears and hence the new shelf price, p^m, illustrated in Figure 7.14 represents the equilibrium price under the tax.

The equilibrium level of quantity after the introduction of tax is q^T, where the difference between $MV\,(= p^C)$ and $MC\,(= p^P)$ is T. The tax creates this wedge between the demand (MV) and supply (MC) schedules in the equilibrium and we call it the **tax wedge**. Both consumers and producers bear the tax burden. The shelf price is equal to the consumer price when producers are legally liable to pay the tax.

7.5.2 The welfare effects of the tax

Before the introduction of the production tax, the total economic surplus the beer market created is represented by the area CBL in Figure 7.15. Let us discuss how the total economic surplus changes after the introduction of the tax.

As we have seen, when the tax is levied, the shelf price rises and the quantity traded in the market decreases. In Figure 7.15, new consumer surplus and producer surplus are depicted. Consumers are facing the higher price p^C and are consuming less, and hence the consumer surplus has decreased. The consumer surplus under the tax is represented by the area $Cp^C D$. Producers are facing the lower price p^P and are producing less, and hence the producer surplus has become smaller. The producer surplus under the tax is represented by the area $p^P BW$. The area $p^C p^P WLD$ shows the burden of the tax on consumers and producers. But part of this burden may be transferred back to the market participants. That is, by taxing the producers, the government raises the **tax revenue**, which is represented by the area $p^C p^P WD$. Let us assume this transfer actually occurs. Then, the total economic surplus under the tax is the sum of the consumer surplus, the producer surplus and the government's tax revenue. It is represented by the area $CBWD$.

We can see that the introduction of a production tax lowers the welfare by the area DWL. Here DWL is the **excess burden of the tax** on consumers and producers in

7.5 The deadweight loss of taxation

this market, often referred to as the **deadweight loss** of taxation. Notice that on the interval from $q = q^T$ to $q = q^*$, $MV > MC$. It means consumers value beer more than is required for producers to supply. When there is no tax, the equilibrium level of quantity is q^* where $MV = MC$. As we can understand from Figure 7.15, the total economic surplus in this market is maximised when $q = q^*$, where $MV = MC$. However, because of the production tax, production of beer stops at $q = q^T < q^*$, where $MV \neq MC$. Because the provision of beer is less than the level that maximises the total economic surplus, we say that there is **under-provision** (or **under-production**) of beer.

Let me give you some examples of calculating the deadweight loss mathematically.

Question A (linear D&S)   Assume that the inverse demand function for a particular good is given as follows: $p = 1000 - q$. The inverse supply function for this good is known as the following: $p = q$. Obtain the deadweight loss when a production tax of $30 per unit is levied. How much tax revenue does the government raise?

Solution   We start with drawing a diagram as usual.

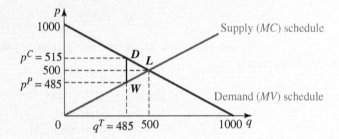

Without the tax, equilibrium is $(p^*, q^*) = (500, 500)$. We need to find q^T at which $MV - MC = 30$:

$$1000 - q^T - 30 = q^T$$
$$q^T = 485.$$

When $q = q^T = 485$, the consumer price and the producer price are $p^C = 515$ and $p^P = 485$, respectively. So the deadweight loss (DWL) and the tax revenue (TR) are:

$$DWL = 30 \times 15 \times \frac{1}{2} = 225,$$

$$TR = 30 \times 485 = 14550 \text{ (dollars)}.$$

Question B (linear D&S, but more elastic supply)   Assume that the inverse demand function for a particular good is given as follows: $p = 1000 - q$ (this is the same as in Question A). The inverse supply function for this good is known as the following: $p = \frac{1}{5}q + 400$. Obtain the deadweight loss when a production tax of $30 per unit is levied.

Solution Notice that everything is the same as in Question A except for the inverse supply function. Without the tax, equilibrium is $(p^*, q^*) = (500, 500)$, which is the same as in Question A.

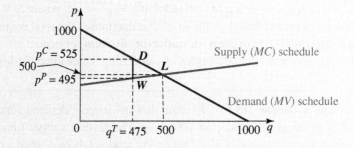

We again need to find q^T at which $MV - MC = 30$:

$$1000 - q^T - 30 = \frac{1}{5}q^T + 400$$

$$q^T = 475.$$

When $q = q^T = 475$, the consumer price and the producer price are $p^C = 525$ and $p^P = 495$, respectively.

$$DWL = 30 \times 25 \times \frac{1}{2} = 375.$$

$$TR = 30 \times 475 = 14250 \text{ (dollars)}.$$

Observation These questions give us an important lesson. Comparing Questions A and B, we can see that more of burden is pushed down on to consumers in Question B. This is because the producer surplus became much less in Question B. In Question A, there was greater producer surplus to absorb the tax.

We can also see that the excess burden (the deadweight loss) is greater in Question B. That is, there is further under-provision of the good in Question B. Note that $q^T = 475$ in Question B, which is 25 units less than $q^* = 500$, where $q^T = 485$ in Question A, which is 15 units less than $q^* = 500$. It also implies that the government is collecting more tax in Question A. By introducing the same tax (that is, a production tax of \$30 per unit), in Question A, the government can collect more tax and there is less under-provision of the good. It appears that if the demand curves are the same, the government should tax the good that has a steeper supply curve.

This statement can be rewritten using the price elasticity we have studied. Let us define the price elasticity of supply μ as follows:

$$\mu = \frac{\text{proportional change in quantity supplied}}{\text{proportional change in the price}}.$$

Mathematically, the price elasticity of supply at (p_0, q_0) is (remember, we need to measure elasticity at a certain point):

$$\mu_{q_0,p_0} = \frac{dq/q_0}{dp/p_0}.$$

Is supply more or less elastic at Point L in Question A? It is less elastic. At Point L, in both examples, $(p^*, q^*) = (500, 500)$. So substituting these into the formula gives:

$$\mu_{500,500} = \frac{dq}{dp}\bigg|_{500,500},$$

where $\frac{dq}{dp}$ is the reciprocal of $\frac{dp}{dq}$ (the slope of the supply schedule with q on the horizontal axis). For Question A:

$$\mu_{500,500} = \frac{dq}{dp}\bigg|_{500,500} = 1.$$

For Question B:

$$\mu_{500,500} = \frac{dq}{dp}\bigg|_{500,500} = 5.$$

Now let me restate what we have observed: (everything else being the same) the government should tax the good whose elasticity is lower (less responsive to the change in the price). There will be less under-provision and hence the deadweight loss will be lower.

In the both questions, the demand schedules were the same. Of course, the difference in demand schedule is important, too. We shall see it in the next subsection as well as in one of the additional exercises at the end of the chapter.

Exercise 7.9 Obtaining the total welfare.

7.5.3 Obtaining the market equilibrium with a tax with perfectly inelastic demand

Let us investigate a special case where the demand is perfectly inelastic, i.e. the demand is constant (the demand schedule is hence vertical). If a production tax is levied, who will bear the tax burden? We proceed as we have done previously, except that we now suppose that both consumers and producers bear some of the tax burden.

In Figure 7.16, Point E shows equilibrium of the market before the tax is levied. The equilibrium price (and the shelf price) of beer per bottle is p^*, and q^* bottles are traded. Now suppose that the production tax of T is levied, and both consumers and producers bear some of the tax burden. Then, the shelf price increases to p^m, but increases by less than T. It implies that, whilst the consumers' demand will be unchanged at q^* – reflecting the infinitely elastic nature of the demand – the suppliers choose quantity q^{**} (where

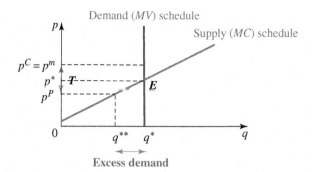

Figure 7.16 There will be an excess demand if producers bear the tax burden.

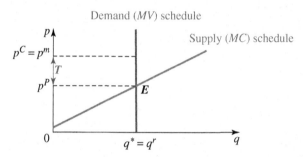

Figure 7.17 The market clears if consumers bear the entire tax burden.

$p^m - T = MC(q^{**}))$. There will be an excess demand for the good (distance $q^{**}q^*$), and so p^m cannot be the equilibrium shelf price.

In this case, as long as the producer price is below the original shelf price (that is, the price before the tax is levied), producers will supply less than q^*. Then we know there will be an excess demand because the demand is always q^*. What it says is that producers cannot bear the tax burden for the market to clear. Consequently we let the consumers bear the entire tax burden (see Figure 7.17 from here on), that is, the shelf price (which is equal to the consumer price) goes up by exactly the amount of the production tax, $p^C = p^m = p^* + T$, and the producers get $p^P = p^*$ per unit (so the producer price is unchanged after the production tax). Therefore the equilibrium shelf price is $p = p^m$. At this price, the producers supply $q^* = q^T$, which consumers are willing to buy at the price $p = p^m = p^C$. This situation is depicted in Figure 7.17.

We saw that when the demand is perfectly inelastic, consumers bear the entire tax burden (even though producers are legally liable to pay the tax, they pass the entire tax burden on to the consumers). There is good intuition for this result. Recall that, in the previous exercise, we related the size of the consumer/producer surplus to the economic incidence of the tax (i.e. who bears the burden). In the above case where the demand is perfectly inelastic, technically speaking, consumer surplus is infinite (although realistically, we should envisage that the demand eventually decreases as the price increases), whereas producers have limited surplus. It means that consumers do not mind bearing the tax burden at all (because they have infinite surplus anyway) but producers do. That is why the entire burden is borne by consumers.

Is there a deadweight loss of taxation in this case? No, there shouldn't be because there is no under-provision of the good in this case. If you look at each of the surplus measures, you can convince yourselves that it must be true. The producer surplus is unchanged because the price the producer receives and the quantity traded are unchanged. The consumer surplus decreases just by the tax revenue the government collected. So, in this example, the tax merely creates the wealth transfers from the consumers to the government. In one of the additional exercises you will see the opposite case, where producers bear the entire tax burden.

7.5.4 Obtaining the deadweight loss with non-linear demand

To conclude this section, let me give you an example to obtain the deadweight loss when one (or both) of the demand and supply curves is (are) non-linear (we need to use the integration technique).

Question (non-linear D&S) Assume that the inverse demand function for a particular good is given as follows: $p = \dfrac{1000}{q}$ $(q > 0)$. The inverse supply function for this good is known as follows: $p = 10q$ $(q \geq 0)$. Obtain the deadweight loss when a production tax of \$150 per unit is levied.

Solution First, let us obtain market equilibrium when there is no tax:

$$\frac{1000}{q} = 10q$$

$$q^2 = 100$$

$$q^* = 10.$$

$$p^* = 10^2 = 100.$$

So $(p^*, q^*) = (100, 10)$. The diagram looks like this.

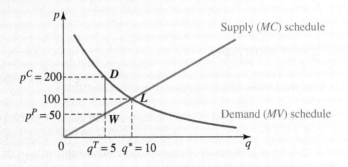

We need to find q^T at which $MV - MC = 150$:

$$\frac{1000}{q^T} - 150 = 10q^T$$

$$10(q^T)^2 + 150q^T - 1000 = 0$$

$$(q^T)^2 + 15q^T - 100 = 0$$

$$(q^T + 20)(q^T - 5) = 0.$$

Ignoring the negative root, we get $q^T = 5$. When $q = q^T = 5$, the consumer price and the producer price are $p^C = 200$ and $p^P = 50$, respectively:

$$DWL = Dq^T q^* L - Wq^T q^* L.$$

The second term of the RHS is the area of a trapezoid:

$$Wq^T q^* L = (50 + 100) \times 5 \times \frac{1}{2} = 375.$$

The first term is the area under the demand curve and above the q-axis on the interval from 5 to 10:

$$Dq^T q^* L = \int_5^{10} \frac{1000}{q} dq$$

$$= 1000 \int_5^{10} \frac{1}{q} dq$$

$$= 1000 \, [\ln q]_5^{10}$$

$$= 1000(\ln 10 - \ln 5)$$

$$= 1000 \ln 2.$$

Therefore:

$$DWL = 1000 \ln 2 - 375.$$

Exercise 7.10 Obtaining the total welfare.

7.6 Additional exercises

1. **(Anti-derivatives)** Answer the following questions.

(1) The marginal cost of producing a certain good is given as $MC(q) = 0.06q^2 - 6q + 175$. Take the anti-derivative of this function (denote a constant of integration by F). What does the anti-derivative represent in this context? Determine F when it costs 672.02 to produce one unit of this good.

(2) Consider a consumer whose level of utility depends on his consumption of x. The marginal utility is given as $MU(x) = \dfrac{1}{2\sqrt{x}}$. Take the anti-derivative of this function (denote a constant of integration by C). What does the anti-derivative represent in this context? Determine C if this utility turns out to be 1 util when $x = 1$.

2. **(The area under the curve)** In the following, use a definite integral to find the area of the region bounded by the given curve, the x-axis, and the given lines. Sketch the area of the region on a diagram.

(1) $y = \dfrac{1}{x}, x = 1, x = 2.$

(2) $y = \sqrt{x} - 1, x = 4, x = 9.$

(3) $y = -(x - 2)^2 + 4.$

(4) $y = \dfrac{1}{2}e^x, x = 0, x = 3.$

3. **(Integration by parts)** Obtain the following definite integrals using integration by parts.

(1) $\displaystyle\int_1^e \dfrac{\ln x}{\sqrt{x}}dx.$ [**Hint.** Set $f(x) = 2\sqrt{x}$ and $g(x) = \ln x$.]

(2) $\displaystyle\int_1^e \ln x\, dx.$ [**Hint.** Set $f(x) = x$ and $g(x) = \ln x$.]

(3) $\displaystyle\int_1^e x \ln x\, dx.$ [**Hint.** Set $f(x) = \dfrac{1}{2}x^2$ and $g(x) = \ln x$.]

4. **(Integration by substitution)** Obtain the following definite integral using integration by substitution.

(1) $\displaystyle\int_0^a xe^{-cx^2}dx.$ [**Hint.** Set $s = -cx^2$.]

(2) $\displaystyle\int_1^e \dfrac{1 + \ln x}{x}dx.$ [**Hint.** Set $s = 1 + \ln x$.]

(3) $\displaystyle\int_0^1 (3x - 1)^5 dx.$ [**Hint.** Set $s = 3x - 1$.]

(4) $\displaystyle\int_0^1 x(3x^2 - 1)^5 dx.$ [**Hint.** Set $s = 3x^2 - 1$.]

5. **(Continuous annuity)** The nominal rate is 10 per cent. Obtain the present value of a continuous (ordinary) annuity whose payments start now and finish at the end of Year 10 when:

(a) payments are constant at $R = 800$; and

(b) payments change according to the following rule: $R = 800t$, where t represents time.

6. **(Market supply)** The supply of 'duck-basil-rice', also known as DBR, on any particular day comprises supplies from three price-taking chefs, A, B and C.

Denoting the price of DBR by p, Chef A's supply function for one day is given as:

$$q_A = \begin{cases} p - 12 & \text{if } p \geq 12, \\ 0 & \text{if } 0 \leq p < 12. \end{cases}$$

Chef B's supply function for one day is:

$$q_B = \begin{cases} p - 20 & \text{if } p \geq 20, \\ 0 & \text{if } 0 \leq p < 20. \end{cases}$$

Chef C is a perfectionist and so he can supply no more than 5 DBRs per day. He does not care about money so much, and he supplies 5 DBRs for any price so long as it is no less than $5 per DBR. However, if it turns out that he gets less than $5 per DBR, he takes it as an insult to his cooking and stops supplying DBR completely.

(a) Specify the daily DBR supply function for Chef C, q_C.

(b) Sketch the daily DBR supply schedule for each of the chefs separately.

(c) Obtain the daily market supply of DBR.

(d) Sketch it on a diagram.

7. **(Obtaining consumer surplus)** A society's demand for a certain good is given as $q = 10 - 2\sqrt{p}$. Answer the following questions.

(a) Sketch the demand curve on a diagram focusing your attention to $0 \leq q \leq 10$.

(b) Calculate the consumer surplus when the market price is $p^* = 1$.

(c) Calculate the consumer surplus when the market price is $p^{**} = 4$.

(d) What is the change in the consumer surplus when the market price changes from $p^* = 1$ to $p^{**} = 4$?

8. **(Obtaining producer surplus)** An inverse market supply function for a certain good is given as $p = q^{3/2} + 6$. Answer the following questions.

(a) Sketch the supply curve on a diagram, focusing your attention to $q \geq 0$.

(b) Calculate the producer surplus when the market price is $p^* = 7$.

(c) Calculate the producer surplus when the market price is $p^{**} = 70$.

(d) What is the change in the producer surplus when the market price changes from $p^* = 7$ to $p^{**} = 70$?

9. **(Calculating surplus for non-linear demand and supply)** A market demand function for a certain good is given as $q = 12 - 2\sqrt{p}$. An inverse market supply function for the same good is given as $p = q^2$. Answer the following questions.

(a) Obtain market equilibrium for this good.

(b) Calculate the consumer surplus, producer surplus and total surplus.

10. **(DWL with different price elasticities of demand)**   Consider a production tax of $2 per unit.

(a) Calculate the economic incidence and the welfare effects of this tax when demand for the good is $q^D = -p + 20$ and the supply of the good is $q^S = p$.

(b) How does your answer change if the demand for the good is $q^D = -\frac{1}{2}p + 15$?

(c) Compare your results for part (a) and part (b). Carefully explain the difference (if any) in the deadweight loss.

11. **(DWL with the perfectly price elastic demand)**   Consider the same tax and the supply of the good as in the previous question. Now suppose that the demand schedule is horizontal to the q-axis at $p = 10$. More specifically, if the price is above 10, there is no demand, but if the price is below 10, the demand is infinite. [**Note.** This is the case where the demand is *perfectly elastic*, i.e. the response to a change in the price at $p = 10$ is infinite.]

(a) Calculate the economic incidence and the welfare effects of the tax.

(b) Who bears the tax burden and why? Is the deadweight loss different from the one you calculated in part (a) in the previous question? Explain your answer referring to the price elasticity of demand.

Appendix A

Matrix algebra

In Chapter 2 we learnt how to find a solution to a system of two linear equations with two unknowns x_1 and x_2. Consider the following system:

$$\begin{cases} a_{11}x_1 + a_{12}x_2 = b_1 \\ a_{21}x_1 + a_{22}x_2 = b_2. \end{cases} \tag{A.1}$$

If a unique solution exists, then it must be that $a_{11}a_{22} - a_{12}a_{21} \neq 0$ and the solution is
$$(x_1^*, x_2^*) = \left(\frac{b_1 a_{22} - b_2 a_{12}}{a_{11}a_{22} - a_{12}a_{21}}, \frac{b_2 a_{11} - b_1 a_{21}}{a_{11}a_{22} - a_{12}a_{21}} \right).$$ You can verify the solution by applying the method of elimination by addition (or substitution) to Equation (A.1).

In turn, consider a solution to the following linear equation:

$$ax = b. \tag{A.2}$$

If $a = 0$ and $b = 0$, then x has infinitely many solutions (because x can be any number), but if $a = 0$ and $b \neq 0$, then the equation obviously has no solution. When $a \neq 0$, to obtain the x that solves the above equation we divide both sides of it by a, or in other words, multiply both sides of it by the inverse of a, a^{-1}:

$$a^{-1}ax = a^{-1}(-b) \tag{A.3}$$

$$x = -\frac{b}{a}.$$

Is there a way to solve Equation (A.1) as we solve Equation (A.2)? In this appendix we will introduce a new idea, which makes it possible for us to solve Equation (A.1) as if we are solving a simple linear equation such as Equation (A.2). Let me foreshadow this process a little bit in a casual manner. We will later see that Equation (A.1) can be described as:

$$\mathbf{Ax} = \mathbf{b}, \tag{A.4}$$

where $\mathbf{A}$, $\mathbf{x}$ and $\mathbf{b}$ show the collection of as, xs and bs, respectively. More specifically, they are described as follows:

$$\mathbf{A} = \begin{pmatrix} a_{11} & a_{12} \\ a_{21} & a_{22} \end{pmatrix}, \quad \mathbf{x} = \begin{pmatrix} x_1 \\ x_2 \end{pmatrix}, \quad \mathbf{b} = \begin{pmatrix} b_1 \\ b_2 \end{pmatrix}.$$

In the above expressions, $\mathbf{A}$ is called a (two-by-two) matrix and the $\mathbf{x}$ and $\mathbf{b}$ are each called a (column) vector. Once we express Equation (A.1) as Equation (A.4), it looks like we can employ the same strategy we used to solve Equation (A.2). That is, we would like to find the inverse of $\mathbf{A}$ and multiply it on both sides of Equation (A.4):

$$\mathbf{A}^{-1}\mathbf{A}\mathbf{x} = \mathbf{A}^{-1}\mathbf{b}$$
$$\mathbf{x} = \mathbf{A}^{-1}\mathbf{b},$$

where $\mathbf{A}^{-1}$ denotes the inverse of $\mathbf{A}$. It turns out that we can obtain the solution $\mathbf{x}$ as above if the inverse matrix $\mathbf{A}^{-1}$ exists.

If you have never seen matrices before, you may be finding it difficult to understand what I'm talking about. There are many things that are unclear. What is meant by the inverse of a matrix? What are matrices in any case? Well, don't worry, we will learn them in the rest of the appendix.

A.1   Matrices and vectors

Suppose a firm hires three workers, $i = 1, 2, 3$. If we denote worker i's monthly pay from January to April by w_{ij} where $j = 1, 2, 3, 4$, the pay information can be expressed using the following array of numbers:

$$\mathbf{W} = \begin{pmatrix} w_{11} & w_{12} & w_{13} & w_{14} \\ w_{21} & w_{22} & w_{23} & w_{24} \\ w_{31} & w_{32} & w_{33} & w_{34} \end{pmatrix}. \tag{A.5}$$

An array of numbers such as $\mathbf{W}$ is called a **matrix**. In $\mathbf{W}$ there are three rows that correspond to workers and four columns that correspond to months, so we call it a 3×4 (three-by-four) matrix. In general, if the matrix has m rows and n columns, then we say its **size** (or **dimension**) is m-by-n and call it an $m \times n$ matrix. Each of the w_{ij}s in $\mathbf{W}$ is called an **entry** (or **element**).

If the firm wants to know how much it paid to each of their workers in a particular month, say in February, it can focus on the second column of $\mathbf{W}$:

$$\mathbf{w}_{i2} = \begin{pmatrix} w_{12} \\ w_{22} \\ w_{32} \end{pmatrix}. \tag{A.6}$$

We can see that $\mathbf{w}_{i2}$ contains only one column. Such a matrix is called a column matrix, or more commonly, a **column vector**. The firm may want to know how much it paid to a particular worker, say Worker 3. In that case, then the third row of $\mathbf{W}$ is the focus:

$$\mathbf{w}_{3j} = \begin{pmatrix} w_{31} & w_{32} & w_{33} & w_{34} \end{pmatrix}. \tag{A.7}$$

Here, $\mathbf{w}_{3j}$ consists of one row only and such a matrix is known to a row matrix or a **row vector**.

We say that two matrices are **equal** if and only if (a) they have the same size; and (b) all corresponding entries are equal. That is, for $m \times n$ matrices $\mathbf{A}$ and $\mathbf{B}$, we have:

$$\mathbf{A} = \mathbf{B} \text{ if and only if } a_{ij} = b_{ij} \text{ for all } i \text{ and } j. \tag{A.8}$$

A.1.1   The transpose of a matrix

If we interchange rows and columns of $\mathbf{W}$ we obtain the following:

$$\mathbf{W}' = \begin{pmatrix} w_{11} & w_{21} & w_{31} \\ w_{12} & w_{22} & w_{23} \\ w_{13} & w_{23} & w_{33} \\ w_{14} & w_{24} & w_{34} \end{pmatrix}. \tag{A.9}$$

Notice now $\mathbf{W}$ is shown with a prime symbol and has become $\mathbf{W}'$. The prime indicates that rows and columns of the original matrix are interchanged. The matrix $\mathbf{W}'$ is called the **transpose** of $\mathbf{W}$. Some people use a superscript T to denote the same thing, that is, $\mathbf{W}' = \mathbf{W}^{\mathrm{T}}$. Note that the size of the transpose $\mathbf{W}'$ (4×3) is different from the size of the original matrix $\mathbf{W}$ (3×4). Quite obviously, we have $(\mathbf{W}')' = \mathbf{W}$.

A.1.2   Special matrices

When we transpose an $m \times n$ matrix, we get an $n \times m$ matrix. The sizes of the two matrices differ if $m \neq n$ but if $m = n$ the sizes are the same. When $m = n$ a matrix is called a **square matrix** of **order** m (or n). For example, $\begin{pmatrix} a_{11} & a_{12} \\ a_{21} & a_{22} \end{pmatrix}$ is a square matrix of order 2.

A matrix that is equal to its transpose is called a **symmetric matrix**. It is obvious that a symmetric matrix needs to be a square matrix (because otherwise the transpose has a different size). For example, $\begin{pmatrix} 1 & 1 \\ 1 & 2 \end{pmatrix}$ is a symmetric matrix but neither $\begin{pmatrix} 1 & 0 \\ 1 & 2 \end{pmatrix}$ nor $\begin{pmatrix} 1 & 0 & 0 \\ 0 & 0 & 1 \end{pmatrix}$ is.

Let's consider a symmetric matrix of order n, $\mathbf{W}_n$. The entries w_{ii}, $i = 1, \ldots, n$ are called the **main diagonal entries** (or more casually the **main diagonals**). A **diagonal matrix** is a square matrix all of whose off-diagonal entries – i.e. w_{ij}, $i \neq j$ – are zero. For example, $\begin{pmatrix} 1 & 0 \\ 0 & 2 \end{pmatrix}$ and $\begin{pmatrix} w_{11} & 0 & 0 \\ 0 & w_{22} & 0 \\ 0 & 0 & w_{33} \end{pmatrix}$ are diagonal matrices but $\begin{pmatrix} 0 & 1 \\ 0 & 0 \end{pmatrix}$ is not.

A special case of the diagonal matrix is when all the main diagonals are unity. In this case we have an **identity matrix**, which we usually denote by $\mathbf{I}_n$, where n shows the order of the matrix. For example, $\mathbf{I}_2 = \begin{pmatrix} 1 & 0 \\ 0 & 1 \end{pmatrix}$ and $\mathbf{I}_3 = \begin{pmatrix} 1 & 0 & 0 \\ 0 & 1 & 0 \\ 0 & 0 & 1 \end{pmatrix}$ are identity matrices of order 2 and order 3, respectively. The identity matrix in matrix algebra is like 'one' in (ordinary) algebra and we shall see how it is used shortly.

A **zero matrix** in matrix algebra is like 'zero' in (ordinary) algebra. It is a matrix all of whose entries are zero. We usually denote it by $\mathbf{O}$. The zero matrix does not have to be a square matrix, e.g. $\mathbf{O}_{2,3} = \begin{pmatrix} 0 & 0 & 0 \\ 0 & 0 & 0 \end{pmatrix}$ is a 2×3 zero matrix. Most of time our focus will

be a zero square matrix $\mathbf{O}_n$ of order n such as $\mathbf{O}_2 = \begin{pmatrix} 0 & 0 \\ 0 & 0 \end{pmatrix}$ and $\mathbf{O}_3 = \begin{pmatrix} 0 & 0 & 0 \\ 0 & 0 & 0 \\ 0 & 0 & 0 \end{pmatrix}$.

A.1.3 Matrix addition and scalar multiplication

Suppose the three workers we previously discussed were employed in another firm for the same duration of time. We denote the pay information for that firm by a different 3×4 matrix X:

$$\mathbf{X} = \begin{pmatrix} x_{11} & x_{12} & x_{13} & x_{14} \\ x_{21} & x_{22} & x_{23} & x_{24} \\ x_{31} & x_{32} & x_{33} & x_{34} \end{pmatrix}. \tag{A.10}$$

In this case – when the size of two matrices are the same – it makes sense to add the two matrices to obtain each worker's aggregate pay for each of the months. It can be done simply by adding each of the corresponding entries in the two matrices. Denoting the sum of the two matrices by $\mathbf{Y} = \begin{pmatrix} y_{11} & y_{12} & y_{13} & y_{14} \\ y_{21} & y_{22} & y_{23} & y_{24} \\ y_{31} & y_{32} & y_{33} & y_{34} \end{pmatrix}$, we can write:

$$\mathbf{Y} = \mathbf{W} + \mathbf{X} = \begin{pmatrix} w_{11} + x_{11} & w_{12} + x_{12} & w_{13} + x_{13} & w_{14} + x_{14} \\ w_{21} + x_{21} & w_{22} + x_{22} & w_{23} + x_{23} & w_{24} + x_{24} \\ w_{31} + x_{31} & w_{32} + x_{32} & w_{33} + x_{33} & w_{34} + x_{34} \end{pmatrix}. \tag{A.11}$$

For example, in March, Worker 2 earned y_{23}, which is the sum of his pay from two firms $w_{23} + x_{23}$.

Subtracting operations can be conducted similarly. For example, suppose the information on the rents three workers paid each month is summarised by $\mathbf{R} = \begin{pmatrix} r_{11} & r_{12} & r_{13} & r_{14} \\ r_{21} & r_{22} & r_{23} & r_{24} \\ r_{31} & r_{32} & r_{33} & r_{34} \end{pmatrix}$, where r_{ij} is the rent Worker i paid in Month j. Then the money that was left in workers' pockets each month after they paid their rents are given by $\mathbf{Z} = \begin{pmatrix} z_{11} & z_{12} & z_{13} & z_{14} \\ z_{21} & z_{22} & z_{23} & z_{24} \\ z_{31} & z_{32} & z_{33} & z_{34} \end{pmatrix}$, where:

$$\mathbf{Z} = \mathbf{Y} - \mathbf{R} = \begin{pmatrix} y_{11} - r_{11} & y_{12} - r_{12} & y_{13} - r_{13} & y_{14} - r_{14} \\ y_{21} - r_{21} & y_{22} - r_{22} & y_{23} - r_{23} & y_{24} - r_{24} \\ y_{31} - r_{31} & y_{32} - r_{32} & y_{33} - r_{33} & y_{34} - r_{34} \end{pmatrix}. \tag{A.12}$$

For example, in April, Worker 1 had z_{14} in his pocket after paying his rent, which is the difference between his aggregate pay for April and his April rent $y_{14} - r_{14}$. As shown above, so long as the sizes of two matrices are the same, you can add them and also subtract one from the other. When these operations are possible, two matrices are said to be

conformable. You cannot add two matrices (or subtract one matrix from the other) if they are not conformable. For example, there is *no* solution to, say, $\begin{pmatrix} 1 & 0 \\ 0 & 1 \end{pmatrix} + \begin{pmatrix} 1 & 0 & 1 \\ 0 & 1 & 0 \end{pmatrix}$.

There may be some cases where you have to scale up (or down) all entries in a matrix by the same number. For example, suppose each of the workers got a discount on their rents by 10 per cent from January to April. The reduced rents they paid are obtained by scaling down the matrix $\mathbf{R}$ by 10 per cent, and we write it as $0.9\mathbf{R}$, or equivalently, $\mathbf{R}0.9$. More specifically,

$$
\begin{aligned}
\mathbf{D} = \begin{pmatrix} d_{11} & d_{12} & d_{13} & d_{14} \\ d_{21} & d_{22} & d_{23} & d_{24} \\ d_{31} & d_{32} & d_{33} & d_{34} \end{pmatrix} &= 0.9 \begin{pmatrix} r_{11} & r_{12} & r_{13} & r_{14} \\ r_{21} & r_{22} & r_{23} & r_{24} \\ r_{31} & r_{32} & r_{33} & r_{34} \end{pmatrix} \\
&= \begin{pmatrix} 0.9r_{11} & 0.9r_{12} & 0.9r_{13} & 0.9r_{14} \\ 0.9r_{21} & 0.9r_{22} & 0.9r_{23} & 0.9r_{24} \\ 0.9r_{31} & 0.9r_{32} & 0.9r_{33} & 0.9r_{34} \end{pmatrix} \quad\quad \text{(A.13)} \\
&= \begin{pmatrix} r_{11} & r_{12} & r_{13} & r_{14} \\ r_{21} & r_{22} & r_{23} & r_{24} \\ r_{31} & r_{32} & r_{33} & r_{34} \end{pmatrix} 0.9,
\end{aligned}
$$

where $\mathbf{D}$ is the matrix whose entries show the discounted rents. For example, d_{32} is the discounted rent Worker 3 paid in February, which is 90 per cent of the normal rent he would have paid in the same month (without the discount). The single number used to scale the matrix – in the above case, 0.9 – is called a **scalar**, and therefore this operation is called the **scalar multiplication**. As stated above, $\theta\mathbf{R} = \mathbf{R}\theta$, where θ is a scalar.

As in (ordinary) algebra, scalar multiplication has to be conducted before matrix addition (or subtraction) unless the latter operation is in brackets. So quite obviously, $\theta\mathbf{Y} - \mathbf{D} \neq \theta(\mathbf{Y} - \mathbf{D})$. The LHS says 'conduct scalar multiplication $\theta\mathbf{Y}$ first then subtract $\mathbf{D}$' whereas the RHS says 'subtract $\mathbf{D}$ from $\mathbf{Y}$ first then multiply the difference by θ'. The subtraction need not be carried out first, however, even when you encounter an expression such as $\theta(\mathbf{Y} - \mathbf{D})$. Another way to calculate it is – just as you would do in (ordinary) algebra – to distribute θ to each of the matrices as follows before taking the difference: $\theta(\mathbf{Y} - \mathbf{D}) = \theta\mathbf{Y} - \theta\mathbf{D}$.

Now let us go through some exercises to consolidate our understanding.

Question Given $\mathbf{X} = \begin{pmatrix} 1 & 1 \\ 1 & 2 \end{pmatrix}$, $\mathbf{Y} = \begin{pmatrix} 1 & 0 \\ 1 & 2 \end{pmatrix}$ and $\mathbf{Z} = \begin{pmatrix} -1 & -2 \\ 3 & 1 \end{pmatrix}$, obtain the following:

(1) $\mathbf{X} + \mathbf{Y}$, (2) $\mathbf{X} + \mathbf{Z}'$, (3) $2\mathbf{X} + \mathbf{Y}$, (4) $3(\mathbf{X} + \mathbf{Y}) - 2\mathbf{Z}$.

Solution

(1)

$$\mathbf{X} + \mathbf{Y} = \begin{pmatrix} 1 & 1 \\ 1 & 2 \end{pmatrix} + \begin{pmatrix} 1 & 0 \\ 1 & 2 \end{pmatrix}$$

$$= \begin{pmatrix} 1+1 & 1+0 \\ 1+1 & 2+2 \end{pmatrix}$$

$$= \begin{pmatrix} 2 & 1 \\ 2 & 4 \end{pmatrix}.$$

(2)

$$\mathbf{X} + \mathbf{Z}' = \begin{pmatrix} 1 & 1 \\ 1 & 2 \end{pmatrix} + \begin{pmatrix} -1 & 3 \\ -2 & 1 \end{pmatrix}$$

$$= \begin{pmatrix} 1-1 & 1+3 \\ 1-2 & 2+1 \end{pmatrix}$$

$$= \begin{pmatrix} 0 & 4 \\ -1 & 3 \end{pmatrix}.$$

(3)

$$2\mathbf{X} + \mathbf{Y} = 2\begin{pmatrix} 1 & 1 \\ 1 & 2 \end{pmatrix} + \begin{pmatrix} 1 & 0 \\ 1 & 2 \end{pmatrix}$$

$$= \begin{pmatrix} 2 & 2 \\ 2 & 4 \end{pmatrix} + \begin{pmatrix} 1 & 0 \\ 1 & 2 \end{pmatrix}$$

$$= \begin{pmatrix} 2+1 & 2+0 \\ 2+1 & 4+2 \end{pmatrix}$$

$$= \begin{pmatrix} 3 & 2 \\ 3 & 6 \end{pmatrix}.$$

(4)

$$3(\mathbf{X} + \mathbf{Y}) - 2\mathbf{Z} = 3\left(\begin{pmatrix} 1 & 1 \\ 1 & 2 \end{pmatrix} + \begin{pmatrix} 1 & 0 \\ 1 & 2 \end{pmatrix} \right) - 2\begin{pmatrix} -1 & -2 \\ 3 & 1 \end{pmatrix}$$

$$= 3\begin{pmatrix} 2 & 1 \\ 2 & 4 \end{pmatrix} - \begin{pmatrix} -2 & -4 \\ 6 & 2 \end{pmatrix}$$

$$= \begin{pmatrix} 6 & 3 \\ 6 & 12 \end{pmatrix} - \begin{pmatrix} -2 & -4 \\ 6 & 2 \end{pmatrix}$$

$$= \begin{pmatrix} 6-(-2) & 3-(-4) \\ 6-6 & 12-2 \end{pmatrix}$$

$$= \begin{pmatrix} 8 & 7 \\ 0 & 10 \end{pmatrix}.$$

(4) Alternatively,

$$3(\mathbf{X} + \mathbf{Y}) - 2\mathbf{Z} = 3 \begin{pmatrix} 1 & 1 \\ 1 & 2 \end{pmatrix} + 3 \begin{pmatrix} 1 & 0 \\ 1 & 2 \end{pmatrix} - 2 \begin{pmatrix} -1 & -2 \\ 3 & 1 \end{pmatrix}$$

$$= \begin{pmatrix} 3 & 3 \\ 3 & 6 \end{pmatrix} + \begin{pmatrix} 3 & 0 \\ 3 & 6 \end{pmatrix} - \begin{pmatrix} -2 & 4 \\ 6 & 2 \end{pmatrix}$$

$$= \begin{pmatrix} 3+3-(-2) & 3+0-(-4) \\ 3+3-6 & 6+6-2 \end{pmatrix}$$

$$= \begin{pmatrix} 8 & 7 \\ 0 & 10 \end{pmatrix}.$$

Exercise A.1 Basic matrix operations.

A.1.4   Matrix multiplication

Let us think about four shops that deal with three goods, pencils, erasers and notebooks. The price information for these goods in each of the shops is given in Table A.1.

If you buy 3 pencils, an eraser and 4 notebooks in Shop A, your expenditure will be: $1 \cdot 3 + (0.5) \cdot 1 + 2 \cdot 4 = 11.5$ (dollars). Using matrices (vectors), this calculation is expressed as follows:

$$(1 \quad 0.5 \quad 2) \begin{pmatrix} 3 \\ 1 \\ 4 \end{pmatrix}, \tag{A.14}$$

so

$$(1 \quad 0.5 \quad 2) \begin{pmatrix} 3 \\ 1 \\ 4 \end{pmatrix} = 1 \cdot 3 + (0.5) \cdot 1 + 2 \cdot 4 = 11.5. \tag{A.15}$$

By the same token, your expenditure if you buy 3 pens, an eraser and 4 notebooks in Shops B, C and D can be expressed, respectively, as:

$$(1.2 \quad 0.5 \quad 1.8) \begin{pmatrix} 3 \\ 1 \\ 4 \end{pmatrix} = (1.2) \cdot 3 + (0.5) \cdot 1 + (1.8) \cdot 4 = 11.3, \tag{A.16}$$

$$(0.8 \quad 0.5 \quad 2.5) \begin{pmatrix} 3 \\ 1 \\ 4 \end{pmatrix} = (0.8) \cdot 3 + (0.5) \cdot 1 + (2.5) \cdot 4 = 12.9, \tag{A.17}$$

Table A.1. The price information on three goods.

Shop	Pencil	Eraser	Notebook
A	1	0.5	2
B	1.2	0.5	1.8
C	0.8	0.5	2.5
D	1.5	0.5	1.5

and

$$\begin{pmatrix} 1.5 & 0.5 & 1.5 \end{pmatrix} \begin{pmatrix} 3 \\ 1 \\ 4 \end{pmatrix} = (1.5) \cdot 3 + (0.5) \cdot 1 + (1.5) \cdot 4 = 11. \tag{A.18}$$

The product of two vectors of the same order is called their **inner product**. In the above examples, the order of the vectors is three, but we can generalise the idea to the inner product of two n-dimensional vectors. For $\mathbf{p}' = \begin{pmatrix} p_1 & \cdots & p_n \end{pmatrix}$ and $\mathbf{q} = \begin{pmatrix} q_1 \\ \vdots \\ q_n \end{pmatrix}$, the inner product $\mathbf{p}'\mathbf{q}$ is:

$$\begin{pmatrix} p_1 & \cdots & p_n \end{pmatrix} \begin{pmatrix} q_1 \\ \vdots \\ q_n \end{pmatrix} = p_1 q_1 + \cdots + p_n q_n = \sum_{i=1}^{n} p_i q_i. \tag{A.19}$$

Putting Equations (A.15), (A.16), (A.17) and (A.18) together, we can summarise the expenditure information as follows:

$$\begin{pmatrix} 1 & 0.5 & 2 \\ 1.2 & 0.5 & 1.8 \\ 0.8 & 0.5 & 2.5 \\ 1.5 & 0.5 & 1.5 \end{pmatrix} \begin{pmatrix} 3 \\ 1 \\ 4 \end{pmatrix} = \begin{pmatrix} 11.5 \\ 11.3 \\ 12.9 \\ 11 \end{pmatrix}, \tag{A.20}$$

or

$$\mathbf{P}\mathbf{q}_1 = \mathbf{x}_1, \tag{A.21}$$

where $\mathbf{P} = \begin{pmatrix} 1 & 0.5 & 2 \\ 1.2 & 0.5 & 1.8 \\ 0.8 & 0.5 & 2.5 \\ 1.5 & 0.5 & 1.5 \end{pmatrix}$, $\mathbf{q}_1 = \begin{pmatrix} 3 \\ 1 \\ 4 \end{pmatrix}$ and $\mathbf{x}_1 = \begin{pmatrix} 11.5 \\ 11.3 \\ 12.9 \\ 11 \end{pmatrix}$.

Now suppose that another person buys 5 pencils, 2 erasers and 10 notebooks from these shops. Let us denote these quantities by $\mathbf{q}_2 = \begin{pmatrix} 5 \\ 2 \\ 10 \end{pmatrix}$. Then this person's expenditure information can be represented by:

$$\begin{pmatrix} 1 & 0.5 & 2 \\ 1.2 & 0.5 & 1.8 \\ 0.8 & 0.5 & 2.5 \\ 1.5 & 0.5 & 1.5 \end{pmatrix} \begin{pmatrix} 5 \\ 2 \\ 10 \end{pmatrix} = \begin{pmatrix} 26 \\ 25 \\ 30 \\ 23.5 \end{pmatrix}, \tag{A.22}$$

or

$$\mathbf{Pq_2} = \mathbf{x_2}. \tag{A.23}$$

Putting Equations (A.20) and (A.22) together, the expenditure information for you and another person can be summarised as follows:

$$\begin{pmatrix} 1 & 0.5 & 2 \\ 1.2 & 0.5 & 1.8 \\ 0.8 & 0.5 & 2.5 \\ 1.5 & 0.5 & 1.5 \end{pmatrix} \begin{pmatrix} 3 & 5 \\ 1 & 2 \\ 4 & 10 \end{pmatrix} = \begin{pmatrix} 11.5 & 26 \\ 11.3 & 25 \\ 12.9 & 30 \\ 11 & 23.5 \end{pmatrix}, \tag{A.24}$$

or

$$\mathbf{PQ} = \mathbf{X}, \tag{A.25}$$

where $\mathbf{Q} = \begin{pmatrix} 3 & 5 \\ 1 & 2 \\ 4 & 10 \end{pmatrix} = (\mathbf{q_1} \quad \mathbf{q_2})$ and $\mathbf{X} = \begin{pmatrix} 11.5 & 26 \\ 11.3 & 25 \\ 12.9 & 30 \\ 11 & 23.5 \end{pmatrix} = (\mathbf{x_1} \quad \mathbf{x_2})$. Check that the

information on quantity and expenditure for you is given in the first column of $\mathbf{Q}$ and $\mathbf{X}$, respectively, and the same is done for the other person in the second column.

Now we have obtained the product $\mathbf{PQ}$ of the two matrices $\mathbf{P}$ and $\mathbf{Q}$, which is $\mathbf{X}$. Notice that x_{ij} of $\mathbf{X}$ is the inner product of Row i of $\mathbf{P}$ and Column j of $\mathbf{Q}$. For example, to calculate x_{21} (your expenditure when you use Shop B), the relevant row of $\mathbf{P}$ is 2 and the relevant column of $\mathbf{Q}$ is 1, as shown below:

$$\begin{pmatrix} 1 & 0.5 & 2 \\ \mathbf{1.2} & \mathbf{0.5} & \mathbf{1.8} \\ 0.8 & 0.5 & 2.5 \\ 1.5 & 0.5 & 1.5 \end{pmatrix} \begin{pmatrix} \mathbf{3} & 5 \\ \mathbf{1} & 2 \\ \mathbf{4} & 10 \end{pmatrix} = \begin{pmatrix} 11.5 & 26 \\ \mathbf{11.3} & 25 \\ 12.9 & 30 \\ 11 & 23.5 \end{pmatrix}, \tag{A.26}$$

and to calculate x_{32} (the other person's expenditure when Shop C is used), the relevant row of $\mathbf{P}$ is 3 and the relevant column of $\mathbf{Q}$ is 2 as shown below:

$$\begin{pmatrix} 1 & 0.5 & 2 \\ 1.2 & 0.5 & 1.8 \\ \mathbf{0.8} & \mathbf{0.5} & \mathbf{2.5} \\ 1.5 & 0.5 & 1.5 \end{pmatrix} \begin{pmatrix} 3 & \mathbf{5} \\ 1 & \mathbf{2} \\ 4 & \mathbf{10} \end{pmatrix} = \begin{pmatrix} 11.5 & 26 \\ 11.3 & 25 \\ 12.9 & \mathbf{30} \\ 11 & 23.5 \end{pmatrix}. \tag{A.27}$$

You should make sure that you can calculate all the other entries of $\mathbf{X}$ as above. Because of the way each of the entries is calculated, the product of the two matrices $\mathbf{PQ}$ can be defined if and only if the number of *columns* of $\mathbf{P}$ is the same as the number of *rows* of $\mathbf{Q}$. We say that $\mathbf{P}$ and $\mathbf{Q}$ are **conformable**. In our example, we have a 4×3 matrix $\mathbf{P}$ and a

3×2 matrix $\mathbf{Q}$. Therefore, $\mathbf{PQ}$ is defined. Notice that the 3 in our example is the number of the goods. It just means that, to define the total expenditure on goods properly, we need to have equal number of prices and quantities. For example, if you only have the price for a pencil, then you won't be able to calculate the expenditure when you buy pencils, erasers and notebooks.

Note also that the size of the product $\mathbf{PQ}$ is 4×2. The number of rows is the same as $\mathbf{P}$ and the number of columns is same as $\mathbf{Q}$. In general, the product of the two matrices $\mathbf{PQ}$, for an $\mathbf{m} \times n$ matrix $\mathbf{P}$ and an $n \times \mathbf{p}$ matrix $\mathbf{Q}$, is an $m \times p$ matrix.

Let us do some exercises.

Question   Given $\mathbf{X} = \begin{pmatrix} 1 & 1 \\ 1 & 2 \end{pmatrix}$, $\mathbf{Y} = \begin{pmatrix} 1 & 0 \\ 1 & 2 \end{pmatrix}$ and $\mathbf{Z} = \begin{pmatrix} -1 & -2 \\ 3 & 1 \end{pmatrix}$, obtain the following:

(1) $\mathbf{XY}$, (2) $\mathbf{YX}$, (3) $\mathbf{YZ}$, (4) $\mathbf{ZY}$.

Solution

(1)

$$\mathbf{XY} = \begin{pmatrix} 1 & 1 \\ 1 & 2 \end{pmatrix} \begin{pmatrix} 1 & 0 \\ 1 & 2 \end{pmatrix}$$
$$= \begin{pmatrix} 1+1 & 0+2 \\ 1+2 & 0+4 \end{pmatrix}$$
$$= \begin{pmatrix} 2 & 2 \\ 3 & 4 \end{pmatrix}.$$

(2)

$$\mathbf{YX} = \begin{pmatrix} 1 & 0 \\ 1 & 2 \end{pmatrix} \begin{pmatrix} 1 & 1 \\ 1 & 2 \end{pmatrix}$$
$$= \begin{pmatrix} 1+0 & 1+0 \\ 1+2 & 1+4 \end{pmatrix}$$
$$= \begin{pmatrix} 1 & 1 \\ 3 & 5 \end{pmatrix}.$$

(3)

$$\mathbf{YZ} = \begin{pmatrix} 1 & 0 \\ 1 & 2 \end{pmatrix} \begin{pmatrix} -1 & -2 \\ 3 & 1 \end{pmatrix}$$
$$= \begin{pmatrix} -1+0 & -2+0 \\ -1+6 & -2+2 \end{pmatrix}$$
$$= \begin{pmatrix} -1 & -2 \\ 5 & 0 \end{pmatrix}.$$

(4)

$$ZY = \begin{pmatrix} -1 & -2 \\ 3 & 1 \end{pmatrix} \begin{pmatrix} 1 & 0 \\ 1 & 2 \end{pmatrix}$$

$$= \begin{pmatrix} -1-2 & 0-4 \\ 3+1 & 0+2 \end{pmatrix}$$

$$= \begin{pmatrix} -3 & -4 \\ 4 & 2 \end{pmatrix}.$$

Exercise A.2   Matrix multiplication.

As you can see in the above exercises, $XY \neq YX$ and $YZ \neq ZY$. There is *no* communicative property in matrix multiplication in general. Therefore when we talk about the product of two matrices X and Y, it can mean two different things, XY and YX. To avoid this ambiguity, to indicate XY we say that Y is **pre-multiplied** by X. Alternatively we can say that X is **post-multiplied** by Y.

Although the communicative property does not hold in matrix multiplication, associative and distributive properties do just as in multiplication of numbers. That is, provided all operations are defined, we have:

$$(XY)Z = X(YZ),$$

and

$$X(Y \pm Z) = XY \pm XZ$$
$$(X \pm Y)Z = XZ \pm YZ.$$

We have just seen the order of matrix multiplication matters, but for some square matrices, it doesn't. The following cases are worth mentioning. Firstly, when a square matrix X is multiplied twice, obviously we have $XX = XX$! The product of two Xs is denoted by X^2 and we say that X is raised to the power of 2. Secondly, when a square matrix X is pre-multiplied (or post-multiplied) by an identity matrix of the same order, we have $XI = IX = X$. As mentioned before, the identity matrix hence plays a role like 'one' in (ordinary) algebra. Thirdly, when a square matrix X is pre-multiplied (or post-multiplied) by a zero matrix of the same order, we have $XO = OX = O$. It is just like a 'zero' in (ordinary) algebra. Regardless of whether X is pre-multiplied or post-multiplied by O, the product is a zero matrix.

A.2   An inverse of a matrix and the determinant: solving a system of equations

From here onwards, we focus only on square matrices because we deal with them most in studying economics or econometrics. In particular, our primary focus will be 2×2 matrices.

A.2 An inverse of a matrix and the determinant

A.2.1   An inverse matrix

In (ordinary) algebra, a reciprocal of a number x, for $x \neq 0$, is defined as $\dfrac{1}{x}$, so the product of the number and its reciprocal is unity. An **inverse** of a matrix plays a similar role in matrix algebra. That is, an inverse matrix of a square matrix $\mathbf{X}$ of order n is, where defined, the square matrix $\mathbf{X}^{-1}$ such that $\mathbf{X}\mathbf{X}^{-1} = \mathbf{X}^{-1}\mathbf{X} = \mathbf{I}_n$.

Let us try to obtain an inverse matrix of $\mathbf{X} = \begin{pmatrix} x_{11} & x_{12} \\ x_{21} & x_{22} \end{pmatrix}$. Suppose that the inverse matrix exists and denote it by $\mathbf{A} = \begin{pmatrix} a_{11} & a_{12} \\ a_{21} & a_{22} \end{pmatrix}$. Then, by definition, we have $\mathbf{X}\mathbf{A} = \mathbf{I}_2$, or equivalently:

$$\begin{pmatrix} x_{11} & x_{12} \\ x_{21} & x_{22} \end{pmatrix} \begin{pmatrix} a_{11} & a_{12} \\ a_{21} & a_{22} \end{pmatrix} = \begin{pmatrix} 1 & 0 \\ 0 & 1 \end{pmatrix}.$$

It follows that:

$$\begin{cases} x_{11}a_{11} + x_{12}a_{21} = 1, & \text{(A.28)} \\ x_{11}a_{12} + x_{12}a_{22} = 0, & \text{(A.29)} \\ x_{21}a_{11} + x_{22}a_{21} = 0, & \text{(A.30)} \\ x_{21}a_{12} + x_{22}a_{22} = 1. & \text{(A.31)} \end{cases}$$

Using Equations (A.28) and (A.30), we can eliminate a_{21} to obtain the following:

$$(x_{11}x_{22} - x_{12}x_{21})a_{11} = x_{22}. \tag{A.32}$$

Likewise, using Equations (A.28)–(A.31), we can obtain the following three equations:

$$(x_{11}x_{22} - x_{12}x_{21})a_{12} = -x_{12}, \tag{A.33}$$
$$(x_{11}x_{22} - x_{12}x_{21})a_{21} = -x_{21}, \tag{A.34}$$
$$(x_{11}x_{22} - x_{12}x_{21})a_{22} = x_{11}. \tag{A.35}$$

So, when $(x_{11}x_{22} - x_{12}x_{21}) \neq 0$;

$$a_{11} = \frac{x_{22}}{x_{11}x_{22} - x_{12}x_{21}},$$
$$a_{12} = -\frac{x_{12}}{x_{11}x_{22} - x_{12}x_{21}},$$
$$a_{21} = -\frac{x_{21}}{x_{11}x_{22} - x_{12}x_{21}},$$
$$a_{22} = \frac{x_{11}}{x_{11}x_{22} - x_{12}x_{21}}.$$

That is, when $(x_{11}x_{22} - x_{12}x_{21}) \neq 0$ the inverse matrix of $\mathbf{X}$ exists and it is:

$$\mathbf{X}^{-1} = \frac{1}{x_{11}x_{22} - x_{12}x_{21}} \begin{pmatrix} x_{22} & -x_{12} \\ -x_{21} & x_{11} \end{pmatrix}. \tag{A.36}$$

However, when $(x_{11}x_{22} - x_{12}x_{21}) = 0$, Equations (A.32)–(A.35) suggest that $a_{11} = a_{12} = a_{21} = a_{22} = 0$, which contradicts Equations (A.28) and (A.30). Hence the inverse matrix of $\mathbf{X}$ does not exist when $(x_{11}x_{22} - x_{12}x_{21}) = 0$.

Question Obtain the inverse matrix for each of the following matrices: $\mathbf{X} = \begin{pmatrix} 1 & 1 \\ 1 & 2 \end{pmatrix}$, $\mathbf{Y} = \begin{pmatrix} 1 & 0 \\ 1 & 2 \end{pmatrix}$ and $\mathbf{Z} = \begin{pmatrix} -1 & -2 \\ 3 & 1 \end{pmatrix}$.

Solution

(1)

$$\mathbf{X}^{-1} = \frac{1}{1 \cdot 2 - 1 \cdot 1} \begin{pmatrix} 2 & -1 \\ -1 & 1 \end{pmatrix}.$$

$$= \begin{pmatrix} 2 & -1 \\ -1 & 1 \end{pmatrix}.$$

(2)

$$\mathbf{Y}^{-1} = \frac{1}{1 \cdot 2 - 0 \cdot 1} \begin{pmatrix} 2 & 0 \\ -1 & 1 \end{pmatrix}.$$

$$= \begin{pmatrix} 1 & 0 \\ -\frac{1}{2} & \frac{1}{2} \end{pmatrix}.$$

(3)

$$\mathbf{Z}^{-1} = \frac{1}{(-1) \cdot 1 - (-2) \cdot 3} \begin{pmatrix} 1 & 2 \\ -3 & -1 \end{pmatrix}.$$

$$= \begin{pmatrix} \frac{1}{5} & \frac{2}{5} \\ -\frac{3}{5} & -\frac{1}{5} \end{pmatrix}.$$

Exercise A.3 Obtaining the inverse matrix (2×2).

A.2.2 The determinant

The term $x_{11}x_{22} - x_{12}x_{21}$ is called the **determinant** of a 2×2 matrix $\mathbf{X} = \begin{pmatrix} x_{11} & x_{12} \\ x_{21} & x_{22} \end{pmatrix}$.

We denote it by $|\mathbf{X}|$ or $\begin{vmatrix} x_{11} & x_{12} \\ x_{21} & x_{22} \end{vmatrix}$. You might encounter the notation $\det\mathbf{X}$ or $\det\begin{pmatrix} x_{11} & x_{12} \\ x_{21} & x_{22} \end{pmatrix}$ in other books, which respectively mean the same thing. Now we can summarise our finding on the inverse matrix as follows.

Consider a 2×2 matrix $\mathbf{X} = \begin{pmatrix} x_{11} & x_{12} \\ x_{21} & x_{22} \end{pmatrix}$. The inverse matrix $\mathbf{X}^{-1}$ exists if and only if $|\mathbf{X}| \neq 0$ and:

$$\mathbf{X}^{-1} = \frac{1}{|\mathbf{X}|} \begin{pmatrix} x_{22} & -x_{12} \\ -x_{21} & x_{11} \end{pmatrix}. \tag{A.37}$$

When the determinant of a matrix is non-zero – i.e. when the inverse matrix exists – the matrix is called **non-singular**. A matrix is called **singular**, on the other hand, when the determinant is zero (so the inverse matrix is undefined).

In passing, the determinant of a 1×1 matrix – which is a scalar – x is defined as $|x| = x$. That is, it is defined as the matrix (scalar) itself. This definition makes sense because, when $x = 0$, its reciprocal (inverse) $\dfrac{1}{x}$ is undefined and we can't find a unique solution to $ax = b$.

A.2.3 Solving a system of equations

Now we are ready to solve the system of Equations (A.1) we saw in the beginning of this appendix. Let me write the system again:

$$\begin{cases} a_{11}x_1 + a_{12}x_2 = b_1 \\ a_{21}x_1 + a_{22}x_2 = b_2. \end{cases} \tag{A.38}$$

It should be straightforward by now that the above system can be represented by the following:

$$\mathbf{A}\mathbf{x} = \mathbf{b}, \tag{A.39}$$

where $\mathbf{A}$, $\mathbf{x}$ and $\mathbf{b}$ are defined as follows:

$$\mathbf{A} = \begin{pmatrix} a_{11} & a_{12} \\ a_{21} & a_{22} \end{pmatrix}, \quad \mathbf{x} = \begin{pmatrix} x_1 \\ x_2 \end{pmatrix}, \quad \mathbf{b} = \begin{pmatrix} b_1 \\ b_2 \end{pmatrix}.$$

To solve for $\mathbf{x}$ we can *pre*-multiply the both sides of Equation (A.39) by $\mathbf{A}^{-1}$, if it exists. That is, if $\mathbf{A}^{-1}$ exists, then there will be a *unique* solution $\mathbf{x}^*$ to Equation (A.39), which is:

$$\mathbf{x}^* = \mathbf{A}^{-1}\mathbf{b}. \tag{A.40}$$

However, if $\mathbf{A}^{-1}$ does not exist, then it means that (A.39) has either (i) *infinitely many* solutions or (ii) *no* solution. Let us see each of these cases using examples from Section 2.10 in the main text.

Question Solve the following systems of equations.

(1) (Same as Equations (2.18) and (2.19))

$$\begin{cases} y = 2x & \text{(A.41)} \\ 4x - 2y = 0. & \text{(A.42)} \end{cases}$$

(2) (Same as Equations (2.20) and (2.21))

$$\begin{cases} y = 2x + 1 & \text{(A.43)} \\ -2x + y = -4. & \text{(A.44)} \end{cases}$$

(3) (Same as Equations (2.22) and (2.23))

$$\begin{cases} y = -x + 5 & \text{(A.45)} \\ y = 3x - 7. & \text{(A.46)} \end{cases}$$

Solution

(1) The equations can be rearranged as follows:

$$\begin{cases} 2x - y = 0 \\ 4x - 2y = 0. \end{cases}$$

Using matrices they can be represented as:

$$\begin{pmatrix} 2 & -1 \\ 4 & -2 \end{pmatrix} \begin{pmatrix} x \\ y \end{pmatrix} = \begin{pmatrix} 0 \\ 0 \end{pmatrix}.$$

The inverse matrix of $\begin{pmatrix} 2 & -1 \\ 4 & -2 \end{pmatrix}$ does not exist because $\begin{vmatrix} 2 & -1 \\ 4 & -2 \end{vmatrix} = 2 \cdot (-2) - (-1) \cdot 4 = 0$.
The two equations in fact are identical and hence any (x, y) that satisfy one equation will satisfy the other. Therefore, there are infinitely many solutions.

(2) The equations can be rearranged as follows:

$$\begin{cases} 2x - y = -1 \\ 2x - y = 4. \end{cases}$$

Using matrices they can be represented as:

$$\begin{pmatrix} 2 & -1 \\ 2 & -1 \end{pmatrix} \begin{pmatrix} x \\ y \end{pmatrix} = \begin{pmatrix} -1 \\ 4 \end{pmatrix}.$$

The inverse matrix of $\begin{pmatrix} 2 & -1 \\ 2 & -1 \end{pmatrix}$ does not exist because $\begin{vmatrix} 2 & -1 \\ 2 & -1 \end{vmatrix} = 2 \cdot (-1) - (-1) \cdot 2 = 0$.
The two equations are parallel in this case (they have the same slope but have different vertical intercepts) and hence there is no (x, y) that satisfies both equations simultaneously. There is no solution.

(3) The equations can be rearranged as follows:

$$\begin{cases} x + y = 5 \\ 3x - y = 7. \end{cases}$$

Using matrices they can be represented as:

$$\begin{pmatrix} 1 & 1 \\ 3 & -1 \end{pmatrix} \begin{pmatrix} x \\ y \end{pmatrix} = \begin{pmatrix} 5 \\ 7 \end{pmatrix}. \tag{A.47}$$

The inverse matrix of $\begin{pmatrix} 1 & 1 \\ 3 & -1 \end{pmatrix}$ exists because $\begin{vmatrix} 1 & 1 \\ 3 & -1 \end{vmatrix} = 1 \cdot (-1) - 1 \cdot 3 = -4$. The inverse matrix is:

$$\frac{1}{-4} \begin{pmatrix} -1 & -1 \\ -3 & 1 \end{pmatrix} = \frac{1}{4} \begin{pmatrix} 1 & 1 \\ 3 & -1 \end{pmatrix}.$$

So by pre-multiplying this matrix on both sides of Equation (A.47), we get:

$$\begin{pmatrix} x \\ y \end{pmatrix} = \frac{1}{4} \begin{pmatrix} 1 & 1 \\ 3 & -1 \end{pmatrix} \begin{pmatrix} 5 \\ 7 \end{pmatrix}$$

$$= \frac{1}{4} \begin{pmatrix} 1 \cdot 5 + 1 \cdot 7 \\ 3 \cdot 5 + (-1) \cdot 7 \end{pmatrix}$$

$$= \frac{1}{4} \begin{pmatrix} 12 \\ 8 \end{pmatrix}$$

$$= \begin{pmatrix} 3 \\ 2 \end{pmatrix}.$$

Hence the system has a unique solution $(x^*, y^*) = (3, 2)$.

Exercise A.4   Solving simultaneous equations using matrices 1.

To conclude the section, let us try solving another problem taken from Section 2.10.

Question   Solve the following system of simultaneous equations (same as Equations (2.24) and (2.25)):

$$\begin{cases} 2y - 3x = 8 \\ -3y + 2x = -7. \end{cases}$$

Solution

The equations can be rearranged as follows:

$$\begin{cases} -3x + 2y = 8 \\ 2x - 3y = -7. \end{cases}$$

Using matrices they can be represented as:

$$\begin{pmatrix} -3 & 2 \\ 2 & -3 \end{pmatrix} \begin{pmatrix} x \\ y \end{pmatrix} = \begin{pmatrix} 8 \\ -7 \end{pmatrix}. \tag{A.48}$$

The inverse matrix of $\begin{pmatrix} -3 & 2 \\ 2 & -3 \end{pmatrix}$ exists because $\begin{vmatrix} -3 & 2 \\ 2 & -3 \end{vmatrix} = (-3) \cdot (-3) - 2 \cdot 2 = 5$. The inverse matrix is:

$$\frac{1}{5} \begin{pmatrix} -3 & -2 \\ -2 & -3 \end{pmatrix} = -\frac{1}{5} \begin{pmatrix} 3 & 2 \\ 2 & 3 \end{pmatrix}.$$

So by pre-multiplying this matrix on both sides of Equation (A.48), we get:

$$
\begin{pmatrix} x \\ y \end{pmatrix} = -\frac{1}{5} \begin{pmatrix} 3 & 2 \\ 2 & 3 \end{pmatrix} \begin{pmatrix} 8 \\ -7 \end{pmatrix}
$$

$$
= -\frac{1}{5} \begin{pmatrix} 3 \cdot 8 + 2 \cdot (-7) \\ 2 \cdot 8 + 3 \cdot (-7) \end{pmatrix}
$$

$$
= -\frac{1}{5} \begin{pmatrix} 10 \\ -5 \end{pmatrix}
$$

$$
= \begin{pmatrix} -2 \\ 1 \end{pmatrix}.
$$

Hence the system has a unique solution $(x^*, y^*) = (-2, 1)$.

Exercise A.5 Solving simultaneous equations using matrices 2.

A.3 An unconstrained optimisation problem

In Section 6.6, we discussed how to solve an unconstrained optimisation problem. We saw that the first-order conditions for a local maximum/minimum of the bi-variate function $f(x_1, x_2)$ are:

$$
\frac{\partial f(x_1, x_2)}{\partial x_1} = \frac{\partial f(x_1, x_2)}{\partial x_2} = 0. \tag{A.49}
$$

The second-order conditions for a local maximum are:

$$
\frac{\partial^2 f(x_1, x_2)}{\partial x_1^2} < 0, \quad \frac{\partial^2 f(x_1, x_2)}{\partial x_2^2} < 0, \tag{A.50}
$$

and:

$$
\frac{\partial^2 f(x_1, x_2)}{\partial x_1^2} \cdot \frac{\partial^2 f(x_1, x_2)}{\partial x_2^2} > \left[\frac{\partial^2 f(x_1, x_2)}{\partial x_2 \partial x_1} \right]^2. \tag{A.51}
$$

For a local minimum A.50 is replaced with the following two inequalities:

$$
\frac{\partial^2 f(x_1, x_2)}{\partial x_1^2} > 0, \quad \frac{\partial^2 f(x_1, x_2)}{\partial x_2^2} > 0. \tag{A.52}
$$

Equations (A.49), (A.50) and (A.52) made sense intuitively, but the justification for (A.51) was hard to provide. In this section, I will show you where (A.51) has come from. In addition, I will represent these conditions by using matrices because the use of them helps us to intuitively understand the second-order conditions for a local maximum/minimum of functions with more than two variables.

A.3.1 Representing unconstrained optimisation using matrices

Consider finding a local maximum (or a minimum) of $y = f(x_1, x_2)$. Taking the total differential of $y = f(x_1, x_2)$ we get:

$$dy = \frac{\partial f(x_1, x_2)}{\partial x_1} dx_1 + \frac{\partial f(x_1, x_2)}{\partial x_2} dx_2. \tag{A.53}$$

Using matrices (or vectors in this case), we can write Equation (A.53) as:

$$dy = \begin{pmatrix} \frac{\partial f(x_1, x_2)}{\partial x_1} & \frac{\partial f(x_1, x_2)}{\partial x_2} \end{pmatrix} \begin{pmatrix} dx_1 \\ dx_2 \end{pmatrix}. \tag{A.54}$$

For a local maximum (or a minimum), we need to have $dy = 0$ for any vector $\begin{pmatrix} dx_1 \\ dx_2 \end{pmatrix}$, so it is necessary that:

$$\begin{pmatrix} \frac{\partial f(x_1, x_2)}{\partial x_1} & \frac{\partial f(x_1, x_2)}{\partial x_2} \end{pmatrix} = \begin{pmatrix} 0 & 0 \end{pmatrix}. \tag{A.55}$$

Hence the first-order condition for a local maximum/minimum is represented by (A.55), which is essentially the same as (A.49). Now, let us think about the second-order conditions for a local *maximum*. The second-order conditions for a local maximum given by (A.50) say that $f(x_1, x_2)$ must be strictly concave at the local maximum with respect to each of x_1 and x_2. That is, they require that the point in question be the local maximum in each of the directions x_1 and x_2. However, we should really consider all the directions to which (x_1, x_2) can move other than these two directions. For example, we can consider moving a bit towards both the directions x_1 and x_2 from the point in question. If $f(x_1, x_2)$ is not strictly concave (say it is strictly convex) *in that direction*, even when it is strictly concave in each of the directions x_1 and x_2, the point in question cannot not be a local maximum because moving a little bit to that direction will increase the value of $f(x_1, x_2)$. If we make sure that the function is strictly concave in all the directions, i.e. 360 degrees in this case, then we can say the point in question is a local maximum. This argument explains why we need (A.51) in addition to (A.50).

The same argument applies to the second-order conditions for a local *minimum*. The second-order conditions for a local minimum given by (A.52) say that $f(x_1, x_2)$ must be strictly convex at the local minimum with respect to each of x_1 and x_2. However, as discussed for a local maximum, we ought to make sure that the function is strictly convex in all the directions. Otherwise we cannot guarantee that the point in question is a local maximum.

To think about the curvature of $f(x_1, x_2)$, we take the total differential of Equation (A.53). It is called the **second-order total differential**, which is denoted by $d^2 y$, because we totally differentiate the total differential dy. The total differential dy we have discussed in the main text (and just before in Equation (A.53)) is therefore sometimes called the **first-order total differential**. Bearing in mind that the two partial derivatives are functions of both x_1 and x_2, let us totally differentiate Equation (A.53) to get the second-order total differential of $y = f(x_1, x_2)$:

$$d(dy) \equiv d^2 y = f_{11} dx_1^2 + f_{21} dx_2 dx_1 + f_{12} dx_1 dx_2 + f_{22} dx_2^2. \tag{A.56}$$

We can use the second-order total differential to assess the curvature of $f(x_1, x_2)$ in the same way that we use the second derivative $f''(x)$ to judge the curvature of a univariate function $f(x)$. Recall that $f(x)$ is strictly concave if and only if $f''(x) < 0$. It turns out that a bi-variate function $f(x_1, x_2)$ is strictly concave if and only if the second-order total differential is negative for all $(dx_1, dx_2) \neq (0, 0)$. On the other hand, a bi-variate function $f(x_1, x_2)$ is strictly convex if and only if the second-order total differential is positive for all $(dx_1, dx_2) \neq (0, 0)$. They are important results so let us highlight them as follows:

- $y = f(x_1, x_2)$ is strictly concave $\Leftrightarrow d^2y < 0 \forall (dx_1, dx_2) \neq (0, 0)$; and
- $y = f(x_1, x_2)$ is strictly convex $\Leftrightarrow d^2y > 0 \forall (dx_1, dx_2) \neq (0, 0)$.

Now, using matrices we can write Equation (A.56) as:

$$d^2y = \begin{pmatrix} dx_1 & dx_2 \end{pmatrix} \begin{pmatrix} f_{11} & f_{12} \\ f_{21} & f_{22} \end{pmatrix} \begin{pmatrix} dx_1 \\ dx_2 \end{pmatrix},$$ (A.57)

or:

$$d^2y = \mathbf{x'Hx},$$ (A.58)

where $\mathbf{x} = \begin{pmatrix} dx_1 \\ dx_2 \end{pmatrix}$ and $\mathbf{H} = \begin{pmatrix} f_{11} & f_{12} \\ f_{21} & f_{22} \end{pmatrix}$.

$\mathbf{H}$'s entry for row i and column j, for $i, j = 1, 2$, is f_{ij}, which is obtained by partially differentiating $f(x_1, x_2)$ with respect to x_i, then x_j. Such a matrix is called the **Hessian matrix** of $f(x_1, x_2)$. Note also that, by Young's Theorem, $f_{21} = f_{12}$, so $\mathbf{H}$ is a symmetric matrix and Equation (A.56) can be written as:

$$d^2y = f_{11}dx_1^2 + 2f_{12}dx_1dx_2 + f_{22}dx_2^2,$$ (A.59)

or:

$$d^2y = \mathbf{x'Fx},$$ (A.60)

where $\mathbf{F} = \begin{pmatrix} f_{11} & f_{12} \\ f_{12} & f_{22} \end{pmatrix}$.

A.3.2　The second-order condition for a local maximum/minimum

By rearranging Equation (A.59), let us investigate the necessary and sufficient condition for $d^2y < 0$. We begin with completing the square on the RHS of Equation (A.60):

$$\begin{aligned} d^2y &= f_{11}dx_1^2 + 2f_{12}dx_1dx_2 + f_{22}dx_2^2 \\ &= f_{11}\left(dx_1 + \frac{f_{12}}{f_{11}}dx_2\right)^2 - \frac{f_{12}^2}{f_{11}}dx_2^2 + f_{22}dx_2^2 \\ &= f_{11}\left(dx_1 + \frac{f_{12}}{f_{11}}dx_2\right)^2 + \frac{1}{f_{11}}\left(f_{11}f_{22} - f_{12}^2\right)dx_2^2. \end{aligned}$$

Both $\left(dx_1 + \dfrac{f_{12}}{f_{11}} dx_2\right)^2$ and dx_2^2 are non-negative (and at least one of them is positive for $(dx_1, dx_2) \neq (0, 0)$), so it is easy to see that it is *sufficient* to have both $f_{11} < 0$ and $f_{11} f_{22} - f_{12}^2 > 0$ for $d^2 y < 0$. That is:

$$f_{11} < 0 \text{ and } f_{11} f_{22} - f_{12}^2 > 0 \Rightarrow d^2 y < 0. \tag{A.61}$$

But is it *necessary* to have both $f_{11} < 0$ and $f_{11} f_{22} - f_{12}^2 > 0$? Indeed it is. Suppose that when $d^2 y < 0$ we have $f_{11} \geq 0$. But, for $dx_2 = 0$ and $dx_1 \neq 0$, we have $d^2 y = f_{11} dx_1^2 \geq 0$. It contradicts $d^2 y < 0$, so for $d^2 y < 0$ it is necessary that $f_{11} < 0$. Also suppose that when $d^2 y < 0$ we have $f_{11} f_{22} - f_{12}^2 \geq 0$. But for (dx_1, dx_2) such that $dx_1 + \dfrac{f_{12}}{f_{11}} dx_2 = 0$, we have $d^2 y \geq 0$ (note that we have already verified $f_{11} < 0$ is necessary). It contradicts $d^2 y < 0$, so for $d^2 y < 0$ it is also necessary that $f_{11} f_{22} - f_{12}^2 > 0$. Hence we have the necessary and sufficient condition for $d^2 y < 0$:

$$f_{11} < 0 \text{ and } f_{11} f_{22} - f_{12}^2 > 0 \Leftrightarrow d^2 y < 0. \tag{A.62}$$

Therefore, the second-order conditions for a local maximum are:

$$f_{11} < 0 \text{ and } f_{11} f_{22} - f_{12}^2 > 0. \tag{A.63}$$

You might wonder why $f_{22} < 0$ (the second inequality in (A.50)) does not appear. In fact, it is implied by (A.63). Notice that when $f_{11} < 0$, for $f_{11} f_{22} - f_{12}^2 > 0$ to hold $f_{22} < 0$ is necessary. Listing $f_{22} < 0$ as one of the second-order conditions is therefore redundant (although it is not incorrect to list it). Despite its redundancy, it was listed in Section 6.6 because my intention there was to graphically explain the second-order conditions.

In any event, you should be able to verify that the second-order conditions for a local *minimum* are:

$$f_{11} > 0 \text{ and } f_{11} f_{22} - f_{12}^2 > 0, \tag{A.64}$$

which are consistent with what we saw in Section 6.6. Note that we have $f_{11} f_{22} - f_{12}^2 > 0$ regardless of whether we look for a local maximum or a local minimum.

A.3.3   Quadratic forms and the definiteness of a matrix

Let me now explain the second-order conditions by using matrices. Look at (A.60). The sign of $d^2 y$ depends on the product of the matrices $\mathbf{x}' \mathbf{F} \mathbf{x}$, which is called the **quadratic form**. Given a matrix $\mathbf{F}$ (which depends on the function in question $f(x_1, x_2)$), the value of the quadratic form depends on $\mathbf{x}$. That is, in general, the quadratic form may be positive, negative or a zero, depending on $\mathbf{x}$. However, for the point that satisfies the first-order condition to be a local maximum, we would like the quadratic form to be negative for *any* $\mathbf{x} \neq \mathbf{0}$. For a local minimum, on the other hand, we would like the quadratic form to be positive for any $\mathbf{x} \neq \mathbf{0}$.

When $\mathbf{x}' \mathbf{F} \mathbf{x} < 0$ for any $\mathbf{x} \neq \mathbf{0}$, then we say that the quadratic form is **negative definite** and that $\mathbf{F}$ is a negative definite matrix. On the other hand, when $\mathbf{x}' \mathbf{F} \mathbf{x} > 0$ for any $\mathbf{x} \neq \mathbf{0}$, then we say that the quadratic form is **positive definite** and that $\mathbf{F}$ is a positive definite matrix. Hence, using the terminology in matrix algebra, the second-order condition for a local maximum (minimum) is that: $\mathbf{F}$ evaluated at the point in question be negative (positive, respectively) definite. The only problem then, is how to tell whether $\mathbf{F}$ is positive definite or negative definite. Well, this job has already been done in the previous subsection!

$$\mathbf{F} = \begin{pmatrix} f_{11} & f_{12} \\ f_{12} & f_{22} \end{pmatrix} \text{ is:}$$

- negative definite if and only if $f_{11} < 0$ and $f_{11}f_{22} - f_{12}^2 > 0$; and
- positive definite if and only if $f_{11} > 0$ and $f_{11}f_{22} - f_{12}^2 > 0$.

A.3.4 Principal submatrices and principal minors: Unconstrained optimisation that involves many variables

The job of finding the second-order condition can be done, as demonstrated in Subsection A.3.2, without the use of matrices. Hence you might wonder why I have bothered to represent the same idea using matrices in Subsection A.3.3. In describing the second-order condition for a local maximum/minimum of a bi-variate function $f(x_1, x_2)$, yes, there seems to be no point using matrices. However, when the function has more than two arguments, the second-order conditions become extremely messy. The use of matrices expedites representing the conditions and also helps to interpret them naturally as an extension of the simplest case (which deals with a function of only two variables). It is beyond the scope of this appendix to deal with optimisation problems that require the use of matrices bigger than 2×2, but I hope that the following discussion at least makes you realise how useful matrices are.[1]

Suppose we have an $n \times n$ matrix. Think about deleting certain rows and the *corresponding* columns of that matrix. For example, for a 3×3 matrix $\mathbf{X} = \begin{pmatrix} x_{11} & x_{12} & x_{13} \\ x_{21} & x_{22} & x_{23} \\ x_{31} & x_{32} & x_{33} \end{pmatrix}$, we can delete row 1 and column 1 to get $\begin{pmatrix} x_{22} & x_{23} \\ x_{32} & x_{33} \end{pmatrix}$. Deleting row 2 and column 2, we get $\begin{pmatrix} x_{11} & x_{13} \\ x_{31} & x_{33} \end{pmatrix}$ and $\begin{pmatrix} x_{11} & x_{12} \\ x_{21} & x_{22} \end{pmatrix}$ can be obtained if we delete row 3 and column 3.

We can delete two rows and the corresponding columns. It yields three matrices – in fact, they are scalars – x_{11}, x_{22} and x_{33}. It is trivial, but by deleting zero rows and columns we have the original matrix $\begin{pmatrix} x_{11} & x_{12} & x_{13} \\ x_{21} & x_{22} & x_{23} \\ x_{31} & x_{32} & x_{33} \end{pmatrix}$. So, in the end, this process yields seven matrices that are called the **principal submatrices**. For example, x_{22} is a principal submatrix of order 1 and $\begin{pmatrix} x_{22} & x_{23} \\ x_{32} & x_{33} \end{pmatrix}$ is a principal submatrix of order 2. The determinant

---

[1] If you would like to study this topic further I recommend that you consult more advanced textbooks in quantitative methods in economics, such as C. P. Simon and L. Blume, *Mathematics for Economists* (Norton, 1994).

of these principal submatrices are called **principal minors**. For example, $\begin{vmatrix} x_{22} & x_{23} \\ x_{32} & x_{33} \end{vmatrix}$ is a principal minor of order 2.

Amongst the principal submatrices, important ones are those that are obtained by deleting the *last k* rows and columns of the matrix, where $k = 0, 1, \ldots, n-1$. For example, for the 3×3 matrix $\mathbf{X}$, by deleting the last 0 rows and columns, we obviously have $\mathbf{X}$ itself; by deleting the last one row and the corresponding column, we have $\begin{pmatrix} x_{11} & x_{12} \\ x_{21} & x_{22} \end{pmatrix}$; and by deleting the last two rows and the corresponding columns, we have x_{11}.

Note that x_{11}, $\begin{pmatrix} x_{11} & x_{12} \\ x_{21} & x_{22} \end{pmatrix}$ and $\begin{pmatrix} x_{11} & x_{12} & x_{13} \\ x_{21} & x_{22} & x_{23} \\ x_{31} & x_{32} & x_{33} \end{pmatrix}$ are called **leading principal submatrices**. The determinant of a leading principal submatrix is called the **leading principal minor**.

Now look at the familiar 2×2 matrix $\mathbf{F} = \begin{pmatrix} f_{11} & f_{12} \\ f_{12} & f_{22} \end{pmatrix}$. There are two leading principal minors: $|f_{11}|$ and $\begin{vmatrix} f_{11} & f_{12} \\ f_{12} & f_{22} \end{vmatrix}$. Notice that $|f_{11}| = f_{11}$ and $\begin{vmatrix} f_{11} & f_{12} \\ f_{12} & f_{22} \end{vmatrix} = f_{11}f_{22} - f_{12}^2$, both of which appear in the definition of the definiteness of $\mathbf{F}$. Therefore, denoting the leading principal minors by $\mathbf{F}_1 = |f_{11}|$ and $\mathbf{F}_2 = \begin{vmatrix} f_{11} & f_{12} \\ f_{12} & f_{22} \end{vmatrix}$, we have the following result.

$\mathbf{F} = \begin{pmatrix} f_{11} & f_{12} \\ f_{12} & f_{22} \end{pmatrix}$ is:

- negative definite if and only if $\mathbf{F}_1 < 0$ and $\mathbf{F}_2 > 0$; and
- positive definite if and only if $\mathbf{F}_1 > 0$ and $\mathbf{F}_2 > 0$.

Now think about a function of n variables $f(x_1, x_2, \ldots, x_n)$ so that $\mathbf{F} = \begin{pmatrix} f_{11} & \cdots & f_{1n} \\ \vdots & \ddots & \vdots \\ f_{n1} & \cdots & f_{nn} \end{pmatrix}$. It is natural to extend the definition of positive/negative definiteness to the $n \times n$ symmetric matrix, and indeed it is known that it depends on signs of the leading principal minors. Denoting the leading principle minor by $\mathbf{F}_k = \begin{vmatrix} f_{11} & \cdots & f_{1k} \\ \vdots & \ddots & \vdots \\ f_{k1} & \cdots & f_{kk} \end{vmatrix}$, $k = 1, \ldots, n$, the following is well established.

A symmetric matrix $\mathbf{F} = \begin{pmatrix} f_{11} & \cdots & f_{1n} \\ \vdots & \ddots & \vdots \\ f_{n1} & \cdots & f_{nn} \end{pmatrix}$ is:

- negative definite if and only if $\mathbf{F}_1 < 0$, $\mathbf{F}_2 > 0$, $\mathbf{F}_3 < 0$, $\mathbf{F}_4 > 0$ and so on; and
- positive definite if and only if $\mathbf{F}_1 > 0$, $\mathbf{F}_2 > 0$, $\mathbf{F}_3 > 0$, $\mathbf{F}_4 > 0$ and so on.

In other words, the necessary and sufficient condition for a symmetric matrix $\mathbf{F}$ to be negative definite is that its leading principal minors alternate in sign, starting with negative (i.e. $\mathbf{F}_1 < 0$); and the necessary and sufficient condition for a symmetric matrix $\mathbf{F}$ to be positive definite is that all of its leading principal minors be positive.

It is extremely difficult to *visualise* the curvature of a function of n variables, but we can naturally extend the two-variable case where we used the second-order total differential d^2y to assess the curvature of $f(x_1, x_2)$. For $f(x_1, \ldots, x_n)$ we can define the second-order total differential:

$$d^2y = f_{11}dx_1 + f_{12}dx_2 + \cdots + f_{1n}dx_n + \cdots + f_{n1}dx_1 + f_{n2}dx_2 + \cdots + f_{nn}dx_n,$$
(A.65)

or:

$$d^2y = \mathbf{x}'\mathbf{F}\mathbf{x},$$
(A.66)

where $\mathbf{x}' = \begin{pmatrix} dx_1 & dx_2 & \cdots & dx_n \end{pmatrix}$.

Just as in the two-variable case, we can focus on the sign of the second-order total derivative to assess the curvature of $f(x_1, \ldots, x_n)$:

- $f(x_1, \ldots, x_n)$ is strictly concave $\Leftrightarrow d^2y < 0 \forall \mathbf{x}' \neq \mathbf{0}'$; and
- $f(x_1, \ldots, x_n)$ is strictly convex $\Leftrightarrow d^2y > 0 \forall \mathbf{x}' \neq \mathbf{0}'$.

From Equation (A.66) $d^2y < 0 \forall \mathbf{x}' \neq \mathbf{0}'$ clearly implies (and is implied by) the negative definiteness of $\mathbf{F}$, and $d^2y > 0 \forall \mathbf{x}' \neq \mathbf{0}'$ implies (and is implied by) the positive definiteness of $\mathbf{F}$. Hence, we now know that the necessary and sufficient condition for $f(x_1, \ldots, x_n)$ to be strictly concave (convex) is that $\mathbf{F}$ be negative (positive) definite.

When we wish to find a local maximum/minimum of $f(x_1, \ldots, x_n)$, for a point that satisfies the first-order condition to be a local maximum/minimum, we need to check the curvature of the function in the neighbourhood of that point. Just as in the two-variable case, we require the function to be strictly concave (convex) in the neighbourhood of the point for it to be a local maximum (or minimum, respectively). We also know that the curvature of the function is summarised by the definiteness of the Hessian matrix $\mathbf{F}$. That is, $f(x_1, \ldots, x_n)$ is strictly concave (convex) if and only if $\mathbf{F}$ is negative (positive, respectively) definite. Hence the second-order condition for the unconstrained optimisation problem involving n variables can be succinctly summarised as follows.

Consider $f(x_1, x_2, \ldots, x_n)$ and a point that satisfies the first-order condition for a local maximum/minimum. The point is:

- a local maximum if and only if $\mathbf{F}$ evaluated at that point is negative definite; and
- a local minimum if and only if $\mathbf{F}$ evaluated at that point is positive definite.

Of course, obtaining the leading principle minors of order n, where $n > 2$, by hand can be a tedious task, which involves calculating the determinant of order $n > 2$ (but there are ways to do it). It is left for interested readers to investigate in other textbooks in quantitative methods.[2]

To close this appendix, let us do the following exercise. It is the same as Exercise 6.6, but try answering the question using matrices.

Question (The profit maximisation problem with two inputs)   Consider a profit maximising competitive firm that produces a certain good denoted by q. The production function is given as

$$q = f(K, L) = K^{\frac{1}{3}} L^{\frac{1}{3}},$$

where K and L denote robots and labour, respectively. Suppose that the price of a robot is $r = 2$ and that labour costs $w = 1$ per unit. Denoting the good's price by p, solve the profit maximisation problem to obtain the amounts of the inputs that the firm hires.

Solution

$$\underset{K,L}{Max}\, \pi(K, L) = \underset{K,L}{Max}\, [pf(K, L) - 2K - L].$$

The first-order condition is:

$$\left(\frac{\partial \pi(K,L)}{\partial K} \quad \frac{\partial \pi(K,L)}{\partial L} \right) = \left(0 \quad 0 \right).$$

Or equivalently,

$$p\frac{\partial f(K, L)}{\partial K} = 2,$$

$$p\frac{\partial f(K, L)}{\partial L} = 1.$$

These equations imply the following:

$$\frac{1}{3}pK^{-\frac{2}{3}}L^{\frac{1}{3}} = 2,$$

$$\frac{1}{3}pK^{\frac{1}{3}}L^{-\frac{2}{3}} = 1.$$

Solving the above for K and L, the input combination that satisfies the first-order conditions is

$$(K^*, L^*) = \left(\frac{p^3}{108}, \frac{p^3}{54} \right).$$

To check this combination is the true local (and global) maximum, we check the second-order condition. That is, we need to verify that the Hessian matrix of $\pi(K, L)$ is negative definite, i.e. we want to check $|\pi_1| < 0$ and $\begin{vmatrix} \pi_{11} & \pi_{12} \\ \pi_{21} & \pi_{22} \end{vmatrix} > 0.$

. . . .

2 *Ibid.*

Or equivalently,

$$\frac{\partial^2 \pi}{\partial K^2} < 0; \text{ and}$$

$$\frac{\partial^2 \pi}{\partial K^2} \cdot \frac{\partial^2 \pi}{\partial L^2} - \left[\frac{\partial^2 \pi}{\partial L \partial K} \right]^2 > 0.$$

Calculating the LHS of them, we have:

$$\frac{\partial^2 \pi}{\partial K^2} = -\frac{2}{9} p K^{-\frac{5}{3}} L^{\frac{1}{3}},$$

$$\frac{\partial^2 \pi}{\partial K^2} \cdot \frac{\partial^2 \pi}{\partial L^2} - \left[\frac{\partial^2 \pi}{\partial L \partial K} \right]^2 = \frac{1}{9} p K^{-\frac{2}{3}} L^{-\frac{2}{3}}.$$

Therefore, given $p > 0$, the the Hessian matrix of $\pi(K, L)$ is negative definite for all $K > 0$ and $L > 0$ (and so of course they are satisfied at the point in question). So $(K^*, L^*) = \left(\frac{p^3}{108}, \frac{p^3}{54} \right)$ is the local (and global) maximum.

Exercise A.6   The profit maximisation with two inputs.

Appendix B

An introduction to difference and differential equations

We have dealt with market equilibrium in various sections of the main text. Our focus has been the mathematical representation of market equilibrium for a particular good – the price level and the quantity traded in the market when they are settled – per se. We did give a verbal explanation as to how the price adjusts when there is excess demand (or excess supply) in the market, but we did not pay much attention to the mathematical representation of the price adjustment process. This appendix provides an introduction to difference and differential equations that will allow us to shed light on such dynamics.

We will start by introducing the cobweb model of price adjustment, which describes the dynamics of the price adjustment. In our example, it turns out the price adjustment can be represented by a linear first-order autonomous difference equation in terms of the price. We will study how to solve this type of difference equation in general. In turn, the linear first-order autonomous differential equation – a continuous-time version of the same form of difference equation – will be introduced and examined in the context of the demand and supply analysis.

B.1 The cobweb model of price adjustment

One of the implicit assumptions in the demand and supply analysis is that sellers make their supply decisions after they know the price of the good. But in reality, in most markets sellers tend to be in the situation where they must commit to a supply decision *before* they know the price of the good in question. What are the implications of this lag on the dynamics of the market price over time?

To think about this matter, let us start by specifying the demand function:

$$q_t^D = 100 - 10p_t, \tag{B.1}$$

where q_t^D is the quantity of the good demanded in Period t and p_t is the market price that prevails in Period t. It is important to notice that there is a subscript t on each variable, indicating that it is time-dependent. For example, q_1^D is the quantity demanded in Period 1, and p_2 is the price that prevails in the market in Period 2. In reality, time is **continuous** but here we assume that it evolves **discretely**. Under this framework, the market clears once per fixed period of time.

In any case, solving (B.1) for p_t the inverse demand function can be written as follows:

$$p_t = 10 - \frac{1}{10}q_t^D. \tag{B.2}$$

Now suppose that the supply decisions are made one period before the goods reach the market. It implies that the supply reaching the market in Period t is decided in Period

Table B.1. The evolutions of p_t and q_t (stable case; $p_0 = 2$).

Period (t)	q_t	p_t
1	35	6.5
2	57.5	4.25
3	46.25	5.375
4	51.875	4.8125
5	49.0625	5.09375
6	50.46875	4.953125
$\vdots$	$\vdots$	$\vdots$
Steady state	$\bar{q} = 50$	$\bar{p} = 5$

$t - 1$ on the basis of what sellers expect the price to be in the next period. To make the story simple, let us assume that sellers expect the next period price to equal the current price. Then we can assume the supply function as follows:

$$q_t^S = 25 + 5p_{t-1}. \tag{B.3}$$

This relationship shows that the quantity supplied in period t, q_t^S, depends on the previous period price p_{t-1} (because sellers believe that the current price will be the same as in the previous period). Accordingly, the inverse supply function is:

$$p_{t-1}^S = -5 + \frac{1}{5}p_t. \tag{B.4}$$

Now, let us suppose that sellers realise that the price in Period 0 is equal to 2, i.e. $p_0 = 2$. What will happen to the quantity supplied in Period 1? We can use Equation (B.3): by setting $t = 1$ and substituting $p_0 = 2$, we can get $q_1^S = 35$.

So in Period 0, the sellers will commit to producing 35 units of the good, which will be supplied to the market in Period 1. Therefore the Period 1 supply is fixed to 35 units at this moment. Accordingly, for the market to clear in Period 1, the quantity demanded must be $q_1^D = 35$ (otherwise, there exists excess demand or excess supply). Equation (B.2) will give us the market clearing level of the price in Period 1: by setting $t = 1$ and substituting $q_1^D = 35$ we can get $p_1 = 6.5$.

Now in Period 1, sellers realise that the price is $p_1 = 6.5$ (not 20 as they expected). When this information is given to sellers, they adjust their expectation and now expect that the price in Period 2 will be $p_2 = 6.5$. Therefore, the quantity supplied in Period 2 will be $q_2^S = 57.5$. Accordingly the market clearing level of price in Period 2 can be obtained by substituting $t = 2$ in Equation (B.2) and substituting $q_2^D = 57.5$: we get $p_2 = 4.25$.

Likewise, the quantity supplied in Period 3 will be determined according to Equation (B.3) (with suppliers expecting $p_3 = 4.25$) as $q_3^S = 46.25$. The market clearing level of price in Period 3 can be obtained by setting $t = 3$ in Equation (B.2) and substituting $q_3^D = 46.25$: we get $p_3 = 5.375$.

We can follow the above procedure forever, but let us summarise the evolution of p_t and q_t over time in Table B.1 (note that $p_0 = 2$).

B.1 The cobweb model of price adjustment

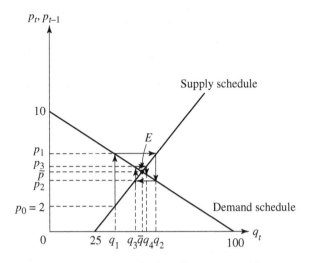

Figure B.1 The cobweb model of price adjustment (stable case; $p_0 = 2$).

The movements in p_t and q_t can also be described by using Figure B.1.

This model is called the **cobweb model** of price adjustment, because the path that (p, q) follows in each period towards Point E looks like a cobweb. Point E is the intersection of the demand and supply schedules in the figure. It shows the **steady state (equilibrium)** of this model because once the price is set at that level, it will rest at that level for all the subsequent periods. In terms of equations, we can obtain the steady state levels of price and quantity by setting $q_t^D = q_t^S = \bar{q}$ and $p_t = p_{t-1} = \bar{p}$ in Equations (B.1) and (B.3), and then solving for $\bar{p}$ and $\bar{q}$ simultaneously. Consequently the steady state values of price and quantity turn out to be $(\bar{p}, \bar{q}) = (5, 50)$.

Given the initial price $p_0 = 2$, in each period, the price that prevails in the market is either above or below $\bar{p}$ and, as time goes on, it *approaches* the steady state price level $\bar{p} = 5$. We say that the cobweb model is **stable** when the price **converges** to its steady state level over time.

Note that if the initial price is different, say $p_0 = 1$, the price will still converge to $\bar{p} = 5$, but the path the price follows will be different to the one we just saw. The table and figure for this path are provided in Table B.2 and Figure B.2, respectively. You can see clearly that the price converges to $\bar{p} = 5$ but the path is different from the one we saw before.

It is also important to understand that not all cobweb models are stable. Suppose instead a different supply function is given as follows:

$$q_t^S = 10 + 20p_{t-1}. \tag{B.5}$$

With the same demand function, for the initial price $p_0 = 2.9$, we can follow the same procedure as before to determine the evolutions of p_t and q_t over time. The evolutions of p_t and q_t are given in Table B.3.

Table B.2. The evolutions of p_t and q_t (stable case; $p_0 = 1$).

Period (t)	q_t	p_t
1	30	7
2	60	4
3	35	6.5
4	57.5	4.25
5	40	6
6	55	4.5
⋮	⋮	⋮
Equilibrium	$\bar{q} = 50$	$\bar{p} = 5$

Table B.3. The evolutions of p_t and q_t (unstable case).

Period (t)	q_t	p_t
1	68	2.9
2	74	3.2
3	62	3.8
4	86	1.4
5	38	6.2
⋮	⋮	⋮
Steady state	$\bar{q} = 70$	$\bar{p} = 3$

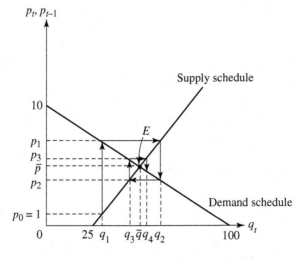

Figure B.2 The cobweb model of price adjustment (stable case; $p_0 = 1$).

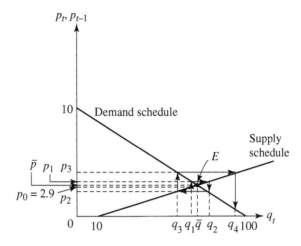

Figure B.3 The cobweb model of price adjustment (unstable case).

The corresponding diagram is provided in Figure B.3.

We can observe that the price is moving further and further away from its steady state level $\bar{p} = 3$ over time. When the price does not converge to its steady state level, we say that the cobweb model is **unstable**.

Is there a way to determine whether a cobweb model is stable or unstable? It turns out that the model's stability depends on the slopes of the demand and supply schedules. More specifically, a cobweb model is stable (unstable) if and only if the absolute value of the slope of the supply schedule is greater (less) than the absolute value of the slope of the demand schedule. The equivalent statement using algebra is given as follows.

The following cobweb model:

$$\begin{cases} q_t^D = A + Bp_t \\ q_t^S = F + Gp_{t-1} \end{cases}$$

- is stable if and only if $|B| > |G|$ $\left(\text{or equivalently } \left|\dfrac{G}{B}\right| < 1\right)$; and

- is unstable if and only if $|B| < |G|$ $\left(\text{or equivalently } \left|\dfrac{G}{B}\right| > 1\right)$.

We will verify this statement in the following two sections where the cobweb model is discussed in the context of the linear first-order autonomous difference and differential equations.

B.2 The linear first-order autonomous difference equation

Let's think about the following cobweb model:

$$
\begin{cases}
q_t^D = A + Bp_t \\
q_t^S = F + Gp_{t-1}.
\end{cases}
\tag{B.6}
$$

In each period, the market must clear so we must have $q_t^D = q_t^S$ for all t. It means that

$$
A + Bp_t = F + Gp_{t-1},
$$

and by rearranging this equation we get

$$
p_t = \frac{G}{B}p_{t-1} + \frac{F - A}{B}.
\tag{B.7}
$$

You can see that the price of the good in Period t, p_t, is expressed as a function of the price of the good in the previous period, p_{t-1}. When the largest difference in time periods for the variable in question – in this case p – is one time period as in Equation (B.7), such an equation is called the **first-order difference equation** in p. Note also that, in Equation (B.7), (a) p_t is linear in p_{t-1}, and (b) terms that contain t do not appear. For these reasons, Equation (B.7) is called the **linear first-order autonomous difference equation**.

Of course, difference equations may take other forms. For example, when the largest difference in time periods for the variable in question is two, then that equation is called the **second-order difference equation**. If p_t is non-linear in p_{t-1} (or p_{t-2}, p_{t-3}, etc.), then it becomes a **non-linear differential equation**. In Equation (B.7), all parameters are constant over time, so time t does not explicitly appear in the equation. If they depend on time (or if there is any term that includes t explicitly), then the equation becomes a **non-autonomous difference equation**. These equations are not our focus in this appendix.[1] For our cobweb model analysis, it suffices to discuss the solution to the linear first-order autonomous difference equation.

B.2.1 Solution to a linear first-order autonomous difference equation

What do we mean by the solution to a difference equation, or to solve a difference equation, such as Equation (B.7)? To think about this matter, let us set $A = 100$, $B = -10$, $F = 25$ and $G = 5$ to match the cobweb model we discussed in the beginning of this appendix:

$$
p_t = -\frac{1}{2}p_{t-1} + \frac{15}{2}.
\tag{B.8}
$$

Substituting $t = 1$ into this equation we get:

$$
p_1 = -\frac{1}{2}p_0 + \frac{15}{2}.
$$

---

1 If you'd like to study differential equations further, you should consult more advanced textbooks on quantitative methods in economics. For example, see Simon and Blume, *Mathematics for Economists*.

B.2 The linear first-order autonomous difference equation

So if we know p_0, then we can calculate the value of p_1 straight away. Indeed if $p_0 = 2$, then $p_1 = 6.5$. You can check that it is consistent with what we have in Table B.1. Now, if we substitute $t = 2$ into Equation (B.8) we get:

$$p_2 = -\frac{1}{2}p_1 + \frac{15}{2}.$$

Hence, likewise, if we know p_1, then we the value of p_2 can be obtained by just substituting the value of p_1 into the above equation. As we have already calculated that $p_1 = 6.5$ (if $p_0 = 2$), we know that $p_2 = 4.25$.

What will be the value of p_{100}? In principle, we can go through this process 100 times to obtain p_{100}. But what happens if you are required to obtain $p_{10\,000}$? It surely takes a long time to obtain it and you may wonder if p_t can be expressed as a function of t (so all you have to do is substitute $t = 10\,000$ into it). It turns out that there exists such a function and it is expressed as follows:

$$p_t = -3\left(-\frac{1}{2}\right)^t + 5. \tag{B.9}$$

In the next subsection, we will learn how to obtain this function, but let me continue discussing this story a little more. What will the path of p_t be if the initial price is given by $p_0 = 1$ – instead of $p_0 = 2$ – in Equation (B.8)? This case corresponds to Table B.2 and we know $p_1 = 7$, $p_2 = 4$ and so on. We can obtain the evolution of p_t for this case step by step like we did above, but is there a function that represents the evolution of the price in terms of t? It turns out that such a function exists and it is:

$$p_t = -4\left(-\frac{1}{2}\right)^t + 5. \tag{B.10}$$

A different initial price gives a different path of p_t, which follows Equation (B.8). For example, Equations (B.9) and (B.10) are two of the different paths of p_t that conform to Equation (B.8). Since we can think about infinitely many p_0, there are infinitely many paths of p_t that conform to Equation (B.8). It turns out that *all* the paths of p_t that conform to Equation (B.8) can be represented by

$$p_t = C\left(-\frac{1}{2}\right)^t + 5, \tag{B.11}$$

where C is a constant. You can see that setting $C = -3$ ($C = -4$) reduces it to Equation (B.9) ((B.10), respectively). It is easy to check that this equation conforms to Equation (B.8).

If p_t is expressed as Equation (B.11), then $p_{t-1} = C\left(-\frac{1}{2}\right)^{t-1} + 5$.

In the meantime, Equation (B.8) can be rearranged as:

$$p_t + \frac{1}{2}p_{t-1} - \frac{15}{2} = 0.$$

The LHS of this equation when $p_t = C\left(-\dfrac{1}{2}\right)^t + 5$ and $p_{t-1} = C\left(-\dfrac{1}{2}\right)^{t-1} + 5$ is:

$$p_t + \frac{1}{2}p_{t-1} - \frac{15}{2} = C\left(-\frac{1}{2}\right)^t + 5 + \frac{1}{2}\left[C\left(-\frac{1}{2}\right)^{t-1} + 5\right] - \frac{15}{2}$$

$$= C\left(-\frac{1}{2}\right)^t + \frac{10}{2} + (-1)\cdot\left(-\frac{1}{2}\right)\cdot C\left(-\frac{1}{2}\right)^{t-1} + \frac{5}{2} - \frac{15}{2}$$

$$= C\left(-\frac{1}{2}\right)^t - C\left(-\frac{1}{2}\right)^t + \frac{10}{2} + \frac{5}{2} - \frac{15}{2}$$

$$= 0.$$

So we have shown that Equation (B.8) always holds when $p_t = C\left(-\dfrac{1}{2}\right)^t + 5$.

We call the equation $p_t = C\left(-\dfrac{1}{2}\right)^t + 5$ the **general solution** to the difference equation (B.8). Solving a difference equation means finding the general solution to the equation, i.e. obtaining all the paths of the variable in question, which conform to the difference equation. In most problems in economics, however, the **initial value** of the variable in question is given, and hence we can typically specify the value of C in the general solution, i.e. we are interested only in obtaining the unique path of the variable, which begins with the specified value. This solution is called the **unique solution** to the difference equation (with the initial value).

B.2.2 Obtaining the general solution

Let me explain how to obtain the general solution to a linear first-order autonomous difference equation. Consider the following difference equation:

$$p_t = ap_{t-1} + b, \tag{B.12}$$

where a and b are constants. It can be rearranged as:

$$p_t - ap_{t-1} = b. \tag{B.13}$$

The solution method will be in two parts and the general solution turns out to be the sum of the solutions we obtain in these parts. We explain them in turn.

Solution to the homogeneous form

$$p_t - ap_{t-1} = 0. \tag{B.14}$$

Equation (B.14) is called the **homogeneous form** of the difference equation (B.13). We will first try to find the (general) solution to this equation and will denote it by p_t^h.

Converting Equation (B.14) into a polynomial expression does the trick. That is, let us set $p_t = Cx^t$, where C is a constant. Then $p_{t-1} = Cx^{t-1}$. Substituting these into

Equation (B.14) we get:

$$Cx^{t-1}(x - a) = 0.$$

Both $C = 0$ and $x = 0$ are trivial solutions, so we must have $x = a$. Recall that we set $p_t = Cx^t$, so with $x = a$, we get the solution to the homogeneous form (B.14) as:

$$p_t^h = Ca^t. \tag{B.15}$$

Now let us look at the second part of the solution.

Particular solution

The **particular solution** to the difference equation (B.13) is *any* solution that solves that equation. If a constant that satisfies $\bar{p} = p_t = p_{t-1}$ exists in Equation (B.13), then you can solve for such a $\bar{p}$ and use it as the particular solution. Indeed, when $a \neq 1$ you can get $p_t^p = \bar{p} = \dfrac{b}{1-a}$, where p_t^p means the particular solution.

Notice that when $a = 1$ this method does not work. When $a = 1$, p_t will never equal p_{t-1} so we need a different way to find the particular solution. Since we know the particular solution will not be a constant, let us assume it depends on t linearly. That is, let us assume that $p_t^p = \alpha t$, where α is a constant. Then $p_{t-1}^p = \alpha(t-1)$ so substituting these into Equation (B.13) (with $a = 1$) we have:

$$\alpha t - \alpha(t - 1) = b.$$

It implies that $\alpha = b$ and so the particular solution is $p_t^p = bt$.

General solution

The general solution to a difference equation is given by adding (a) the solution to the homogeneous form of that equation, and (b) the particular solution to that equation. That is, $p_t = p_t^h + p_t^p$.

Hence for Equation (B.12) (or equivalently (B.13)) we have:

$$p_t = \begin{cases} Ca^t + \dfrac{b}{1-a} & \text{if } a \neq 1, \\ C + bt & \text{if } a = 1. \end{cases} \tag{B.16}$$

In (B.16), the constant C is unspecified, i.e. the solution covers all the paths of p_t. However, when the initial value p_0 is given, then it is possible to specify the value of C. That is, for the case $a \neq 0$ in (B.16) we have:

$$p_0 = Ca^0 + \dfrac{b}{1-a},$$

which means that $C = p_0 - \dfrac{b}{1-a}$. Likewise when $a = 1$, we have $C = p_0$.

So, when the initial value p_0 is given we can get the unique solution to the difference equation:

$$p_t = \begin{cases} \left(p_0 - \dfrac{b}{1-a}\right)a^t + \dfrac{b}{1-a} & \text{if } a \neq 1, \\ p_0 + bt & \text{if } a = 1. \end{cases} \tag{B.17}$$

Let us do some exercise to get used to going through the above steps.

Question A   Solve $p_t = -\dfrac{1}{2}p_{t-1} + \dfrac{15}{2}$ when $p_0 = 2$.

[**Note.** This question corresponds to the case where $A = 100$, $B = -10$, $F = 25$ and $G = 5$ in Equation (B.6). The price path is also described in Table B.1 and Figure B.1.]

Solution   The homogeneous form of the equation is

$$p_t + \frac{1}{2}p_{t-1} = 0.$$

Setting $p_t = Ca^t$, we get:

$$Ca^t + \frac{1}{2}Ca^{t-1} = 0.$$

This equation implies $a = -\dfrac{1}{2}$. So the solution to the homogeneous form of the equation is

$$p_t^h = C\left(-\frac{1}{2}\right)^t.$$

In the meantime, the particular solution can be obtained by setting $\bar{p} = p_t = p_{t-1}$ in the equation in question. We get $\bar{p} = 5$ and use it as the particular solution, p_t^p.

Therefore, the general solution is:

$$p_t = p_t^h + p_t^p = C\left(-\frac{1}{2}\right)^t + 5.$$

Since we know that $p_0 = 2$, it follows that:

$$p_0 = 2 = C + 5,$$

which means that $C = -3$. So the unique solution to the difference equation is:

$$p_t = -3\left(-\frac{1}{2}\right)^t + 5.$$

Question B   Solve $p_t = -2p_{t-1} + 9$ when $p_0 = 2.9$.

[**Note.** This question corresponds to the case where $A = 100$, $B = -10$, $F = 10$ and $G = 20$ in Equation (B.6). The price path is also described in Table B.3 and Figure B.3.]

Solution   The homogeneous form of the equation is

$$p_t + 2p_{t-1} = 0.$$

Setting $p_t = Ca^t$, we get:

$$Ca^t + 2Ca^{t-1} = 0.$$

This equation implies $a = -2$. So the solution to the homogeneous form of the equation is:

$$p_t^h = C(-2)^t.$$

In the meantime, the particular solution can be obtained by setting $\bar{p} = p_t = p_{t-1}$ in the equation in question. We get $\bar{p} = 3$ and use it as the particular solution, p_t^p.

Therefore, the general solution is:

$$p_t = p_t^h + p_t^p = C(-2)^t + 3.$$

Since we know that $p_0 = 2.9$, it follows that:

$$p_0 = 2.9 = C + 3,$$

which means that $C = -\dfrac{1}{10}$. So the unique solution to the difference equation is:

$$p_t = -\frac{1}{10}(-2)^t + 3.$$

Exercise B.1   Solving linear first-order autonomous difference equations.

B.2.3   The steady state and convergence

Now we are in a position to verify the claim we made about the stability of the cobweb model. Let us consider the cobweb model as in Equation (B.6). The **steady state** of the model, where both p and q come to rest, exists if and only if $\dfrac{G}{B} \neq 1$. Denoting the steady state value of price by $\bar{p}$, we can obtain $\bar{p}$ by setting $\bar{p} = p_t = p_{t-1}$ in Equation (B.7). We get $\bar{p} = \dfrac{F - A}{B - G}$.

Does the price converges to this steady state value as in Figure B.1? Or does it diverge from it as illustrated in Figure B.3? To examine this matter, let us look at the difference equation (B.7), which we have obtained from our cobweb model. The unique solution to that equation given p_0 shows the paths of the price in our cobweb model over t. We know the unique solution to Equation (B.7) is the following (you can easily verify that it is consistent with the solutions in Exercise B.1):

$$p_t = \begin{cases} \left(p_0 - \dfrac{F - A}{B - G}\right)\left(\dfrac{G}{B}\right)^t + \dfrac{F - A}{B - G} & \text{if } \dfrac{G}{B} \neq 1, \\[4mm] p_0 + \dfrac{F - A}{B}t & \text{if } \dfrac{G}{B} = 1. \end{cases} \tag{B.18}$$

We will focus on the case where the steady state exists, i.e. when $\dfrac{G}{B} \neq 1$. Using the fact that $\bar{p} = \dfrac{F - A}{B - G}$ when $\dfrac{G}{B} \neq 1$, we can rewrite Equation (B.18) as follows:

$$p_t = (p_0 - \bar{p}) \left(\frac{G}{B} \right)^t + \bar{p} \quad \text{if } \frac{G}{B} \neq 1. \tag{B.19}$$

So whether p_t converges to $\bar{p}$ (of course if p_0 is different from $\bar{p}$) depends solely on the value of $\dfrac{G}{B}$. If $\left| \dfrac{G}{B} \right| < 1$, then $\lim\limits_{t \to \infty} \left(\dfrac{G}{B} \right)^t = 0$. For example, if $\dfrac{G}{B} = -\dfrac{1}{2}$ (corresponding to Question A in Exercise B.1), then you can see below that the magnitude of $\left(-\dfrac{1}{2} \right)^t$ becomes smaller and smaller:

$$-\frac{1}{2}, \frac{1}{4}, -\frac{1}{8}, \frac{1}{16}, -\frac{1}{32}, \frac{1}{64}, -\frac{1}{128}, \frac{1}{256}, \ldots$$

Therefore, if $\left| \dfrac{G}{B} \right| < 1$:

$$\lim_{t \to \infty} p_t = \lim_{t \to \infty} (p_0 - \bar{p}) \left(\frac{G}{B} \right)^t + \lim_{t \to \infty} \bar{p}$$

$$= (p_0 - \bar{p}) \lim_{t \to \infty} \left(\frac{G}{B} \right)^t + \bar{p}$$

$$= (p_0 - \bar{p}) \cdot 0 + \bar{p}$$

$$= \bar{p}.$$

You can see that p_t approaches $\bar{p}$ because the first term of the RHS of Equation (B.19) becomes closer and closer to zero. You can also see that, when $\dfrac{G}{B} = -\dfrac{1}{2}$, whilst the magnitude of the first term decreases, it alternates in sign. For this reason, p_t converges to $\bar{p}$ in oscillation. In fact, we can state that we have **convergence in oscillation** if $-1 < \dfrac{G}{B} < 0$.

In contrast, if $\left| \dfrac{G}{B} \right| > 1$, then $\lim\limits_{t \to \infty} \left(\dfrac{G}{B} \right)^t \neq 0$. For example, if $\dfrac{G}{B} = -2$ (corresponding to Question B in Exercise B.1), then you can see below that the magnitude of $(-2)^t$ becomes larger and larger:

$$-2, 4, -8, 16, -32, 64, -128, 256, \ldots$$

Since the magnitude of the first term of Equation (B.19) increases, p_t does not converge to $\bar{p}$ when $\left| \dfrac{G}{B} \right| > 1$. When $\dfrac{G}{B} = -2$, p_t moves away from $\bar{p}$ in an oscillating fashion. More generally, we have **divergence in oscillation** if $\dfrac{G}{B} < -1$.

If $0 < \dfrac{G}{B} < 1$ we know p_t converges to $\bar{p}$ from the previous analysis, but the path does not oscillate. In this case, we have **monotonic convergence**, i.e. p_t will approach $\bar{p}$ either from above or below monotonically. On the other hand, we have **monotonic divergence** when $\dfrac{G}{B} > 1$.

B.3 The linear first-order autonomous differential equation

In the difference equations we looked at in the previous section, our focus was how the variable in question changes between discrete time periods such as years, months, etc. In other words, time was modelled discretely, but we can model it continuously as well. Here we take the duration of such a period to be infinitesimally small, i.e. we consider an *instantaneous* change in the variable. Consider the following model where the variable of focus is the price, p:

$$\dot{p} = \theta\left(q^D - q^S\right),\ \theta > 0. \tag{B.20}$$

where $\dot{p} \equiv \dfrac{dp}{dt}$ is the time derivative of p and shows the *instantaneous* change in p. The quantity demanded and the quantity supplied are given by q^D and q^S, respectively, and both of them depend on p (specified shortly). Equation (B.20) says that when there is excess demand $\left(q^D - q^S\right) > 0$, the price will instantaneously adjust upwards because θ – which represents the speed of the price adjustment; the greater θ is, the faster the price adjusts – is also positive. On the other hand, when there is excess supply $\left(q^D - q^S\right) < 0$, the price will fall instantaneously. Hence Equation (B.20) is consistent with the demand and supply analysis we discussed in the various parts of the main text. When the price is at the level where the market clears, i.e. $\left(q^D - q^S\right) = 0$, we have $\dot{p} = 0$, so the price comes to rest. This price level is called the **steady state** price level.

Now, let's suppose that the demand and supply functions are given as follows, at all times:

$$\begin{cases} q^D = A + Bp \\ q^S = F + Gp, \end{cases}$$

where A, B, F and G are constants. Substituting these into Equation (B.20), we get:

$$\dot{p} = \theta(B - G)p + \theta(A - F). \tag{B.21}$$

Setting $a = \theta(B - G)$ and $b = \theta(A - F)$, it reduces to

$$\dot{p} = ap + b. \tag{B.22}$$

Equation (B.22) contains the time derivative $\dot{p}$, hence it is called the **differential equation**. Note also that, in Equation (B.22), (a) $\dot{p}$ is linear in p, (b) the time derivative that has the highest order is $\dot{p}$ (the first-order time derivative), and (c) t does not explicitly appear, e.g. a and b are constant over time. For these reasons, respectively, Equation (B.22) is called the **linear first-order autonomous differential equation** in p. As is the case for difference equations, differential equations can take other forms. For example, $\dot{p}$ may not be linear in p, in which case such an equation is called the **non-linear differential equation**. When the the time derivative that has the highest order is $\ddot{p}$ (the second-order time derivative), then the equation is called the **second-order differential equation**. When t appears in the equation explicitly, e.g. a and/or b may be time-dependent and so they are $a(t)$ and/or $b(t)$, then we have a **non-autonomous differential equation**. Our focus in this appendix will be the linear first-order autonomous differential equation as in Equation (B.22).[2]

B.3.1   Obtaining the general solution to a linear first-order autonomous differential equation

The same method we used to obtain the solution to the same form of the difference equation applies. Namely, we will first obtain the (general) solution to the homogeneous form of the differential equation. Then we will obtain the particular solution of the differential equation. The general solution to the differential equation turns out to be the sum of these solutions. Let us look at them in turn.

Solution to the homogeneous form

We have:

$$\dot{p} - ap = 0. \tag{B.23}$$

Equation (B.23) is called the **homogeneous form** of the differential equation B.22. We will first find the (general) solution to this equation and will denote it by p^h.

We can solve Equation (B.23) for p by applying the integration technique. That is:

$$\dot{p} = ap$$

$$\frac{1}{p}\frac{dp}{dt} = a$$

$$\int \frac{1}{p}\frac{dp}{dt}dt = \int a\,dt$$

$$\int \frac{1}{p}dp = \int a\,dt$$

$$\ln p = at + C_1,$$

where C_1 is a constant of integration. Solving this equation for p, we get the solution to the homogeneous form p^h:

$$p^h = Ce^{at}, \tag{B.24}$$

where $C = e^{C_1}$.

---

2 If you are interested in different forms of (and obviously more advanced) differential equations, you should consult more advanced textbooks in quantitative methods in economics. See, for example, Simon and Blume, *Mathematics for Economists*.

Particular solution

The idea of the **particular solution** to the differential equation (B.22) is the same as in the case for solving difference equations: it is *any* solution that solves that equation. You can use the steady state value of p in Equation (B.22), $\bar{p}$, as the particular solution when it exists. The steady state exists when $a \neq 0$ and you can obtain $\bar{p}$ by setting $\dot{p} = 0$ in Equation (B.22).[3] We get $p^p = \bar{p} = -\dfrac{b}{a}$. Because the time derivative of p^p is zero, it is easy to see that $p^p = -\dfrac{b}{a}$ satisfies Equation (B.22) (and hence we know it is actually the particular solution).

General solution

As said before, the **general solution** to a differential equation is given by the sum of (a) the solution to the homogeneous form of that equation, and (b) the particular solution to that equation. That is, $p = p^h + p^p$.

Hence for Equation (B.22) we have:

$$p = \begin{cases} Ce^{at} - \dfrac{b}{a} & \text{if } a \neq 0, \\ C + bt & \text{if } a = 0. \end{cases} \tag{B.25}$$

As in the general solution to a difference equation, in Equation (B.25), the constant C is unspecified. Therefore this solution covers all the paths of p, which depend on the initial value $p(0)$. When $p(0)$ is given, we can nail down the value of C. That is, for the case $a \neq 0$ in Equation (B.25), we have

$$p(0) = Ce^0 - \frac{b}{a},$$

which means that $C = p(0) + \dfrac{b}{a}$. Likewise when $a = 0$, we have $C = p(0)$.

So, when the initial value p_0 is given, the **unique solution** to the differential equation (B.22) is:

$$p = \begin{cases} \left(p(0) + \dfrac{b}{a} \right) e^{at} - \dfrac{b}{a} & \text{if } a \neq 0, \\ p(0) + bt & \text{if } a = 0. \end{cases} \tag{B.26}$$

Let us do some exercises to get used to going through the above steps.

---

3 When $a = 0$ then the general solution to Equation (B.22) can be obtained simply by taking the integral of both sides of the equation: $p = C + bt$ if $a = 0$.

Question A   Solve $\dot{p} = -3p + 15$ when $p_0 = 2$.

[**Note.** This question corresponds to the case where $A = 100$, $B = -10$, $F = 25$, $G = 5$ and $\theta = \dfrac{1}{5}$ in Equation (B.21).]

Solution   The homogeneous form of the equation is:

$$\dot{p} + 3p = 0.$$

After rearranging this equation we can integrate both sides by t:

$$\dot{p} = -3p$$

$$\frac{1}{p}\frac{dp}{dt} = -3$$

$$\int \frac{1}{p}\frac{dp}{dt}dt = \int (-3)dt$$

$$\int \frac{1}{p}dp = \int (-3)dt$$

$$\ln p = -3t + C_1,$$

where C_1 is a constant of integration. So the solution to the homogeneous form of the equation is:

$$p^h = Ce^{-3t},$$

where $C = e^{C_1}$.

In the meantime, the particular solution can be obtained by setting $\dot{p} = 0$ in the equation in question. We get $\bar{p} = 5$ and use it as the particular solution, p^p.

The general solution, therefore, is:

$$p = p^h + p^p = Ce^{-3t} + 5.$$

Since we know that $p(0) = 2$, it follows that:

$$p(0) = 2 = C + 5,$$

which means that $C = -3$. So the unique solution to the differential equation is:

$$p = -3e^{-3t} + 5.$$

Question B   Solve $\dot{p} = 3p - 15$ when $p_0 = 2$.

[**Note.** This question corresponds to the case where $A = 100$, $B = -10$, $F = 175$, $G = -25$ and $\theta = \dfrac{1}{5}$ in Equation (B.21).]

Solution   The homogeneous form of the equation is:

$$\dot{p} - 3p = 0.$$

After rearranging this equation we can integrate both sides by t:

$$\dot{p} = 3p$$

$$\frac{1}{p}\frac{dp}{dt} = 3$$

$$\int \frac{1}{p}\frac{dp}{dt}dt = \int 3dt$$

$$\int \frac{1}{p}dp = \int 3dt$$

$$\ln p = 3t + C_1,$$

where C_1 is a constant of integration. So the solution to the homogeneous form of the equation is:

$$p^h = Ce^{3t},$$

where $C = e^{C_1}$.

In the meantime, the particular solution can be obtained by setting $\dot{p} = 0$ in the equation in question. We get $\bar{p} = 5$ and use it as the particular solution, p^p.

The general solution, therefore, is:

$$p = p^h + p^p = Ce^{3t} + 5.$$

Since we know that $p(0) = 2$, it follows that:

$$p(0) = 2 = C + 5,$$

which means that $C = -3$. So the unique solution to the differential equation is:

$$p = -3e^{3t} + 5.$$

Exercise B.2   Solving linear first-order autonomous differential equations.

B.3.2   The steady state and convergence

Now let us focus on the case where the steady state exists for Equation (B.22). The steady state value of p is $\bar{p} = -\dfrac{b}{a}$ and so the unique solution to Equation (B.22), given p_0, can be rearranged as:

$$p = (p(0) - \bar{p})e^{at} + \bar{p}. \tag{B.27}$$

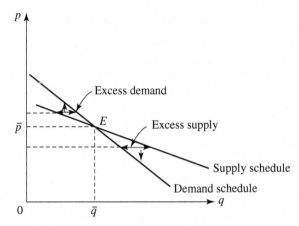

Figure B.4 The demand and supply model (unstable case).

If the first term of the RHS of the equation tends to zero as t goes to infinity, then we have p converging to its steady state value $\bar{p}$. Whether $(p(0) - \bar{p}) e^{at}$ converges to zero depends on the value of a. For p to converge to $\bar{p}$ it is necessary (and sufficient) to have $a < 0$; and otherwise we have divergence from $\bar{p}$ (unless $p_0 = \bar{p}$ of course).

Bearing this result in mind, let us examine the demand and supply model. When the steady state exists, i.e. $B - G \neq 0$, the unique solution to Equation (B.21), given $p(0)$, is:

$$p = \left(p(0) + \frac{A - F}{B - G} \right) e^{\theta(B-G)t} - \frac{A - F}{B - G}. \tag{B.28}$$

Since $\bar{p} = -\dfrac{A - F}{B - G}$, it can be written as:

$$p = (p(0) - \bar{p}) e^{\theta(B-G)t} + \bar{p}. \tag{B.29}$$

Given $\theta > 0$ (by assumption), whether p converges to $\bar{p}$ depends on the sign of $B - G$. For convergence we need to have $B - G < 0$, i.e. $G > B$. For a downward sloping demand schedule and an upward sloping supply schedule, we have $B < 0$ and $G > 0$, respectively, so the necessary and sufficient condition for convergence will be met for sure. For $p(0)$ the market price will converge to its steady state level $\bar{p}$. We say that the steady state is **stable** when convergence occurs. Question A in Exercise B.2 ($B = -10$ and $G = 5$) corresponds to this case.

In contrast, when we have $G < B$, the price diverges from $\bar{p}$ unless $p(0) = \bar{p}$. We say such a steady state is **unstable**. The relevant situation can be observed in Question B in Exercise B.2 ($B = -10$ and $G = -25$). As you might have noticed, in this case both the demand and supply schedules are downward sloping as depicted in Figure B.4.[4] Note also that $G < B$ means that the supply schedule is flatter than the demand schedule.

You can see in the figure that when the initial price is above $\bar{p}$, there is excess demand. In this model, as specified in Equation (B.20), when there is excess demand the price adjusts upwards. So the price moves away from the steady state level (and never comes back). On the other hand, if the initial price turns out to be below $\bar{p}$, there is excess supply. The price moves downwards according to Equation (B.20) and so we observe divergence from $\bar{p}$ as well. The steady state illustrated in Figure B.4 is unstable because the price never reverts to its steady state unless the initial value happens to coincide with it.

------

4 We have not dealt with a downward sloping supply schedule throughout this book. What might give rise to it? It is difficult to provide a proper explanation without using some knowledge from intermediate microeconomics, but you can imagine the following case to get a sufficient idea. Suppose you are supplying your labour (q hours per day) and the price you get paid is the hourly wage (p). Suppose at the current wage, you are working 8 hours per day. If the wage increased, would you work more? On one hand, the rise in the wage makes working more attractive (than spending your time on other things), but on the other hand, it means you needn't work as much as before to make the same earnings. If the latter factor outweighed the former, then your labour supply would be less at the higher wage.

Index

Printed in the United States
by Baker & Taylor Publisher Services